KU-262-995

Why Everything Is Going To Get Worse Before It Gets Better

Books by Vernon Coleman

The Medicine Men (1975)
Paper Doctors (1976)
Everything You Want To Know About Ageing (1976)
Stress Control (1978)
The Home Pharmacy (1980)
Aspirin or Ambulance (1980)
Face Values (1981)
Guilt (1982)
The Good Medicine Guide (1982)
Stress And Your Stomach (1983)
Bodypower (1983)
An A to Z Of Women's Problems (1984)
Bodysense (1984)
Taking Care Of Your Skin (1984)
A Guide to Child Health (1984)
Life Without Tranquillisers (1985)
Diabetes (1985)
Arthritis (1985)
Eczema and Dermatitis (1985)
The Story Of Medicine (1985, 1998)
Natural Pain Control (1986)
Mindpower (1986)
Addicts and Addictions (1986)
Dr Vernon Coleman's Guide To Alternative Medicine (1988)
Stress Management Techniques (1988)
Overcoming Stress (1988)
Know Yourself (1988)
The Health Scandal (1988)
The 20 Minute Health Check (1989)
Sex For Everyone (1989)
Mind Over Body (1989)
Eat Green Lose Weight (1990)
Why Animal Experiments Must Stop (1991)
The Drugs Myth (1992)
How To Overcome Toxic Stress (1990)
Why Doctors Do More Harm Than Good (1993)
Stress and Relaxation (1993)
Complete Guide To Sex (1993)
How to Conquer Backache (1993)
How to Conquer Arthritis (1993)
Betrayal of Trust (1994)

Know Your Drugs (1994, 1997)
Food for Thought (1994, revised edition 2000)
The Traditional Home Doctor (1994)
I Hope Your Penis Shrivels Up (1994)
- People Watching (1995)
Relief from IBS (1995)
The Parent's Handbook (1995)
Oral Sex: Bad Taste And Hard To Swallow? (1995)
Why Is Pubic Hair Curly? (1995)
Men in Dresses (1996)
Power over Cancer (1996)
Crossdressing (1996)
How to Conquer Arthritis (1996)
High Blood Pressure (1996)
How To Stop Your Doctor Killing You (1996, revised edition 2003)
Fighting For Animals (1996)
Alice and Other Friends (1996)
Spiritpower (1997)
Other People's Problems (1998)
How To Publish Your Own Book (1999)
How To Relax and Overcome Stress (1999)
Animal Rights – Human Wrongs (1999)
Superbody (1999)
The 101 Sexiest, Craziest, Most Outrageous Agony Column
       Questions (and Answers) of All Time (1999)
Strange But True (2000)
Daily Inspirations (2000)
Stomach Problems: Relief At Last (2001)
How To Overcome Guilt (2001)
How To Live Longer (2001)
Sex (2001)
How To Make Money While Watching TV (2001)
We Love Cats (2002)
England Our England (2002)
Rogue Nation (2003)
People Push Bottles Up Peaceniks (2003)
The Cats' Own Annual (2003)
Confronting The Global Bully (2004)
Saving England (2004)
Why Everything Is Going To Get Worse Before It Gets Better (2004)

novels
The Village Cricket Tour (1990)

The Bilbury Chronicles (1992)
Bilbury Grange (1993)
Mrs Caldicot's Cabbage War (1993)
Bilbury Revels (1994)
Deadline (1994)
The Man Who Inherited a Golf Course (1995)
Bilbury Country (1996)
Second Innings (1999)
Around the Wicket (2000)
It's Never Too Late (2001)
Paris In My Springtime (2002)
Mrs Caldicot's Knickerbocker Glory (2003)

short stories
Bilbury Pie (1995)

on cricket
Thomas Winsden's Cricketing Almanack (1983)
Diary Of A Cricket Lover (1984)

as Edward Vernon
Practice Makes Perfect (1977)
Practise What You Preach (1978)
Getting Into Practice (1979)
Aphrodisiacs – An Owner's Manual (1983)
The Complete Guide To Life (1984)

as Marc Charbonnier
Tunnel (novel 1980)

with Alice
Alice's Diary (1989)
Alice's Adventures (1992)

with Dr Alan C Turin
No More Headaches (1981)

With Donna Antoinette Coleman
How To Conquer Health Problems Between Ages 50 and 120 (2003)

Why Everything Is Going To Get Worse Before It Gets Better

(And What You Can Do About It)

Vernon Coleman

BLUE
BOOKS

Published by Blue Books, Publishing House, Trinity Place, Barnstaple, Devon EX32 9HG, England.

This book is copyright. Enquiries should be addressed to the author c/o the publishers.

© Vernon Coleman 2004. The right of Vernon Coleman to be identified as the author of this work has been asserted in accordance with the Copyright, Designs and Patents Act 1988.

Printed 2004 (twice), reprinted 2005

ISBN: 1 899726 75 6

All rights reserved. No part may be reproduced, stored in a retrieval system or transmitted, in any form or by any means, electronic, mechanical, photocopying, recording or otherwise without the prior written permission of the author and publisher. This book is sold subject to the condition that it shall not by way of trade or otherwise be lent, re-sold, hired out or otherwise circulated without the publisher's prior consent in any form of binding or cover other than that in which it is published.

A catalogue record for this book is available from the British Library.

Printed by J.W. Arrowsmith Limited, Bristol

Dedication

This book is dedicated to my wife, my friend, my love and my playmate: Donna Antoinette, the Welsh Princess.

She shares my fury at the way our nation has been taken from us and sold into corporate slavery; my indignation at the way our corrupt politicians lie to us as they tear from us every last fragment of our privacy and our liberty; my anguish as our society becomes increasingly brutal and uncaring; my pain as I watch the weakest and most vulnerable citizens of the world abused by the hate and rage-filled fanatics who ignore our voices, tear from us the power which is ours and thrust us into corporate sponsored wars; my bewilderment as they create a fake war on terrorism and use the resultant excuse of 'State security' as a corrupt reason to replace a thousand years of democracy with the vilest form of fascism and my determination to stand up for those intangible but invaluable benefits which we take for granted and do not miss until they are gone: our freedom, our rights as individuals, our privacy and our dignity.

I dedicate this book to her.

And I add my thanks and my respect to the countless thousands of readers who have honoured me with their support and encouragement.

We will win because we have no choice.

Vernon Coleman, May 2004

Chapter 1

Reasons For Discontent

I am neither right wing nor left wing. I'm not anything-wing. I really just want to be left alone to get on with my life in peace.

I want the Government to do what it should be doing – providing a safe environment, protecting me and my family from danger wherever it can, and running a secure, efficient and safe infrastructure. I don't expect any of this for free. I am perfectly prepared to pay for the essential services which are part of a civilised society.

But...

* * *

My two previous books on politics, *England Our England* and *Rogue Nation*, arose out of a genuine sense of anger and frustration.

I started to write *England Our England* when I first realised just how the bureaucrats of the European Union were interfering with my life and my country. I became furious when I realised that, thanks to the EU, it would soon be impossible for me to campaign about any of the things I care passionately about. The EU is, for example, making it impossible for animal lovers to campaign for animals. And it is, I believe, the EU which will eventually lead to the demise of the NHS. The more I learnt about the EU the more alarmed I became. When I discovered that the EU was planning to remove England from maps (and the history books) I was horrified.

I wrote *England Our England* because I felt I had to. (Readers frequently ask why I didn't call it *Britain Our Britain*. The answer is simple. Scotland and Wales will become mere regions of the EU but they will continue to exist. England will completely disappear.)

People feel unwanted in their own country today. 'It's our country, and we want it back,' wrote one reader of *England Our England*. But those of us who care have no party representing us in Parliament and no real voice in London or Brussels. Soon we will have no country.

I wrote *Rogue Nation* partly because I was appalled at the way America was riding roughshod over the rest of the world, partly because I was horrified at the way Britain was being dragged into America's wars and also because it seemed to me (and still seems to me) that America is, of all the nations in the world, the main and most significant threat to world peace. America is the Rogue Nation.

This book is about Britain – what has gone wrong, why it's gone wrong, how we can survive and what we can do about it.

The quality of life in Britain is rapidly deteriorating and will continue to do so, in every possible way, for the foreseeable future – or at least until the people of Britain stand up and say 'Enough!'. Under New Labour traditional legal and human rights have been redefined as privileges; to be withdrawn on the whims of New Labour Ministers. We have far too much law and far too little justice.

I have explained in this book why I think everything has gone so badly wrong. This is a book in defence of freedom, independence and privacy and since no large, existing political party supports those ideals this isn't a book about politics so much as a book against politics.

I want less government. And I want politicians to do the things they are supposed to do with more efficiency and more honesty. I want them out of my hair. I want them to get on with providing roads, schools, hospitals and national defence. I want them to pick up my rubbish and to have men in uniforms patrol my neighbourhood to deter and catch criminals. I don't want the Government interfering with every aspect of my life, poking their noses into my wallet and my home. I want them to have respect for the country they are supposed to be administering; not to give it away. I want our so-called leaders to have respect for our history and our heritage. And I want them to do what we, the people, want them to do, not what they want to do. I don't want to live in a country led by people who believe in lies, corruption and nepotism rather than honesty, integrity and justice.

Actually, except at time of (genuine) war we don't need a leader. We need and want good administrators. Modern politicians want to be leaders but they have none of the required qualities. Sadly, they also have no experience of, or patience for, running anything; they are incompetent at administration.

If you feel disillusioned by politics, and frustrated by what is happening around you, you are not alone.

* * *

It is natural (and easy) to see problems in isolation, not to realise just how many things have gone wrong, and not to see the underlying causes for the confusion and despair we feel. Britons don't usually like to speak out too much, or to try and interfere. We like to leave things to the politicians. We want to trust them.

But it's too late for trust. And we have to know what's gone wrong in order to put things right.

Until you know how and why things have gone wrong (and what is likely to go wrong in the future) it is difficult to know what to do to defend yourself. Information itself is of no value unless you know that it's accurate and trustworthy, but even information that is accurate and trustworthy has no real worth unless you know how it might affect your life, what you can do with it and how you can respond to it.

When you look past the lies which have been used so consistently by politicians trying to hide the truth, and understand what really is happening to our world, you will be in a strong position to prepare for the future – and to help fight to get your country back.

This book has three purposes.

First, to remind you (or tell you if you haven't noticed) of some of the main ways in which our world has deteriorated; to try to explain why the world is the way it is today; to show that you aren't alone in feeling that the world has gone mad and to provide some explanations. It is, perhaps, a comfort to know that most people think like you and I do.

My second aim is to show how you can best protect yourself and your family during the coming months and years. Things are going to get worse before they get better. (But I have no doubt that they will eventually get better.) If you don't know what is going on you can't plan. And if you don't plan and know how to look after yourself – well, the future will be even bleaker.

The final purpose of this book is to point out that there is light at the end of the tunnel. Britain isn't ready yet for a revolution. But the revolution will come and it will come suddenly and quickly. It will be unlike other revolutions because there will be no rioting in the streets, no shooting, no violence. This will be a bloodless revolution.

There are some substantial changes ahead.

* * *

Why should you believe my predictions for the future? Well, for over thirty years I have been making predictions based on my interpretation of the available evidence and my track record is considerably better than that of any Government department and, as far as I am aware, a match for that of any other commentator. (There is, for example, a list of a few dozen of my forecasts in the field of medicine and health care in the latest edition of my book *How To Stop Your Doctor Killing You*.)

The revolution, an uprising of right minded citizens who care about their freedom, their identity, their privacy, their history and their country, will probably come in a very unexpected way and at an unexpected time.

* * *

Don't be afraid to be angry. It is your right and your duty to be very, very angry. The world's current problems have accumulated because dishonest, greedy, corrupt people have taken advantage of our fear, apathy, indifference and trust. It is often said that people get the government they deserve. In general that may be true. But no one deserves the governments we've had recently. Our governments have created a world in which it is seen as weak to be well intentioned, honest or sensitive. They simply want us to obey, conform and consume.

It is time for us all to stand up and be counted.

* * *

It is, of course, safer and easier to do nothing.
But the cost is just too great.

Before It Gets Better

* * *

'A government big enough to give you everything you want is a government big enough to take from you everything you have.'
Gerald R. Ford, former President of the USA

* * *

Life gets on top of us all these days. Like the white rabbit, we are always hurrying. And, much of the time, what goes on in our world makes about as much sense as what went on in Wonderland. Freedom and privacy are disappearing fast and being replaced as guiding principles by aggression, hypocrisy and oppression. Our taxes go up and up but the quality of the services we pay for goes down and down. Even people who were quiet and disinterested in politics are beginning to sit up and take notice. They feel unwanted and unloved by their own country. They feel that everything is changing so quickly that they no longer recognise the world around them.

* * *

In theory, the Government is there to make life safer and easier for us; so that we can go about our daily business and pleasure with greater comfort and security.

But in practice that's no longer what happens. When people were recently asked if they thought the Government controlled too much of their daily lives two thirds of respondents answered 'yes'. The same percentage also said they thought the Government was wasteful and inefficient in everything it did.

Instead of making our lives safer and easier the Government now makes everything harder and more dangerous. Whose side are they on? Why does Blair keep taking us to war? Why are the British people being denied an opportunity to vote on their own future constitution? Why does Britain remain a member of the EU when membership costs the country a small fortune and the majority of people want to leave? Why, when most people want hunting banned and the Government promised to ban it, is hunting still legal? Why is the NHS such a mess? Why, when most people want immigration controlled does the Government do nothing? Why did the Government start a war against

Iraq when a vast majority of the British electorate didn't want to go to war at all? Why, when it can't run anything properly, does the Government insist on interfering in almost every aspect of our lives?

Too much government and too much government control means that no one succeeds but that all will eventually fail equally.

George Orwell showed the way in which patriotism can degenerate into totalitarianism. Orwell invented 'newspeak', a deliberate creation by a totalitarian state which precludes the possibility of dissent. The goal of the government is to force the people into submission through fear and to force them to love (or, at least, accept) the State through the absence of any other alternative. It has happened.

We are, we are told, living in a parliamentary democracy. Really? It's an easy claim to make. Saddam Hussein claimed to be a democratic leader. Stalin claimed his Russia was democratic. Mugabe claims to run Zimbabwe democratically. It is worth remembering that Blair, like his friend Bush, was not elected by a majority of the people.

A true nation is a community of people, an extended family if you like. A state is a political and administrative entity. Today, we have a lot of the latter but none of the former. Your country doesn't love you any more because your country doesn't really exist any more – not in the way we used to think of it.

* * *

'For the fascist everything is in the state, and nothing whether of the mind or body exists, and still less has value, outside the state.'
BENITO MUSSOLINI

* * *

Our New Labour leaders are fond of describing their opponents as fascists, and the proponents of the EU tend to describe all those who question the value of the United States of Europe as fascists. But the truth is that we already live in a fascist state. It happened quietly, without fuss, and without storm-troopers marching through the streets; but it happened.

There is a great misunderstanding about what fascism is but there really shouldn't be. Mussolini, the man who invented fascism, described it as the right of the state to express the real essence of the individual. That is exactly how we now live.

Before It Gets Better

Mussolini's fascism ruled that the state must of necessity embrace all the activities of the citizens; it must be a corporate state, with the right to the last word on every subject.

Fascism is a socialist marriage of big government and big business, where the state is paramount. That is what fascism was in Germany and Italy in the 1930s and 1940s.

The truth is that we, like the Americans, now have a fascist government. And the EU is a fascist organisation.

All governments have a natural leaning towards fascism. Ours has got there.

* * *

There is no discernible difference between communism (or socialism) and fascism. Fascism sucks the very life out of a country.

* * *

To take the country to war against the wishes of the people, and to ignore the public clamour for a referendum on the new EU constitution, were acts not of the leader of a democracy but of an old-fashioned, unreconstructed fascist dictator.

It doesn't really matter what you call it – a totalitarian state, Marxist socialism, state control, a bureaucratic state or just straight, simple, unadorned socialism – we are living under fascist rule.

In politics if you go to the left far enough you will reach the same place that you will reach if you go to the right far enough. Our centralised government believes that its main purpose is to defend itself and its own position, wealth and status, rather than to serve the electors. New Labour should rename itself the National Socialist Party. How long will it be before they reintroduce the jackboot as an essential fashion accessory?

* * *

'One of the things the government can't do is run anything. The only things our Government runs are the Post Office and the railroads and both of them are bankrupt.'
LEE IACOCCA

* * *

Much of what has happened (and is happening) in Britain is the sort of thing Britons found repulsive about what we used to refer to as 'banana republics'.

It was New Labour which in February 2004 proposed keeping evidence from selected defendants, reducing the burden of proof required by courts and having secret trials before vetted judges. They were, they added, thinking of having trials at which verdicts could be taken on the 'balance of probabilities'. (So much easier than having to prove a charge beyond reasonable doubt.) New Labour want to allow intelligence information to be used as acceptable evidence and to have trials without bothering to have the defendant present. Accused individuals can now be kept in prison indefinitely. Public stonings and the building of concentration camps surely cannot be far behind.

Each new, small erosion of our civil liberties, and of the normally accepted standards of a civilised society, is accepted and allowed to pass by because it is small and, to a population which has grown accustomed to allowing the Government and the courts a free hand, does not seem too alarming. But the small erosions accumulate. And already the tenets upon which our brand of civilisation was founded are fast disappearing.

* * *

We live in a rich, allegedly developed country, but our government treats the ill, the poor and the unfortunate with derision and contempt. The National Health Service, once glorious, once the envy of the world, has been more or less destroyed. Our leaders have for years been busy closing down mental hospitals and throwing the patients out into the urban wilderness. It is politically incorrect to keep people in long-stay institutions, argue the new bureaucrats. It's also cheaper to dump them on the streets.

How do our leaders get away with it?

Because we let them get away with it.

* * *

Why does the Government seem determined to destroy British industry by introducing a constant avalanche of absurd rules and regulations? Why does Britain have the worst transport system in the developed world? Why is Britain now inextricably linked to the USA when the Government is also committed to our becoming part of a European superstate (the other parts of which loathe America so much that some experts have claimed that the next Cold War will be between the USA and the EU)?

Why do even young people believe that everything is worse than it used to be? Why do politicians never apologise or admit that they have made a mistake? Why is it not treason when a Prime Minister takes his country to war (and exposes to danger the citizens who have entrusted their welfare to him) and does so on the basis of false information? Why are hundreds of British politicians and civil servants not locked in the Tower of London for their part in taking Britain into the EU under false pretences?

Politicians have a great deal of authority, why do they no longer have any sense of responsibility?

* * *

'Few of us can easily surrender our belief that society must somehow make sense. The thought that the state has lost its mind and is punishing so many innocent people is intolerable. And so the evidence has to be internally denied.'
ARTHUR MILLER

* * *

Why is all this happening? Is it an accident? Or could it be (as conspiracy theorists believe) part of a plot to depress (and therefore oppress) us? A growing number of people firmly believe that we are the victims of a conspiracy and that unseen, shadowy figures (politicians, bankers and industrialists) are busy taking control of our lives (and everyone's money) in some search for global supremacy.

The cock-up theorists believe that everything that is happening is just a result of chaos and staggering incompetence.

Both of these theories are partially right. There are conspiracies. And there is a lot of cocking-up going on. Indeed, I doubt if there has ever been quite so much cocking-up as there is these days. Most of our leaders are too stupid to find the light switch and too inept to know how to turn it on even if they came across it by accident.

But there is a third explanation for the way things are.

There is something else going on which is outside the control of the Government and the conspirators. There is something happening that is outside everyone's control.

WHY EVERYTHING IS GOING TO GET WORSE

The institutions which we are supposed to run for our benefit are now controlling us and the way we do things – for their own benefit.

I first realised how and why this happens after studying the health service, and the drug companies, for several decades. I really couldn't understand why our health care system continued to be so badly organised. I found it difficult to understand why doctors, administrators and drug company bosses all kept ignoring the obvious medical truths. There is, for example, clear unequivocal evidence showing that heart disease can be treated safely and effectively without drugs or surgery. But doctors and hospitals persist in using drugs and surgery. Why? Are they all blind, stupid or stark raving bonkers?

And then I saw the light – and realised that the NHS (and the drug companies and the medical establishment) are no longer being run for people or even by people. The organisations are in charge. The NHS operates the way it does because that makes the NHS a more powerful institution. The bureaucrats do the things they do because that increases the power of the organisation they serve. The medical establishment rejects new advances which threaten doctors' power because the medical establishment has acquired a purpose of its own.

Individual doctors who have read the appropriate research know that it is crazy to continue to perform open heart surgery. Individual doctors who have looked at the evidence know that most drugs are useless and do more harm than good. But the medical establishment doesn't consist of individual doctors; it is an entity with a life of its own. The medical establishment knows that in order for it to survive certain truths must be suppressed or scorned. And so that is exactly what happens. The institution thrives. The patients die.

Much the same thing happens in business. The world's biggest and richest drug companies are for ever selling drugs which do no good and which, indeed, kill people. Are these companies run by psychopaths? It's a thought which has its attractions but I don't really think that's the case.

The fact is that the people who work for big companies aren't in charge; they merely run things for the benefit of the company which employs them. The individuals working for the company make decisions which benefit the company, rather than the human race. Effectively, this means that the company is in charge. The big drug companies have to make quarterly profits. The company's objectives and needs come first.

It took me another year or two to realise that what has happened in the world of medicine has also happened everywhere else. Big arms companies aren't all run by sadistic psychopaths who like the idea of small children being blown up by landmines and cluster bombs. Food companies aren't all run by ignorant mass murderers who deliberately make sure that they sell products which cause cancer and heart disease. In every case things are the way they are because that's the way the company needs them. The people who *think* they are in charge aren't really in charge at all. The people who *think* they are in charge are merely serving the needs of the corporation which pays them.

The world has, in fact, gone completely bonkers. The lunatics aren't running the asylum. The asylum is running the lunatics.

* * *

*'The bureaucrat's first objective, of course, is preservation of his job –
provided by the big government system, at the taxpayers' expense.
Whether real world problems get solved or not is of secondary importance.
It doesn't take much cynicism, in fact, to see that the bureaucrats have
a vested interest in not having problems solved. If the problems did not exist
(or had been invented) there would be no reason for the bureaucrat to have a job.'*
WILLIAM SIMON, FORMER USA TREASURY SECRETARY

* * *

Britons are suffering a triple whammy: first, there are the problems caused by the EU; second, there are the problems caused by our close relationship with the USA and third, there are the problems caused by our own Government: possibly the most incompetent and corrupt Government Britain has ever had.

The nation (and, indeed, the world) is heading for the biggest economic crash we've ever known.

* * *

It is not difficult to compare Britain today with the final years of the Roman Empire. In the final years of the Roman Empire the middle-classes were battered into extinction but the poorer folk were becoming increasingly dependent on, and loyal to, a Government which kept them happy with bread and an unending supply of brutal and barbaric circus entertainments. Today, the Government hands out cash and the people

19

are entertained with *Big Brother*, *Eastenders* and *I'm A Celebrity Get Me Out Of Here*.

* * *

'I hate causes, and if I had to choose between betraying my country and betraying my friend, I hope I should have the guts to betray my country.'
E. M. FORSTER

* * *

The politicians think we haven't noticed.

They still think they can trick us into believing that life is better than ever before.

No more.

A growing number of people want a better life. They want lives with more meaning, less pressure and more time. They want a return to real values.

More than half the population of the UK recently agreed that they regularly dream of doing something completely different with their lives.

Most people are unhappy about what is happening to their country. Hundreds of thousands are voting with their feet; taking their families and their savings and moving abroad. Some go in search of sunshine. Most don't. Most of those abandoning the country of their birth do so because they are dissatisfied with what they see happening around them. Resentful, angry youths who feel outlawed and unwanted vandalise the streets and fight one another. Resentful, angry workers who feel outlawed and unwanted simply leave and go somewhere else; they have sensed, perhaps, that when a just law isn't enforced it will never be respected and when unjust laws are enforced the law loses respect. Most don't speak out because they feel intimidated by our politically correct society as much as by the thugs who now roam and rule our streets.

Hundreds of thousands no longer want to live in a country where it is unsafe to walk the streets at night. They don't want to live in a country where the sick must wait months for treatment and where the elderly are left dying in hospital corridors because there are no beds for them. They don't want to stay in a country where the public services aim for mediocrity and rarely reach their target. And they don't want to live in a country where they know they will be condemned as racist bigots simply for caring about their nation's heritage.

They don't want to live in a country which is rapidly dividing into two: those who have authority and those who have responsibility. Responsibility and authority used to go together. Those who had the latter also had the former. Separating authority from responsibility is one of the main reasons why our nation is now in such a mess.

* * *

The number of Britons leaving the country is rising rapidly.

Around 300,000 a year sell their homes, say goodbye to their friends and relatives and leave. Most used to go to Australia, the USA or South Africa. Today most go to Europe: France or Spain in particular. Most are middle-class, middle-age and simply seeking a better life. Most are good workers and good earners, the sort of people who contribute to society. But they've had enough of a failing infrastructure and rising taxes.

The British Government has said that it expects 20 million people to move into Britain during the next 20 years. Most of the immigrants will want to live in England; a nation which is already one of the most crowded countries in the world – four times as crowded as France, for example. (The population of Scotland is in decline and is forecast to continue to decline for the foreseeable future. The immigrants simply don't want to go that far north.) Migrants are coming into the country far faster than new babies are being born, and immigrants tend to have far more children than long-term residents. More than half of all new Britons will soon be the children of new immigrants. Since New labour took power Britain has consistently been the world's favourite destination for asylum seekers.

The Government is not worried by the expected influx of new migrants. This flood of new people will, they say, be balanced by the fact that a similar number of native Britons will leave. The New Labour Government expects 15 million Britons to move out of Britain during the next decade or so – either to Europe or to Old Commonwealth countries. (If those are the Government's figures then we can be pretty sure that they are a grotesque under-estimate. The one thing the Government is good at is getting its figures wrong.)

A survey conducted by the British Government itself showed that 54% of the British population would like to settle in another country. In other words most British people don't like living in Britain any more.

They aren't on their own. A recent survey for the magazine *International Living* put Britain well down the list of favourite destinations for people who earn their own living. The United Kingdom is level with Slovakia, just above Panama and Slovenia and only three percentage points above Estonia and Lithuania on the list. The UK is, however, very definitely No 1 on the list of favourite nations among those seeking Government handouts.

* * *

Three quarters of the people who want to quit Britain believe that the quality of life in Britain is deteriorating. They are going because of the high cost of living, the rise in crime, the traffic jams, the soaring council taxes and the lack of space.

Well over one million affluent older Britons now live abroad. They have emigrated, they say, in search of a better infrastructure and lower taxes. They have gone looking for lower crime rates, better transport, better housing, better food and better health care. The weather, they insist, is a bonus. Independent experts reckon that one in five Britons are planning to leave the country. By 2020, around 5 million older – and richer – Britons will live abroad. Naturally, they will have taken their money with them.

Other governments (including some of those from which asylum seekers are currently coming to the UK) are falling over themselves to offer tax breaks and other incentives to attract rich Britons to their countries.

It isn't difficult to deduce from all this that the nature of our population is changing dramatically.

You might imagine that the Government would be concerned. Not a bit of it. They are encouraging well-off Britons to leave.

Have they really not yet realised that if you, every year, replace 300,000 to 500,000 hard-working tax paying citizens with a similar number of non-earning immigrants you might have a problem? Either they have not, or else they realise that the people emigrating are largely Tory voters while the people coming in will probably vote for the Government which hands out the benefits. (Or could the Government simply want to weaken and dilute traditional British values – and, especially, English values – in order to prepare the nation for its new role as a series of anonymous regions within the European Union?)

BEFORE IT GETS BETTER

The sums don't add up. The future is chaos. But the Government doesn't care. Whatever happens it will be someone else's problem in a few years' time.

* * *

'I fear for our nation. Nearly half of our people receive some kind of government subsidy. We have grown weak from too much affluence and too little adversity.'
ROMAN SENATOR, SPEAKING IN AD 63

* * *

There are over 1,000 families in Britain receiving over £36,000 a year in benefits. The money comes from British taxpayers. Many of these families do not include a single member who has ever paid tax. Many are not British. In October 2003 a newspaper found a couple with four children (one aged 17) receiving a tax-free benefits package of £46,712. The family would have needed to earn £70,723 if they had been working full-time and paying taxes. Tax and rate payers were forking out over £600 a week for them to live in a hotel.

There are many families with an income (composed entirely of benefit payments) which is two or three times the average wage. This is clearly absurd (and is one of the reasons why the UK is so popular with asylum seekers). Politicians have deliberately forgotten that benefits are paid to keep people alive, not to make them rich.

Millions now expect and believe that the world owes them a living (plus a TV set, a DVD player, and a new car every two years). The demands and expectations of those receiving benefits are now so huge that, absurd as it may sound, people receiving benefits have on several recent occasions actually threatened to go on strike.

The workers, who are gradually beginning to realise that it is them and not the Government which pays for all this, are getting restless; arguing that the benefits system was designed to make sure that no one went without food, clothing, shelter and heat. It was not, they say, designed to make sure that no one went without a subscription to several satellite channels.

The Government is not impressed by these worries. According to the New Labour Government, families are living in poverty if they do not have friends or family in for a drink or a meal at least once a month, if they have any worn-out furniture in their home and if they don't have annual holidays. It is, of course, the Government's policy to eradicate poverty by boosting benefits.

No one would argue with that aim, though some might argue with the definition of poverty. Those hard-working Britons who don't hold regular parties, can't remember their last holiday and have furniture which would be rejected if they tried to give it away to a charity shop might find this rather alarming.

'I don't want to oppress anyone,' wrote one reader, 'but I am fed up with living in a lazy, dirty, greedy, resentful society.'

The unfairness of all this is producing clear signs of unrest and discontent.

Back in the early 1990s, the number of people who thought that the Government should spend more money on benefits for the poor, and should redistribute incomes from better-off to poorer people, was over 50%. By the early part of the 21st century that figure had fallen to around a third. And it's dropping fast.

In 1993 less than 30% of the population agreed with the statement: 'Around here, most people could find a job if they really wanted one.'

By 2003 70% of the population agreed with the statement.

In a book called *The Health Scandal* (first published in 1988) I forecast that by the year 2020 Britain would be facing an enormous demographic problem. That was, I estimated, the date when the number of people dependent on the State (either as pensioners or as disabled beneficiaries of Government money) would exceed the number of tax paying employees. At that point, I forecast, the whole system would finally begin to crumble. There would be a revolution as taxpayers objected to having to support so many other people.

At the time my fears were dismissed as nonsense. But it is becoming increasingly clear that the fear was justified. More than half of all Britons are now on social security and the situation is getting worse.

There are far too few people to pay for all this; the number of people who are actually working; doing real jobs, creating wealth, is diminishing every year.

Worse still the workers, the poor sorry souls who struggle to pay for the Government's largesse, must battle through miles of red tape, rows of speed cameras, real stress and the very real perils of overwork. Heart disease, cancer and stroke have replaced simple calluses and sunburn for the modern slave.

Britain has become flabby, out-of-condition and headed for the knackers yard. It is no consolation to know that the rest of Europe is in much the same condition. Nor is it any consolation to know that America has also become grotesquely flabby and is headed for even greater disaster.

As the cost of paying out benefits increases, taxes will continue to have to rise. As the number of tax payers goes down so the taxes paid by those remaining will have to rise still more. The future looks bleak. If things go on at this rate then the last Briton leaving the country will have to turn the lights out. The ones remaining (asylum seekers and those unwilling or unable to work) will, sadly, be unable to afford to pay the electricity bills.

***

The big question, of course, is why, when the economy is in such a mess, does New Labour continue to hand out so much money in benefits? The answer is simple and can be summed up in one word: votes.

With a 60% turn out of the electorate (by no means unusual these days) New Labour needs the votes of (at most) 51% of those who turn out (i.e. around 30% of the total possible vote) to win.

As the number of people receiving benefits rises steadily so New Labour can survive and stay in power without getting one vote from a taxpayer. All New Labour has to do is to make sure that they offer those on benefits more money than the other parties are offering. They can fund this by pushing up taxes without worrying. I repeat: New Labour can stay in power for ever without ever having a single vote from a taxpaying citizen.

The principle of 'one man one vote' has been corrupted by the number of people who are now dependant on the State. Britain, it seems to many, is being run by and for the people who live on the hard work of others. An overly generous benefits system means that people are encouraged to do nothing – and to allow the State to look after them. The do-nothings, who are in the majority, then vote in a Government to suit them.

It is a bizarre situation

The drones have never had it so good. The workers have never had it so bad.

WHY EVERYTHING IS GOING TO GET WORSE

* * *

The growing levels of resentment are aggravated by the Government's enthusiasm for means testing.

It is (exactly) as though householders who paid premiums to an insurance company were told that they could never claim anything back because the insurance company had given every penny it had to people who wanted 'things' but had never bothered to work or to save for them.

It is hardly surprising that the hard-working, over-taxed middle-classes are getting angry.

* * *

This book is not simply an attack on New Labour. It's an attack on all modern Governments and on (nearly all) modern politicians. I don't have any reason to believe that the Tories or the Liberals would be any better than New Labour.

Indeed, the starting point for what has gone wrong with Britain goes back beyond the beginnings of New Labour.

In some ways it really all started to go wrong in the 1980s. In 1984 Margaret Thatcher said she wanted to change the country 'from a dependent to a self-reliant society, from a give-it-to-me to a do-it-yourself nation; to a get-up-and-go instead of a sit-back-and-wait-for-it Britain'. However, although she realised how important it was to her philosophy to curb public spending she failed at this.

And it was Thatcher who strengthened the transatlantic alliance (and prepared the way for Blair's love affair with Clinton and Bush) by her relationship with Ronald Reagan.

Finally, it was Thatcher who established a presidential style government – having little regard for the views of other ministers.

The New Labour Government which is wrecking Britain so rapidly is the natural successor to the Tory Governments of the 80s and 90s. Blair is Thatcher's natural successor in every conceivable way.

* * *

'Once upon a time government budgets were balanced, our money was sound, the streets were safe and taxes imposed by all levels of government took less than 10% of our income.'
HARRY BROWNE

BEFORE IT GETS BETTER

* * *

We live in strange, difficult and confusing times.

In some ways – largely material – we are richer than any of our ancestors. In other ways – largely spiritual – we are infinitely poorer.

Superficially, we live in a wealthy, civilised society. We have motorways, nuclear power, colour television, aeroplanes, vitamin pills and microwave ovens. We have motor cars which nag us and remind us to put on our seat belts. We have central heating systems which automatically turn themselves on when the temperature falls, windscreen wipers which automatically clean away raindrops the moment they start to fall and running shoes with lights fitted into the heels. Surgeons can transplant hearts, livers, lungs, kidneys and pieces of brain and they can make large breasts smaller and small breasts larger.

Most of us live in well-equipped homes which our great grand parents would marvel at. We have access to (relatively) clean drinking water at the turn of a tap. At the flick of a switch we can obtain light to work by and heat to cook by. We have automatic ovens, washing machines, tumble-dryers, dishwashers, food blenders, vacuum cleaners, television sets, video recorders and a whole host of other devices designed either to make our working lives easier or our leisure hours longer or more enjoyable. We have computers that can perform thousands of calculations in the time it takes us to find a pencil. We can travel thousands of miles in a matter of hours.

But the world you and I live in has become a cold, cruel, brutal, heartless place. Every standard of propriety has been trashed. Politicians lie and corporate bosses cheat their customers, their shareholders and their staff; marriage is dismissed as old-fashioned and unnecessary; mainstream television shows are based on sexual excess and violence and producers vie with one another to plumb new depths of tastelessness, stupidity and irrelevance; art has been devalued so much that major prizes are awarded to talentless buffoons while genuinely creative individuals are dismissed as out-of-date and irrelevant. Today you don't have to do anything, achieve anything or create anything in order to be a television star: you just have to be vulgar and there. There are, it seems, no limits, no ethics and no rules (other than the rules the Government chooses to impose upon us). We are in decline and the fall is inevitable. Remember the Roman Empire? France before the

Revolution? Germany between the two world wars – forced to print money in vast quantities in order to pay off its debts?

Today, sadism seems endemic, resentment widespread and the notion of nationality, once regarded as a comfort, is derided as intolerably racist. Our apparent prosperity has brought with it great anxieties and insecurities. We may work fewer hours but for many commuting takes several hours a day. And then there is the endless paperwork. The demands for more and more information from statutory and commercial bodies means that we have all become professional form fillers. Just telephoning the bank to remonstrate about an error can take an hour. Many labour saving devices promise much but in reality take up more labour, time and money. The workmen who mend them know that their specialist skills are in great demand. They charge huge fees and turn up if and when it suits them. Is it hardly surprising that we live in an age of anger, frustration, anxiety and intolerance. In one recent survey of motorists, four out of every ten said they had been involved in at least one road rage incident in the previous twelve months.

In the shops, customers are now expected to do more of the work themselves. At the garage they must put the petrol in their car. When shopping they must collect the groceries from the shelves themselves. Furniture has to be assembled by hand, with the aid of incomprehensible instructions. At the bank we have to fill in our own deposit slips. At fast-food restaurants we're expected to collect our own food and clear away our own plates.

It's a long time since the corner grocery store had a chair for customers to sit on while their order was put together. And a long time since there was a boy to walk back home behind the customer, carrying the brown paper bags containing her groceries.

The incidence of violence in our society is increasing faster than at any previous time. No country in Europe (with the possible exception of Sweden) now has more crime than Britain. Just walking down a British street can be a frightening and disturbing experience and although this may be, in part, a consequence of the fact that many young British men shave their heads and tattoo themselves as though they belonged to a primitive tribe rather than to a once civilised society, there is no doubt that many young men (and women) don't just like brutality and violence but are brutal and violent.

The incidence of child abuse is on the increase. Vandalism is now so common in all our major cities that no one takes any notice any more. The incidence of baby battering is on the increase. There are now more alcoholics in Britain than ever before. And the incidence is increasing every year. Drunkeness is now widespread at sporting venues. In a wonderful piece of commercially inspired hypocrisy the authorities search spectators when they enter a sportsground and confiscate any alcohol they are carrying. But once the spectators get into the ground the authorities sell them as much alcohol as they can afford to buy. (Naturally, the alcohol inside the ground is sold at a much higher price than alcohol sold outside the ground). Women in Britain now drink far more than women anywhere else in Europe. Young women aged 18 to 24 consume, on average, more than five bottles of wine a week. That's three times the average in France. The future health problems are phenomenal. In ten years time alcohol related disease will be endemic in Britain. Why do so many drink so much? They drink because it is a way to escape from despair, disillusionment and distrust. Young people today are putting their money into the pockets of publicans and club owners rather than into pension funds. And who can blame them? They know that the money spent on alcohol will disappear but they suspect, probably with justification, that any money they put into a pension fund will probably disappear too. They are hiding from reality. And who can blame them for that?

Cruelty to animals has become so common that no one really bothers any more. Scary movies have to be made scarier than ever because the new generation of children have been desensitised to violence. One popular Web site now offers a wish list of 'Scary and Disturbing Movies, Books and Video Games'. If that doesn't scare you then it should. The incidence of serious mental illness in Britain is increasing rapidly. Millions of women and old people no longer dare to go out onto the streets after dark. Vandalism is commonplace in all our cities. No one in authority seems to care.

We have polluted our environment, fouled our seas and filled our island with indestructible rubbish. We're so used to toxic waste that we now import shiploads of it from the USA. A study of the air quality on the underground in London found that breathing the air for 20 minutes on the northern line is the equivalent of smoking one cigarette. The air at a northern line station was 70 times more dirty than the air at street level.

Why Everything is Going to Get Worse

Our roads are more congested than ever before. And dangerous, too. My wife and I don't drive very much on motorways. Twice a month or so. But three times in the last years our lives have been endangered. Once a passenger in a car travelling in front of us threw a bottle out of his window. The bottle smashed on the motorway in front of us. We were travelling in the fast lane at the time. Twice, people standing on bridges have thrown bricks at our car. The police are too busy changing the film in the speed cameras to concern themselves with such dangerous behaviour. The police force, like hospitals, railways and the Post Office, has to make money. Where is the point in trying to catch criminals when you can make a much bigger profit out of fining motorists?

(It seems as though the whole British Government is now run for profit. Just before Christmas 2003, Britain's Ministry of Defence applied to register the trademark 'British Army' so that it could be used to sell Christmas decorations and cuddly toys. Police cars in several parts of Britain now carry commercial advertisements and logos.)

* * *

The people we pay to look after us when the fates are against us, to take care of us when we most need support and help and to protect us from cruelty and injustice – politicians, judges, lawyers, doctors and clergy – have, by and large, abandoned and betrayed us.

The politicians no longer do the things they should do (the things they were put in place to do) and they interfere where they shouldn't, constantly introducing new laws which impinge upon our freedom.

The Government doesn't even trust us to run a bath without their help. In 2006 New Labour plans to introduce legislation forcing us to have temperature controlling devices on our hot water taps.

A perfect example of the stupidity and pointlessness of Government interference is provided by the fluoridation of water – allegedly done to stop tooth decay. Fluoride is added to the water supply of around 60% of the USA population but only to the water of 2% of the European population. And yet European citizens have a much lower rate of dental caries. Despite all the clear evidence opposing the use of fluoride, the New Labour Government is desperate to put fluoride into every Briton's drinking water.

The Government is constantly keen to interfere in the minutiae of our lives and yet their own collective incompetence is staggering. The disaster that was The Dome was perhaps the best example of their failure to understand the most fundamental principles of organisation. They cannot even run an efficient Post Office.

A civilised society is supposed to provide a government which is appointed by, and responsive to, the electors. It is supposed to provide protection for life and property. It is supposed to provide justice, protection from illness, education for all its citizens, health care for them when they are sick, transport and a fair, just, effective, polite and humane administrative infrastructure. In return for providing this, the government is entitled to receive tax payments from its citizens.

* * *

Our contract with the State should be null and void. According to every piece of consumer legislation in existence we have been betrayed and abandoned. Our trust has been abused. It would be arguable that we would be within our rights to refuse to pay our taxes. When you take the trust out of politics there isn't much of anything left.

The irony is that the New Labour Government now claims it has the right to interfere in states which have 'failed'. By any stretch of anyone's imagination the UK, now run by mendacious, hypocritical, secretive, duplicitous, dishonourable politicians, fits that description only too well.

In Britain today responsibility has been divorced from authority; there is no accountability and no incentive. In principle, the state machinery exists only to make life safer and better for the citizens. But today's state machinery exists to exist – and to defend itself.

New Labour ministers constantly refuse to take responsibility for their own actions; it is hardly surprising that no one else in the country seems to want to take responsibility either.

* * *

Our so-called leaders have lost their way and they're taking us with them. Most politicians don't give a damn about the people they are paid to represent. They are inspired only by self-interest, lust and greed. It is hardly surprising that Britons have lost pride in themselves and their country. The vulgarians now rule.

The law has become a discredited, distrusted sick joke. Policemen, lawyers and judges constantly abuse their authority. Their primary instinct is not to protect us but to abuse, arrest and imprison us. Everyone is guilty until proved innocent.

Political correctness, the new cover for censorship, leads to the victim being punished and the criminal being given compensation and counselling. Our courts are clogged with people suing the council because they tripped over an uneven paving slab. The UK has adopted the litigation habits of the USA and the rules and bureaucracy of the EU. (Unlike others in the EU we are made to stick to all the new regulations.) As more and more people refuse to take any responsibility for their own lives, so the amount of litigation rises. (Much of the litigation is inspired by people who are receiving government benefits and who regard litigation as a chance to earn a little extra. They are accustomed to getting money-for-nothing and it never occurs to them that money has to come from somewhere.)

* * *

Our public services are appalling.

1. On the whole doctors now do more harm than good. Iatrogenesis – doctor-induced disease – is now recognised (alongside cancer and circulatory disease) as being one of the big three killers in the developed world. The medical establishment has been bought by the drug industry and today's men and women in white coats are an insult to the memory of Hippocrates and Paracelsus. Managers, not doctors or nurses, now run hospitals. Most know as little about management as they know about health care. Caring doctors have become depressed, disillusioned and have retired. Younger doctors, exhausted but unfulfilled, now see medicine as a business not a vocation. Within a few years it will be virtually impossible to get a night visit from a doctor in Britain. When I was a young GP I would never have dreamt that family doctors would ever accept, or be allowed to accept, a contract which did not include, as its basis, 24 hour responsibility.

2. There is little discipline in our schools. The Government admits it has made exams easier so that everyone can pass them. Illiteracy levels are rising dramatically.

3. The post is getting worse and more unreliable year by year. When the penny post was first invented people in England could rely on getting their mail the next day – or sometimes even the same day. Today, even

first-class mail can arrive days late. The Royal Mail is no longer run as a service. Like the railways, the hospitals and every other public service it is expected to make a profit. When British postal workers went on strike in the autumn of 2003 they had already been offered a 15% pay rise by a company which was losing £750,000 a day. (Naturally, the government did nothing to stop the strike.)

4. There is no sense of service any more among public employees. A survey showed that three quarters of emergency workers admit that in a real emergency they would abandon their official work in order to aid their own families. Compare that to the orchestra on the Titanic.

* * *

We have access to sophisticated communications systems and we have far more power over our environment than our ancestors ever had and yet we are regularly reminded of our vulnerability and our dependence on the system we have created. We are materially wealthy but spiritually deprived. We have conquered most of our planet, and some of the space which surrounds it, but we are woefully unable to live peacefully with one another.

As we become materially richer so we also seem to become more fearful and spiritually poorer. In the 1960s people feared the bomb. Today we fear everything. The more we have the more we seem to need, and the more we learn the greater our ignorance. (And the more people there are who are prepared to take advantage of our ignorance.) The more control we have over our environment the more damage we do to it. The more successful we become the more miserable we are. The more we learn the more we forget about our duties and responsibilities to one another.

As manufacturers and advertisers have deliberately translated our wants into needs so we have been encouraged to exchange generosity and caring for greed and self-concern. Politicians and teachers, scientists and parents have encouraged each succeeding generation to convert simple dreams and aspirations into fiery no-holds-barred ambitions. In the name of progress we have sacrificed goodwill, common sense and thoughtfulness and the gentle, the weak and the warm-hearted have been trampled upon by hordes who think only of the future. Our society is a sad one; the cornerstones of our world are selfishness, greed, anger and hatred. Those are the driving forces which society teaches us to respect.

WHY EVERYTHING IS GOING TO GET WORSE

Am I the only person to have noticed drivers deliberately accelerating towards pedestrians daring to cross the road?

A survey showed that over half the cars which carry one of those absurd 'Baby on board' stickers have no baby on board. If these stickers are there (as the users often claim) to help the emergency services then these people are at best selfish and at worst criminally negligent since a fireman or ambulance man could die trying to rescue a non-existent baby.

Over half of the cars which have disabled cards on the windscreen do not contain anyone in them who is disabled. (Relatives of the disabled person use the card to get free or more convenient parking.)

* * *

We are surrounded by the gaudy signs of our wealth and the physical consequence of human ambition and endeavour. But we have created a world in which loneliness, unhappiness, anxiety and depression are commoner than at any previous time in our history. Never before has there been so much sadness, dissatisfaction and frustration as there is today.

The demand for tranquillisers and sleeping tablets has steadily increased as our national and individual wealth have increased. A huge proportion of our population cannot sleep at night without drugs. It is often said (frequently by people who really should know better) that we can only feel our own sadness. This is true only of psychopaths. The rest of us have imaginations and we can (and do) empathise with those around us.

Elderly taxpayers who need nursing care have to sell their homes and use up their savings before the State will help. (That is the same State which generously provides homes and benefits to alleged asylum seekers.) Students have to borrow relatively huge sums of money in order to pay their tuition fees at college. (In Scotland the elderly and the students are not penalised in this way. Thanks to money provided by the English these facilities are provided free of charge.)

* * *

During the last few decades we have changed our world almost beyond recognition. Advertising agencies, television producers and newspaper editors have given us new aims to strive for, new hopes, new

34

ambitions and new aspirations. At the same time they have also given us new fears and new anxieties. With the aid of psychologists, clever advertising copywriters have learned to exploit our weaknesses and our natural apprehensions to help create demands for new and increasingly expensive products. Our world has changed dramatically. Values and virtues have been turned upside down and inside out. Tradition, dignity and craftsmanship have been pushed aside in the search for ever greater productivity and profitability.

If these ever become the 'good old days' then we are really in trouble.

It is hardly surprising that all these changes have produced new stresses and strains of their own. The pressure to succeed joins with the pressure to conform and the pressure to acquire and as a result we live today in a world where the base levels of stress are fixed at dangerously high levels. Millions feel constantly stressed, tired and too busy. There is always too much to be done and too little time in which to do it. Most people run their lives at 900 m.p.h. and not infrequently find themselves fighting the urge to run away from it all.

Despite the speed of life, and the energy expended, poverty is commonplace in 21st century Britain. Thousands of old people are struggling to live on pensions that will not pay their heating bills and food bills. Pensioners struggling to survive on fixed pensions and their savings are the new poor. For thousands of old people the only choice is whether to freeze to death or to starve to death. Every winter in Britain 50,000 old people die because they cannot afford to feed themselves and keep themselves warm. While Blair keeps busy starting wars the electors who gave him power are dying of cold and hunger. In the bad old days the elderly were respected. Old age offered freedom, time and relief from the driving forces of youth. Today, our older citizens are seen as a nuisance. We ignore them as much as we can. Doctors kill them off when they can get away with it.

The elderly and the genuinely infirm are at the back of the queue in today's society; struggling to cope on inadequate pensions and never daring to make a peep of protest because they really aren't the sort to complain, even when they know that they are getting a raw deal.

These are the people who have worked hard all their lives and who thought that their work would one day entitle them to a decent pension. To the New Labour Government these are the dross; politically, economically and socially insignificant. They can be ignored because they are too proud to ask for that to which they are legally entitled let alone to demand that to which they are morally entitled. The politically correct find nothing distasteful about neglecting the elderly; many of whom probably (quite wrongly) thought that their taxes and national insurance contributions were being put on one side so that they could be given adequate pensions in their needy years.

Our politicians and the media have forgotten to care. Talking about poverty doesn't win votes and writing about it doesn't sell newspapers.

* * *

The new greed is exemplified daily by the unending stream of television shows revealing how smug property developers and bargain hunters have made money out of the rising property market (rather than out of exploiting their own entrepreneurial skills) and flogging off heirlooms to the next layer in a pyramid selling scheme for ersatz antique dealers. On one random day recently I counted the programmes on Britain's four main terrestrial channels which dealt with houses (usually as a way to making money) and antiques (invariably as a way to making money). In a single day's programming there were nine programmes dealing with property and six dealing with antiques.

* * *

Most of us are in a state of constant pertubation. Three out of every four women in Britain visit their GP with a psychiatric problem at least three times in their lifetime. One in every six women will, at some time or other, have to be admitted to a psychiatric hospital for in-patient care. The figures for men are much the same.

Depression and anxiety are the two commonest mental problems – they are responsible for at least a fifth of *all* consultations in the GP's surgery so if there are five people in a doctor's waiting room then it's a safe bet that at least one of the people sitting there will be suffering from either anxiety or depression.

Suicide rates among men (not just young men) are rising dramatically. Every year, in Britain, over 100,000 people become so disenchanted with life that they choose death instead.

* * *

Many of those who successfully commit suicide leave notes blaming their decisions on the failure of their businesses – ruined by bureaucrats. The Government seems to regard 'profit' as a dirty word (though, curiously, they expect State run operations to make a profit); fascist to their fingertips, they regard the needs of society as infinitely more important than the needs of the individual. The battle to decide whether the state is more important than the individual (or vice versa) is as old as politics. I think it is fair to say that there is not now a leading government anywhere in the world which believes that the individual is more important than the state.

Governments are there to provide a background; to oil the workings of the nation. But our Government wants to interfere with everything and, eventually, to control everything. Since most of the politicians now ruling us have never even had a job (and virtually none of them have ever run a business) they aren't very good at the controlling and, most important of all, they don't understand that individual self-interest is good for society. A baker doesn't sell bread because it's good for his customers but because it's good for him. (That's not my observation. It was first noted by Adam Smith, writing in *Wealth of Nations*). The baker wants satisfaction from his work but he also needs profit. Profit gives him a living and an incentive.

* * *

'It is not from the benevolence of the butcher, the brewer or the baker that we expect our dinner, but from their regard to their own interests.'
ADAM SMITH

* * *

Mediocrity is rapidly becoming acceptable in public life. We accept mediocre politicians, mediocre transport, mediocre food and mediocre service everywhere. Even our sportsmen have become mediocre.

'I thought we did enough to win,' has become a mantra among professional sportsmen.

We don't like it. But we don't like to say anything about it. There are two reasons for our silence.

First, we suspect that whatever we say nothing much will change.

Second, we are frightened to show our heads above the parapet.

And so mediocrity rules.

WHY EVERYTHING IS GOING TO GET WORSE

* * *

The UK is the second largest supplier of arms to developing countries. Every year British companies sell arms worth £3 billion to other countries. The New Labour Government provides arms exporters with subsidies worth £420 million a year.

Both Britain and America have for decades deliberately exaggerated the military threat (first from the USSR and now from terrorists) in order to justify spending massive amounts on arms. The arms industry is kept happy by the constant demand for new and more powerful armaments.

The new war against terror provides a great excuse for increased spending on arms. No one bothers to explain how nuclear submarines and atomic weapons can be used to quell city centre terrorists, suicide bombers and guerrillas.

* * *

We live in a world in which people are encouraged to think mainly (or only) of themselves. We stop caring because every day there are fresh outrages and frustrations to take the sting out of yesterday's angers. We are constantly shocked and bewildered, feeling more and more that we are alone, unprotected and uncared for by the people (and the society) we have been taught to respect.

Frustration and dissatisfaction are now much commoner than at any time in history. Our complex and ever changing world is constantly creating new pressures and stresses.

We are all totally dependent on other people and quite unable to control our own destinies. If someone else's motor car breaks down on our route to work and causes a blockage then we will be late. Our reliance on others means that our lives can be devastated by strikes. The postman who goes on strike, and causes heartache to millions, has his holiday ruined when the air traffic controllers strike. The air traffic controllers suffer when hospital staff go on strike. And on the cycle goes. We are all dependent on one another. None of us is immune. Frustration (a major cause of stress, anxiety and depression) is now inevitable.

* * *

Fear, jealousy, greed, dishonesty, suspicion, socially inspired ambitions and endless layers of guilt create physical disorders such as irritable bowel syndrome, asthma and high blood pressure as well as mental disorders such as anxiety and depression. Millions of women suppress their innate gentleness and femininity and struggle to acquire male-like toughness in order to succeed in a harsh and cruel world. A real vicious circle has developed: people are aggressive because the world around them is so terrible. And the world is awful because people are so aggressive.

* * *

The ultimate purpose of living now often seems to be simply to keep living. We spend much of our energy struggling to find ways to live longer and forgetting to live the lives we have.

We are constantly vulnerable to the lies of the pseudo-scientists and the media manipulators whose agendas are so well hidden. Life is now so complicated that only the specialists understand what is going on in any particular area of life. Finding the truth is nigh on impossible. Perception is now everything. We are constantly being tricked by propaganda and sophistry.

We look at where we are going but rarely at where we are. We are encouraged to think always of the joy that will come tomorrow (for example, when we retire) because this distracts us from the pain and disappointment of today.

Self-satisfied and ignorant teachers kill creativity and teach their students to imitate. Originality is punished as dangerous and subversive. We are all taught to distrust our own opinions and to respect the voice of authority.

We are in such a hurry that we never get a chance to talk. We live monotonous shallow lives, constantly hurrying but for ever wondering where all the time went: we go through life as spectators. The pressures to succeed, conform and acquire ensure that the base levels of daily stress are fixed at dangerously high levels. But on top of all this, life is full of exhausting daily trivia as European, national, regional and local bureaucrats constantly add new layers of legislation to the existing mess of red tape. Bureaucracy has a natural tendency to spread. It is the cancer of our institutions, both private and public.

* * *

WHY EVERYTHING IS GOING TO GET WORSE

People who care about what they do are regarded as eccentric. We are taught to be afraid (and even ashamed) of emotions and passions – even though there is clear evidence to show that suppressing emotion is a short cut to stress-related illness such as anxiety and depression.

Many people have completely lost their faith in the future of mankind. The world is increasingly seen as a dangerous and violent place. We have no privacy. Ugliness is all around us and contaminates our lives so that we suffer spiritually and aesthetically.

We have created a world in which we are strangers to ourselves and prisoners of the expectations of others. Millions feel isolated and lonely. Old, simple truths are constantly being replaced with new, complex, half-truths.

***

Our 'leaders' tell us that we have never had it so good; that we have more time than our ancestors ever had and that productivity is rising. We are told that health care is better than ever and that we're healthier and fitter than our parents or our grandparents.

We want to believe these lies. But we know they are lies.

There were 66,000 officially reported incidents of anti-social behaviour in the United Kingdom on just one day in September 2003. That's Britain 2003 style. Britain could win gold medals for yobbishness.

Public agencies now spend £3.5 billion a year clearing up the mess caused by vandals. But our cities are still defaced.

Our football hooligans and holidaymakers are now notorious. Britain, once great, has become squalid. Our citizens are famous the world over for unacceptable public behaviour. England football fans are so infamous that other countries regard us all as hooligans. On a trip to watch a match in Turkey, fans of the England team pulled down their trousers, shouted rude comments to Turkish women and urinated on Turkish flags in the street. The British authorities seemed surprised when fighting started. Fighting and violence between professional footballers is now commonplace. The authorities condone violence on the pitch and then seem surprised when there is violence on the terraces. Even crowds at cricket match are now infected with yobbishness.

***

Britons now top the world league for binge drinking. At the start of

40

the 1980s just 2% of deaths among young men were the result of binge drinking. Today that figure is 7%. Children of six are now routinely admitted to hospital after bingeing on lager or alcopop drinks.

Feminism seems to have encouraged modern British girls to behave like sluts. Girls claim that it is their right to behave like men. But they choose to behave like louts. Did the suffragettes really die so that young women could vomit in the streets and then offer themselves to be 'roasted' or gang banged by crowds of drunken footballers? Afterwards, these liberated women sell their stories to the Sunday newspapers. No one seems to think there is anything wrong in this. Everyone gets publicity. Everyone makes money. No one cares.

* * *

The insolvency business is one of the few booming industries in the UK. Personal and corporate bankruptcies are running at record levels – and rising annually.

* * *

Rail travel in Britain has become a dirty and dangerous (and unpredictable) business. Late night trains (when they run) are hideously dirty and covered with the remains of fast-food meals. The statistics show that trains in Britain are delayed, dirty and more prone to accidents than at any time in the history of the railways. Passengers suffered a 92% fall in reliability of the rail network but a 70% increase in costs between 2000 and 2003. When announcing this the rail regulator warned that passengers could not expect service reliability to return to pre-2000 levels until after 2013. In 1999-2000 passengers waited 7.8 million minutes for late trains but in 2002-3 they waited 14.9 million minutes for delayed trains. Network rail doesn't think it can do better than bring delays down to 8.4 million minutes by 2012- 2013.

In 2004 it was announced (quite seriously) that the failure of trains to arrive on time would in future be solved by changing the timetables and making train journeys longer. Yet another example of Britain's constantly deteriorating infrastructure.

After the Government confiscated the rail operator from its shareholders (many of whom were already impoverished pensioners) it has poured billions of pounds of taxpayers' funds into the black hole that is railway transport in Britain. Things have continued to get worse.

41

Why Everything is Going to Get Worse

***

In Britain, as in the old USSR, there is plenty of money for administration but little or no money for maintenance or for improving the infrastructure. (And, as in the old USSR, although there are armies of pen pushers on hand there are very few skilled workmen available.) In the first six years since Labour came to power the number of direct public sector jobs rose by 354,000. Today around one in four of the working population work for the Government. (And remember that most of the public sector corporations – British Telecom, British Rail and so on – have been privatised.). The British figure isn't as bad as the one in France (where one in three of the working population work for the Government) but it is clearly unsustainable in an allegedly capitalist economy.

And yet despite this army of workers nothing seems to work any more. Our infrastructure is a global joke. When there is half an inch of snow the nation grinds to a halt. When there is rain the country is flooded. When there is sunshine there is a water shortage. When leaves fall the trains are halted. When there is wind the power lines come down.

The chaos spreads from Government-controlled parts of the nation to privately-controlled parts of the nation and back again. The only certainty is that if it is British then it probably isn't working properly.

Britain's electricity strategy is a shambles and as power stations come to the end of their working lives the country is close to a crisis. Our gas network is, if possible, in an even more perilous condition. And the nation's sewage system, largely built in Victorian times is on the point of collapse. One of the reasons for the water shortages which now bedevil Britain every summer (despite the heavy rain we still get) is the fact that vast quantities of water leak out of burst mains and ageing pipework.

Under New Labour, public spending has risen by 50% but the value we get has fallen dramatically. The quality of all public services (health, education, police etc.) has deteriorated rapidly since Blair took over. We are paying more for less.

A huge percentage of our taxes now goes to pay for the inflationary pay rises and massive incomes given to people who work for the Government in meaningless, undemanding pseudo-jobs; these people have little or no sense of public service but are greedy and quick to take advantage of the compensation culture and they see Government employment only a route to wealth and security. When assistant photocopier operators in public offices are paid more than nurses in private hospitals (as they are) then you know that there is something badly wrong with the system.

It's all getting so bad that thoughtful, caring, taxpaying Britons are leaving the country in droves. Just before Christmas 2003 the Confederation of British Industry announced that one in three British firms had already started moving parts of their businesses abroad because of extra red tape and higher taxes and what they politely called 'dissatisfaction' with schools, hospitals and transport.

Voters are fed up with ever rising taxes and ever falling standards. At national and local levels taxpayers get less for more. 'Less for more' is the modern politician's catchphrase.

What a bloody country.

What's happened? Who did this to us?

We want our country back.

* * *

The trains are terrible but so are our roads where jams are created by speed restrictions designed not to make the roads safer but to increase the revenue from the speed cameras.

Ah, the speed cameras.

Speed cameras have superseded motorway marking cones as our great national achievement. There are more cameras littering our verges than you'd find in a Nikon warehouse. The Government lies and says the cameras are to keep us safe. Like starting a war against Iraq was to keep us safe. But, of course, everyone knows the cameras are nothing to do with road safety. The speed cameras are simply another way of taxing motorists and keeping down the wear and tear on the crumbling roads.

In towns and cities parking fees and fines rise at multiples of inflation as local authorities use the motorist as a cash cow. The Mayor of London introduced a new tax on motorists wanting to drive into the city. (The tax has been described as one of the few in the world which brings in less than it costs to administer. When does a tax stop being a tax and start becoming vengeance?)

WHY EVERYTHING IS GOING TO GET WORSE

***

The medical profession, pockets of which used to treat the Hippocratic Oath seriously, has sold out and become a marketing arm of the pharmaceutical industry. Doctors, nurses and other health care professionals have become a part of the selfish, uncaring society. Britain's health care is now unquestionably the worst in the so-called 'developed' world. Our medical care is now even worse than America's for heaven's sake! The evidence shows that doctors are now one of the three big modern killers; up there alongside cancer and heart disease.

We have never spent so much on health care, but our health care is poorer than it has been for decades. We are getting sicker not better. The NHS now employs more people than at any time in its history but waiting lists are getting longer and thousands of people die because they cannot get the treatment to which they are entitled. There isn't much curing going on and there certainly isn't any caring. Street crime used to be blamed on drug addicts stealing to pay for drugs. Soon people will be stealing to have their teeth done, their varicose veins repaired or their husband's cancer cut out.

Could the ever lengthening waiting times possibly be related to the fact that there are now more administrators than beds and more administrators than nurses?

Naturally, neither the politicians nor the administrators think there is a link.

Social workers are a sick joke; so obsessed with incest, daily meetings and their own sense of importance that they have completely lost touch with the real world and forgotten what compassion means. We now have more social workers than ever before but social problems are endemic in many areas of our nation. The incidence of baby battering is on the increase.

Lawyers, schoolteachers and others who might have been expected to fight for freedom are now interested only in preserving their own professional status.

Religious leaders now abstain from moral authority – they have presumably been told by their public relations people that morality is no longer a marketable commodity. It seems that Nietzsche got it right when he forecast that by the start of the 21st century moral values would be no more than a memory.

BEFORE IT GETS BETTER

* * *

Revolutionaries who dreamt of freedom, peace and compassion when they were twenty dream today of new triple tufted carpets, double glazing and ABS brakes. Today's twenty-year-olds have missed out the dreams of freedom, peace and compassion and gone straight to the dreams of triple tufted carpets, double glazing and ABS brakes.

* * *

Whatever happened to respect?

Gone.

Respect for others seems to be regarded as a weakness. Today sensitive, decent, respectful folk are constantly bullied and cheated. Teenagers proudly walk around wearing T-shirts carrying the message: 'No Respect'; as though respect was something of which to be ashamed. (I fully realise that I am beginning to sound like an old Indian Army Colonel. I don't care.)

No one ever expected respect from civil servants (who have, probably since their inception, been neither civil nor regarded themselves as anyone's servants) but these days we don't even get respect from the people whose goods we buy or whose services we hire.

'If you want someone to love you be nice to them', said one leading politician speaking off the record. 'If you want someone to respect you, punch them on the nose.'

* * *

The concept of public service no longer seems valued. The honours list was originally devised to reward individuals who had made a special, selfless, voluntary contribution to our society. These days, awards are routinely handed out to overpaid sportsmen, civil servants who have simply done their (well-rewarded) jobs and show business entertainers who have made huge sums of money out of their work. Who will be the first empty-headed bimbo to receive an honour for services to breast enlargement and topless modelling?

The honours system is now utterly pointless and corrupt and is used by the leaders of political parties to reward their financial backers, to advance their chums, to gain influence and to make themselves look good by associating themselves with popular entertainers and sports stars. In the days when sports stars performed as amateurs it made sense for them to be rewarded for representing their country. But today's athletes are, like all sportsmen and women, professionals. They don't do it for England, Scotland or Wales, they do it for £1,000,000, a flash car, and wealth beyond their wildest dreams. It's a hell of a lot easier to become a millionaire kicking a football or running round a track than it is working hard in a factory. And yet who is really doing more for their country? The millionaire tax exile athlete or the constant and hard-working man who gives his life, his health and a good chunk of his earnings to his country?

* * *

One of my readers gave up a protected job and chose to fight for his country at the outbreak of the Second World War. His health was ruined by five years in the Royal Navy. He and his wife, now both over 80 and crippled, reluctantly asked for a disabled badge for their car so that they could continue to do their own shopping. An anonymous local council employee arbitrarily turned down their request (which had been supported by their doctor) and told them bluntly that they had no right of appeal.

When the same reader needed medical help he was told that there was a 12 month waiting list for an essential investigation needed to tell him whether or not he had cancer. He was expected to use his pension to pay for a private consultation. Five days after sending his massive bill the consultant rang my reader's wife and threatened to send a debt collector if he wasn't paid promptly. They hadn't posted his cheque because neither of them was fit enough to walk to the nearest postbox.

* * *

What happened to politeness?

Do you remember politeness?

People used to be polite to one another. Or, at least, most of them did anyway. Politeness may have been a veneer of respect but it was a veneer which was valuable. When roundabouts were designed it was assumed that motorists would offer one another a certain amount of courtesy. These days, at busy times, roundabouts simply don't work and huge queues develop as motorists struggle to join the speeding circus. One expert has already suggested that roundabouts be replaced by traffic lights.

When I was a child I was taught to send a 'thank you' note if I attended a party or received a gift. How many children (or adults) bother to send 'thank you' notes these days? I regularly receive requests for signed books from charities (and even from statutory organisations). When I send the books (at my own expense, of course) I almost never receive an acknowledgement (let alone a 'thank you').

A friend of mine visited her doctor recently and was shocked to see that he had a kitchen clock on his desk. When she sat down he pressed a button. 'What's that for?' she asked. 'It buzzes when your ten minutes is up,' he told her.

These days millions of people do things which they know to be immoral or unethical. Millions are too weary and too frightened to fight against corruption or oppression. At work people are encouraged not to get involved. 'Don't commit, think short-term, think of yourself only,' is the new standard mission statement for 21st century mankind. Trust, loyalty and mutual obligation have disappeared. That sense of community which was once one of our greatest values has gone – destroyed in just a few years. Any society desperately needs the glue of fraternity that the French revolutionists added to liberty and equality. We have lost ours.

What happened to that old adage that 'the customer is always right'? It sounds comical now. But shops assistants used to be taught not to argue with customers. These days it's been turned round. 'The shop assistant is always right' makes more sense. ('And probably too busy to bother serving you' would make a good addition except that it is now probably illegal to use the word 'serve'.)

What the hell happened to civilisation? In what sense is the Britain of Tony Blair more 'civilised' than the Britain of Queen Victoria? The worst thing about New Labour is that they promised to be different. They are different only in that they are worse than any of their predecessors; more corrupt, more uncaring and more fascist.

* * *

What happened to freedom?

It has been taken away from us by people who tell us (and genuinely expect us to believe them) that the only way for us to preserve our freedom is for us to hand it over to them. How absurd. How can you preserve something by destroying it? They have taken away our choices and our freedom to run our own lives. They want to take away our initiative and our responsibility and make us totally dependent on the bureaucrats. For heaven's sake, they are even planning to make it illegal for an honest, innocent man to walk down the street with a penknife in his pocket. All this suits the politicians perfectly, of course. They want us to be dependent, compliant and quiet.

It has become nigh on impossible for Britons to protest in the streets. (According to new legislation planned by New Labour it will soon be impossible.) Those who do have the courage to protest know that they may be videotaped and photographed by the police, put into the police computer and, subsequently visited at home by the police.

We have even lost the freedom to move about freely. Travel, once one of man's great joys and privileges, has become unpleasant, difficult and, often, nigh on impossible. Travel has been made miserable (and dangerous) by the platoons of rude, aggressive, humourless guards who now infect our airports and railway stations. The terrorists have killed relatively few people but since 11/9 they have, nevertheless, affected all our lives for the worse. (The attack on the USA took place on the 11th September 2001 and should, therefore, be referred to as 11/9 not 9/11.) Travel is a fundamental necessity for education and wisdom. 'Without change our brains and bodies rot,' wrote Bruce Chatwin. The street thugs who seem to rule our cities are an immediate threat to our safety, but the biggest threat to our freedom comes from our own Government. The people whom we pay to make our lives easier are taking from us the very things we pay them to protect.

When brain specialists took encephalograph readings of travellers they found that changes of scenery (not to mention an awareness of the passage of seasons through the year) stimulated the rhythms of the brain. The stimulation eventually contributed to a sense of well-being and a feeling of purpose in life. On the other hand, tedious routine and monotonous surroundings produced apathy, fatigue and a variety of nervous disorders.

'Notre nature,' wrote Pascal, 'est dans le mouvement...la seule chose qui nous console de nos misères est le divertissement.'

I bet Pascal never had his nail clippers confiscated by a stony-faced, overweight guard with halitosis.

It isn't just the physical danger of being shot or mugged (and the risk from the police authorities is in many countries as great as the risk from robbers) it is the pre-meditated rudeness which makes travel unbearable. Flying has been a relatively unpleasant experience for decades but the expanding layers of officious guards hired to search for nail files and other dangerous weapons have downgraded the pleasure of travel by plane; it is these days far quicker and infinitely more civilised to travel by train if travelling less than 500 miles or so. (Naturally, the 'authorities', having spotted this, are now installing guards at railway stations.) Governments seem to vie with one another in producing absurd restrictions – invariably in the name of preventing terrorism. Few can match the Americans for arrogance and stupidity. When the American authorities ordered airlines around the world to stop passengers queuing up at lavatories, or walking up and down the aisle, experts struggled to find a logical explanation for the order. One analyst suggested (apparently quite seriously) that the Americans were worried that terrorists might meet up outside the loo to plot a takeover of the plane. No one seemed too bothered about the fact that standing up and moving about is the best way to avoid a deep vein thrombosis while flying. No one mentioned that deep vein thrombosis probably kills a thousand times more people than terrorists have ever killed.

* * *

Whatever happened to patience?

Gone.

Today everything has to be done in a rush, whether there is any real urgency or not.

What could need urgency less than a funeral?

I went to one recently where a car full of close relatives were, because of a road accident, a few minutes late arriving. The funeral director was asked to wait five minutes. He waited exactly five minutes and then, when the missing relatives had still not arrived, his driver raced through a 30 m.p.h. limit at 40 m.p.h. in order to make up the five minutes.

The journey was a nightmare. We didn't know our way to the crematorium and so tried to keep in line behind the hearse. There were half a dozen cars in the cortege. We were all wearing black and easily identified. But other motorists still barged in, forcing their way into the cortege, breaking up the line of cars and adding chaos and frustration to the sadness. Even a police car bullied its way into the cortege.

* * *

Whatever happened to responsibility?

Gone.

No one wants to take responsibility these days.

They will accept the authority. With glee.

But not the responsibility. Politicians don't resign these days. They laugh, shrug and turn away.

Workmen make easy promises but don't bother to keep them – causing enormous problems and endless days of disruption.

The feeling of public responsibility, and a need to put something back (which was best exemplified by the Victorians) is absent in our society. Bank employees and sports stars who earn obscene amounts of money rarely, if ever, set up charitable foundations, as so many Victorians did. Why should they? They don't feel part of a community. And they will get mentioned in the honours list without giving away any of their money. (If a knighthood is the real aim, then a donation to the Government would do far more good than a donation to charity.)

* * *

Whatever happened to justice? The linking of worth and reward, as well as legal justice.

All gone.

Our society has abandoned individual justice for collectivism. This is just another example of the state taking precedence over the individual. Another example of fascism in action.

* * *

Whatever happened to kindness?

People have been taught to see kindness as weakness. Since they have been taught to despise weakness they despise kindness too. People are fined, or sent to prison, for feeding the birds. Woe betide any modern day St. Francis of Assisi.

Somewhere we are breeding people tougher and nastier than I ever imagined people could be. These individuals despise the generous-spirited for not having covered up and disguised a trait which is widely seen as a weakness.

A survey for a women's magazine found that 70% of people think that people are ruder now than they were just five years ago.

I'm surprised only that the other 30% haven't spotted the change.

Fight with compassion and people assume you are odd. Tell the truth and you will be labelled controversial. Stand up for others and you will be sneered at because most people fight only for themselves.

Mental illness is now commoner than physical illness but the stigma is worse than ever. Prejudices against the mentally ill (and, indeed, against the elderly) seem to be the politically acceptable replacements for sexism and racism – and are much more potent for being unnoticed. We really haven't moved very far on from the days when lunatics were locked up in Bedlam and the public invited in to watch them. You think I'm exaggerating? Consider this: when, in 2003, a former world champion heavyweight boxer called Frank Bruno was admitted to a hospital suffering from depression the headline in Britain's biggest selling newspaper, *The Sun*, was 'Bonkers Bruno Locked Up'. One suspects that given half the chance *The Sun* might have offered its readers cut price day trips to see Bruno fighting with his demons or strapped in a straitjacket, preferably frothing at the mouth. Other branches of the media (including television, which usually likes to sneer at tabloid newspapers but is, in reality, usually far more intrusive and judgmental) were little better.

In a decent civilised society the editor of *The Sun* would have been placed in the stocks and pelted with eggs. But, of course, no one dares criticise *The Sun* for fear of the consequences.

Public employees in particular seem to have lost all understanding of the words 'compassion' or 'kindness'. Many readers have reported that traffic wardens deliberately hang around outside doctors' surgeries, hospitals and pharmacies so that they can 'catch' drivers who are easy prey. A man who stopped because his wife, receiving chemotherapy, felt sick, was given a ticket within sixty seconds of stopping the car. One woman who visited her dying husband in hospital was given a ticket daily after struggling to find somewhere to park. Another reader reports when she stopped her car in a church driveway so that she could give cardio-pulmonary resuscitation to a man who had collapsed in the street she asked an approaching traffic warden to call an ambulance. 'That's not my job,' responded the traffic warden, writing out a ticket and sticking it on her car.

Parking a car in Britain has become a nightmare. Evade the speed cameras and keep your licence and there is still the problem of how and where to dispose of your car legally once you get into town to do your shopping or go to work. Council and government employees get special parking areas, but the rest of us must take pot luck. Councils have turned car parking into a major source of revenue in several ways. They constantly push up the cost of parking well above the rate of inflation. Knowing that they have a monopoly they can charge what they like. I have seen no parking signs fixed two feet off the ground so that motorists can't see them. A traffic warden can then walk along a whole line of cars handing out parking tickets. I've even seen motorists issued with tickets while parked on grass verges.

It has been reported that in Manchester the authorities have put car parking regulations on posts which are passed by motorists coming into town. Visitors approaching the city at a perfectly legal 40 m.p.h. (and perhaps hunting for the appropriate turn off) are expected to spot notices, in writing just two inches high, telling them what the parking restrictions are for the town. There are no signs within the town telling motorists where or when they can park (or for how long) The same is true of many other British towns. In Wales I visited a car park where it is illegal to hand your car park ticket over to another motorist if there is unexpired time on it when you leave. The responsible Council is legislating against kindness, thoughtfulness and generosity.

The parking gestapo have become absurd. A warden recently gave a ticket to a bus at a bus stop and car owners with their cars parked in their private driveway have found tickets stuck on their windscreens. Parking attendants who give out the most tickets are, in some towns, given prizes. (Top prize in London recently was a motor car. Clearly, those selecting the prize had a sense of humour.)

Car parking regulations used to be designed to 'promote the free flow of traffic and to enhance to safety of road users and pedestrians'. No more.

A friend who knows a traffic warden socially says her personality changes when she puts on a uniform. In her civilian clothes she is kindly, courteous and gentle. Once she puts on her uniform and becomes a traffic warden she becomes officious, humourless, self-important and unthinking.

It is hardly surprising that out-of-town shopping centres are booming and town centres everywhere are filling up with charity shops and deserted premises. A combination of absurdly high rates, an endless series of local business taxes and punitive parking regulations designed simply to raise money are dealing a death blow to town centres.

* * *

What happened to quality?

We have exchanged it for speed. Not the speed of doing a good job quickly but the speed of doing any job in haste.

Whatever happened to dignity?

It has been stripped away from us. But why? And where did it go?

Whatever happened to charity?

Ah, that one is easy.

Charity got hijacked by commerce.

At one end of the scale there are huge charities which spend 75% of their income on salaries and expenses and much of the remainder on marketing and advertising to pull in more money. At the other end of the scale there are the professional street beggars.

Nothing exemplifies our something-for-nothing society better than those modern beggars who don't really need the money to avoid starvation but want it to satisfy wants for beer or drugs, and who have devalued the concept of charity.

Whatever happened to the difference between 'right' and 'wrong'? Whatever happened to truth, humility, honesty, privacy and integrity?

Whatever happened to pride and self-esteem?

Pride really isn't the sin it is usually made out to be. Pride is as constructive and valuable as any of the virtues.

'Pride, then, seems to be a sort of crown of virtues,' said Aristotle, 'for it makes them greater, and it is not found without them. Therefore it is hard to be truly proud; for it is impossible without nobility and goodness of character.'

Pride and self-esteem are today regarded as sinful and politically incorrect.

If someone does anything different, original or (heaven help them) successful they get sneered at by endless rows of jealous non-entities.

Chapter 2

Whatever Happened To Service And Customer Care?

Advertising is designed to make you feel dissatisfied. Advertising succeeds by making people unhappy. That's how it works. You see an advert and if the advert is powerful enough you feel you have to buy the product. Until you have bought whatever it is they are selling you remain unsatisfied.

The professionals who prepare the advertisements with which you are confronted are only too aware of the fact that it is no longer enough for them to tell you of the value of the product that they are selling. These days advertising agencies know very well that in order to succeed in the modern market place they must create new needs; their advertising must create wants and desires, hopes and aspirations and then turn those wants, desires, hopes and aspirations into needs.

Advertising agencies know (because they've done the research) that it is impossible to sell anything to a satisfied man. But, in order to keep the wheels of industry turning, in order to keep the money coming in, in order to ensure that society continues to expand, the advertising agencies must keep encouraging us to buy; they must constantly find new and better ways to sell us stuff we don't really need.

Any fool can sell us products and services that we need. If your shoes wear out then you will buy new ones or have the old ones repaired. If you are hungry and there is only one restaurant for miles then that restaurant will get your service. As far as the advertising agencies are concerned the trick is to get you to buy shoes when you don't need to, and to buy shoes that are more expensive than they need be; to buy food when you are not hungry and to fill your car with petrol long before its tank is empty simply because you are attracted by the offer that accompanies a particular brand of fuel. If your car is about to run out of petrol then a garage doesn't need to offer you free drinking mugs or a chance to win a holiday in Benidorm in order to get your custom.

The trick is in turning our most ephemeral wants into basic needs. In order to do this advertising agencies must use all their professional skills to make us dissatisfied with what we already have. Contented, happy people don't buy things they don't need.

The deceit isn't confined to international advertising agencies. Spin has trickled down from the top.

When, one evening, with water pouring through the ceiling, I telephoned a 24 hour plumber, I found myself speaking to a call centre receptionist who offered me an appointment four days ahead.

'But you advertise a 24 hour service,' I pointed out. 'That's right,' replied the receptionist. 'Our phones are answered 24 hours a day.'

'When I tried a competitor, also advertised as a 24 hour a day plumber, I got an answering machine. 'I'm a plumber 24 hours a day,' said this second advertiser when I eventually tracked him down on his mobile phone the next day. 'But you can't expect me to be going out in the evenings and at nights.'

We are dependent upon one another as never before. How many people can repair their own car, dishwasher and television set? But finding help (even when you are offering to pay for it) has become increasingly difficult. The deceitful advertising simply adds to the frustration and disappointment.

*** ✳ ***

'No man ever stood the lower in my estimation for having a patch in his clothes; yet I am sure that there is greater anxiety, commonly, to have fashionable, or at least clean and unpatched clothes, than to have a sound conscience.'
HENRY DAVID THOREAU

WHY EVERYTHING IS GOING TO GET WORSE

* * *

The frustration doesn't stop even when you've bought whatever it is you've been persuaded to think you need.

The manufacturer's instructions are often incomprehensible. Computers are particularly bad in this respect. The manual for one computer I bought contained no advice on how to turn it off. (There was an 'on' switch but that didn't turn the computer off.) When I telephoned the helpline a tired sounding woman told me that she dealt with several hundred people a day asking the same question. 'Why don't you suggest that someone puts a line about this in the manual?' I asked. 'That's not my department,' she replied.

Perhaps it would be cynical to point out that manufacturers make money when consumers call their helplines.

Does anyone ever find out how to use all the expensive gadgetry in modern cars? Even after several years there are dozens of knobs and switches in my car for which I know of no use. The other night I had to stop the car and leaf through the handbook to find out which switches operated the fog lights.

Little things that go wrong are exhausting and stressful and cause irritation way beyond their size. We know that repairing the dishwasher will require several frustrating telephone calls and hours spent sitting waiting for the repairman to turn up.

If you buy furniture you'll probably have to build it yourself. The huge fold-out sheet of instructions will be printed in 12 languages but none of the 12 languages will be English, or indeed anything you recognise or were taught at school.

Buy a video recorder and it will take you days to set it up. The last time I bought one the salesman insisted it was 'self-setting' and that a child could set it up in ten minutes. Not having a child handy, I paid extra to have an expert come round and set it up. In the end it took four experts three days to make it work. The fourth expert succeeded because he threw away the book of instructions and simply worked his way through all the possibilities.

To all the problems raised by over-complicated or badly designed products must be added the problems created by the packaging in which the products are sold. Shrink-wrap, in particular, can be a nightmare. It is, for example, almost impossible to open a shrink-wrapped video without the aid of a sharp knife. Getting through the packaging has become one of life's most hazardous activities and 'unwrap rage' is commonplace. A survey of 2000 over 50s showed that 71% had suffered cuts, sprains or bruises trying to open food packaging. Ring pull cans (with the ring pull fastened too tightly to the lid) and 'childproof' caps are, along with blister packs and shrink-wrapped anything, the most troublesome items.

* * *

I went into a Post Office yesterday. There were five counters. The assistant at one was chatting to a friend. At the second the assistant was very slowly sticking stamps on a parcel. (When I left nearly ten minutes later she was still sticking the stamps on the same parcel.) One assistant was explaining a passport application form to a British national who clearly didn't speak any English. A fourth counter was closed. The queue was huge.

The queues in town and city post offices will grow longer because post offices in villages are closing down at a startling rate. Villages which already have no train, no bus, no shop and no policeman will soon have no post office.

* * *

I visited three towns recently where there are more charity shops than 'real' shops. Charity shops (which get their stock free and much of their labour at considerably below the market rate) are ubiquitous – though not thriving. In order to pay their rates and insurance and their own administrative overheads, some charity shops are now having to charge so much that ordinary people can't afford to buy from them. Owner-occupied shops are now a rarity. A generation ago a shopkeeper would know about the products he sold. He would care about them too. Today's shop assistant knows nothing and cares less. Small cafes and restaurants are as rare as cheery traffic wardens. More and more small hotels are being converted into apartments as hoteliers find high rates and Government red tape a twin burden too heavy to bear. How much longer will small hairdressing salons be able to hold out? Many small shops now have to break the law (commonly by not having insurance) in order to stay in business. The combination of high rates and draconian regulations mean that it is nigh on impossible to run a

57

proper shop and make a profit. Older shopkeepers can just about struggle on for a year or two because they own their building. Those lovely little shops, run by people who cared, are disappearing rapidly. It all happens so easily. The supermarket starts to sell books. They only sell the books that they decide will be best-sellers. Because the supermarket is selling those books they become best-sellers. But the small bookshop in your town cannot compete with the price offered by the supermarket. In fact, the small bookshop probably cannot buy books at the price for which they are being sold in the supermarket. And so the bookshop, losing the sales of the most wanted books, goes bust. And next time you want to buy a book that isn't in the supermarket's chosen top few (and, therefore, isn't available at the supermarket) you won't be able to buy a copy because there will be no local bookshop.

* * *

A 1940's council house will probably last 200 years before it has to be knocked down. But today's soft wood timber-framed and breeze block constructions will probably be uneconomic to repair and will simply collapse in a generation or so's time. This rather undermines the whole idea of housing having a real value. 'As safe as houses' rather loses its meaning when you know the house will fall down before you can pass it on to the next generation. Instead of going up in price houses should (and in the future may well) go down, just as the value of modern cars falls rapidly after they are driven out of the showroom. This will completely change the economic structure of the country.

* * *

Do you remember the days when shops and businesses regarded customer loyalty as a valuable asset?

Those days have gone.

Today's successful firms no longer have the time or the money to care about customer loyalty – not unless you are a very special customer.

Big companies know exactly how good a customer you are. If you aren't rich and spending huge amounts of money on their products they would probably rather lose your custom than spend money fixing your problem.

Complaining used to bring results. No more. You're more likely to be ignored.

BEFORE IT GETS BETTER

At one big company the top 350 customers (themselves all large or medium-sized companies) are served by six people in customer service. The next biggest 700 customers are looked after by another six people. The next 30,000 customers have just two people to look after their problems. And the 300,000 small customers at the bottom of the pile have a telephone number to call. When they call the number they get a recorded message.

Dissatisfaction with airlines, banks, stores, hotels, phone companies, computer companies and just about every other type of service company you can think of is rising. If complainants ever get through to a real person they often complain that they are treated brusquely, or even rudely; they may be put on hold or simply cut off.

All this is happening because companies can easily collect information about their customers. They know what every customer is worth to them. They know that 80% of their profits come from 20% of customers and that 80% of the complaints come from 20% of the customers. They also know that the two groups aren't the same. Low margin customers simply aren't wanted.

At one stockbroker, clients who trade 12 times a year and have £75,000 in assets don't wait more than 15 seconds to deal. Other customers can wait 10 minutes or more.

Many companies use a system which enables them to identify, and then avoid, unprofitable groups of people or neighbourhoods. The companies can tell from your telephone number whether you are (or are likely to become) a good customer. When you call for the first time you will be classified before you place an order but you won't know whether you are getting directed to good or bad service and you won't know what benefits you are missing. If you are ringing a bank, for example, your ability to negotiate a deal will depend on the code the computer has given you. When you telephone an airline the company will know what sort of customer you are. If you are important they will look after you, if you're not then hard luck. When good customers telephone, a light will flash on the screen to tell the company's representative that you should be treated well. The service you get depends on your perceived value to the company.

There is no longer any such thing as loyalty to customers (though businesses expect customers to be loyal to them – and have devised a whole raft of cynical ploys to achieve this).

Central and local government offices are just as indifferent to the needs of customers. One Council I know advertises the fact that it has a 'noise complaints hotline'. This, they claim, shows how much they care about their ratepayers' needs. But if you ring the hotline you will find yourself listening to a recorded message telling you that if you wish to make a complaint and speak to a live human being you must ring back on Mondays between 10 am and 11 am.

To a small extent this is our fault, as customers. We have chosen price, choice and convenience over service. We have chosen the supermarket over the village shop because it is cheaper. Supermarkets, with our support, have destroyed and are destroying whole communities.

* * *

Advice To Help You Protect Yourself As A Consumer

1. Before buying anything ask yourself the following simple questions:
   - Why?
   - What for?
   - What do I want from this?
   - Is it genuinely beautiful, useful or fun?

2. If you buy things you don't really need or want you will have to work harder than you want, possibly doing things you don't really want to do, in order to pay for them. Life has its own bunkers and burdens. Why add more trouble to your life by accumulating too much stuff? Refuse to allow yourself to be trapped by society's lunatic values. Many people do things – and buy things – because they are trying to impress people they don't even know. Don't let that happen to you. When you find yourself buying something you know you don't need ask yourself who you are trying to impress. And then ask yourself whether or not you really care what they think about you.

   Many people are 'dead' at twenty-five: their ambitions, hopes and aspirations confined to acquiring a car with 'genuine' vinyl seats and a conservatory with electrically-operated blinds. They won't be buried for another half a century but they are doing little more than killing time until life runs out. They watch life drift by; never grasping their destiny or taking control. Thoreau was right when he wrote that 'the mass of men lead lives of quiet desperation'.

How many of your friends do jobs that they hate – and then excuse themselves by arguing that they need the money to pay for the stuff with which they have littered their lives. And how much of that stuff – paid for with blood, sweat and tears – is worth the price that has been paid? Too many people sell their bodies, souls and minds so that they can buy an ice cream maker, a timeshare apartment in Marbella and a three-piece suite in mushroom velour. Don't make the mistake of wasting your life on low expectations. Don't let your possessions own you and direct your life. The less you consume the less you need to work.

3. Keep your life as simple as you can. There are difficult times ahead.

4. Don't allow yourself to be tricked into following fashion – when it isn't going anywhere you want to go. Be particularly careful of new technology. Much new computer equipment, for example, is expensive, difficult to use and likely to break down frequently. Do the benefits outweigh the problems? Will the new equipment really make your life easier? Or will it merely add more irritation?

5. If you have a complaint about a large organisation (and you are not a favoured customer) prepare yourself for a long battle. If you want to get anything done you will have to make a nuisance of yourself – and probably make yourself unpopular with at least three people. Keep copies of all your correspondence. Keep details of the names and titles of everyone you speak to. Keep a diary of the dates and times when everything happened. And don't bother complaining unless it's a major issue – which is genuinely worth your time and effort. Most large organisations are too afraid of litigation ever to admit that they have made a mistake. The days when companies would apologise and send along a bouquet of flowers or a box of chocolates seem distant. Sadly, in my view, it is now probably not worth complaining about large State organisations such as the NHS. Such organisations have official complaints procedures but these seem to me to be designed to defend staff rather than to protect the rights of patients.

6. Obtain the name, telephone number and fax number of the bosses of companies with which you do regular business. For example, if you regularly travel with one airline take with you the name and office details of the chairman and chief executive. If you have

trouble while travelling call the boss. Most company bosses have efficient and careful secretaries or personal assistants who will be of far more assistance to you than the customer service department will ever be.

7. Electrical equipment is coming down in price so fast that malfunctioning equipment is not usually worth having repaired. When a cassette recorder stopped working I took it to a dealer's shop. They quoted £20 more for a preliminary repair assessment than the price for a brand new, much more impressive replacement. This is a scandal but in this case you can't beat the system so take advantage of it. Take a deep breath, throw away your malfunctioning whatever and buy a new one.

8. Never buy a piece of kitchen equipment or a tool that doesn't have the maker's name permanently engraved upon it. If the maker isn't proud enough to identify himself he probably doesn't expect the item to last long enough for you to be satisfied with it.

9. Be a truly discerning customer. We all like to think we are cautious customers. When making a major purchase we collect piles of catalogues, look through all the promises and try to compare the benefits of a seven speed flooter against the benefits of a titanium microskeleton. But being a discerning customer doesn't just mean making a rational decision about which gizmo to buy – it also means trying to make a rational decision about whether you really need to buy one at all. Remember that spending vast amounts of money unnecessarily doesn't make you look rich, but it does make you become poor.

10. When you find a product which works efficiently, effectively and economically the manufacturer will stop making it. So buy a few more and put them away somewhere, dry and safe.

11. We now expect the things we buy to break down within months or even weeks. Motor cars, washing machines, television sets and so on are all built with obsolescence their only real guarantee. Expensive pieces of equipment invariably break down the day after the guarantee runs out. So give them a good work-out as the final day of the guarantee approaches.

12. There is little point in asking shop assistants for help. Most have not

been trained and know very little about the products they sell. (They are usually far more interested in selling extended warranties.)

13. When you have a difficult problem to deal with at a bank, courthouse or utility company, try to deal with someone of the opposite sex.

14. We live in a world which is run by (and for) bureaucrats. Petty-minded men and women (often in uniforms) have state sponsored power which they wield with relish. This can be extremely annoying, but never try to fight a bureaucratic organisation. You can't beat a large organisation because it will always have more time, more patience and more money than you have. Organisations don't get tired, they don't feel guilty and they don't become embarrassed. Nor do they worry about losing their jobs. If you want to win, pick a fight with a specific individual within the organisation.

15. Whenever you can, choose to travel by train rather than by aeroplane.

16. Don't buy brand new products. Wait for the 'second generation' of products. If you buy a brand new gadget there will probably be teething troubles. If you wait for the second version then the teething troubles may have been sorted out.

17. Simplify your life in order to allow for the daily problems which will be created by your dependence on so many other people. Our lives are organised in such a sophisticated and complicated way that we must, inevitably, rely on other people's honesty and goodwill. Sadly, that honesty and goodwill isn't always apparent. If people all did what they said they were going to do life would be a doddle – but most of them don't and won't. Lazy, lackadaisical workers who simply don't care about anything other than their weekly pay cheque can bring chaos into the lives of thousands. Militant workers who strike at the drop of a hat can bring cities and industries to a halt. The truth is that we are all slaves in one way or another and we will drive ourselves insane if we struggle against forces which are beyond our power. The answer is to be prepared. Keep torches and candles in your home. Keep a bicycle in the garage. And learn how to deal with minor emergencies around the home yourself.

Chapter 3
The Law Is An Ass

Much unhappiness and frustration is caused by the fact that in our society the law is commonly confused with justice, liberty, freedom and equality.

In truth the law has very little to do with these fundamental principles.

Nor has the law anything to do with morality as a concept of right or wrong. The law changes according to public perception of acceptable morality.

At the end of the 19th century Oscar Wilde was imprisoned and ruined for having had sexual relationships with men. At the same time Lewis Carroll, whose hobby, as Charles Dodgson, was photographing small girls in various states of undress, was honoured by the Queen. Today it would be Dodgson who would be in prison and ruined, and Wilde queuing up to meet the Queen at Buckingham Palace.

It's important for us to know in our hearts what we think of as right or wrong because the law cannot be relied upon to give us any guidance in this area.

* * *

'Must the citizen ever for a moment, or in the least degree, resign his conscience to the legislator? Why has every man a conscience then? I think that we should be

men first, and subjects afterwards. It is not desirable to cultivate a respect for the law, so much as for the right. The only obligation which I have the right to assume, is to do at any time what I think right. Law never made men a whit more just; and by means of their respect for it, even the well disposed are daily made the agents of injustice.'

HENRY DAVID THOREAU

* * *

We like to think that the law exists to protect us as individuals. It doesn't.

Today, few individuals can afford to take advantage of the protection offered by the law. The law oppresses the weak, the poor and the powerless and sustains itself and the powers which preserve it.

The cost of litigation (and the availability of legal aid) means that there is one law for the rich and the very poor and no law for the hard-working millions in the middle – unable to afford lengthy legal battles and yet not poor enough to qualify for legal aid. The result is that the law threatens and reduces the rights of the weak and strengthens and augments the rights of the powerful.

Our arbitrary and costly legal system seems designed to disadvantage the vocal middle-classes, lest they ever dare stand up and try to speak out on behalf of their principles. Modern governments don't approve of principles. And they don't approve of freedom or free speech either.

* * *

Our misconceptions about the purpose of our law lead to much disappointment, frustration and stress. We all like to forget it but the law represents (and is backed up by) violence. The law exists and thrives because we all know that if we don't do what the law says we must do then paid law enforcement officers will beat us up, lock us up or kill us.

That, like it or not, is the way the law works and without that ever present threat of violence the law wouldn't work at all. Indeed, crime is increasing in our society because criminals know that there is very little chance of their being caught and punished.

* * *

In recent years it has become increasingly apparent that offences against the state are treated far more seriously than offences against the individual. The law, it has become clear, is primarily concerned with protecting society (and those who are in positions of influence) than in protecting ordinary citizens.

For example, those who dare to demonstrate because they disagree with the Government's policies are far more likely to be arrested or beaten up by policemen than those who break into the private homes of citizens to steal their belongings.

* * *

The Terrorism Act 2000 allows the police to lock people up simply for belonging to an organisation that the Government has decided to classify as terrorist (for example, animal rights organisations are officially classified as 'terrorist' organisations since they are a threat to big business) or for wearing the wrong clothes. Anyone who opposes the Government for any reason is likely to be regarded as a terrorist or a supporter of terrorism.

Demonstrating in Britain has been a dangerous activity for some years and things are getting worse. Demonstrations are about to be banned completely on the dubious and utterly indefensible grounds that they are a threat to our national security. (Many might argue that the illegal invasion of Iraq was a much greater threat to our national security.)

And the Government is pushing through the Civil Contingencies Bill (little more than a lowlife dictator's bill) which allows ministers to change or abolish Acts of Parliament without asking Parliament. The new bill allows New Labour Ministers to seal off areas of the country completely, to stop people moving about (or to force them to move about), to ban public gatherings, to set up special courts, to destroy or seize property without compensation and to deploy the armed forces to control the civilian population.

The new legislation will, in other words, allow Blair and his fellow party members to do what they like, when they like. The new Bill allows them to take charge of the country (and abolish Acts of Parliament which offer protection to citizens) if they think the environment, national security of human welfare 'may be endangered'. Who decides if the environment, national security or human welfare may be endangered? Blair, Straw, Blunkett and Prescott, of course.

* * *

The law exists to help society defend itself; it is used by those who represent society as a weapon with which to dominate and discriminate against individual powers and freedoms.

The law is man's inadequate attempt to turn justice – a theoretical concept – into practical reality. Sadly, our modern legal system is invariably inspired more by the prejudices and self-interest of the lawmakers than by respect or concern for the rights of innocent individuals.

The one person who really needs a good lawyer in our justice system is the innocent person. The habitual offender, the professional criminal, knows the rules, and knows how to manipulate the system. The wholly innocent citizen knowing nothing, understanding nothing and not yet knowing that police officers now lie as routinely and as cold-bloodedly as politicians, is lost.

* * *

Fortunately, most citizens are not quite innocent enough to think that the police always tell the truth.

The police are now widely regarded (even by law abiding middle-classes) as the enemy. Twenty years ago the majority of people felt reassured and comforted when they saw a police uniform. Today most people feel afraid. Not many people would dare ask a policeman the time these days.

Newspapers are constantly full of horrific stories showing that the police really no longer have a proper sense of responsibility to their employers (the public).

When police in London arrested a young man for suspected drink driving they left his 27-year-old girlfriend alone on a housing estate. It was 4 am. She had no keys, telephone or purse and spoke little English. She was raped by a man who offered her a lift and then attacked again after the first man had dumped her. When a complaint was made the police put an initial inquiry into the hands of an officer who had been at the scene of the arrest. Not surprisingly, the officer made no recommendations and did not consider disciplining himself or anyone else. The woman's boyfriend, the driver whom the police had taken away, was later found not to be over the limit and was not charged with drunken driving. The police logo in the area is '*Working for a safer London*'.

* * *

It seems to many that the police are too busy arresting the wrong people for the wrong things.

In early 2004 it was reported that the police had arrested a man who had fallen asleep at a football match. If falling asleep at a sporting event is now to be an arrestable offence then half the members in the pavilion at Lords Cricket Ground will end up snoozing in the local magistrates' court.

The police may be mere tools employed to put policies into practice but as those policies become increasingly unpopular so the police themselves lose the trust and respect of the ordinary citizens. Inevitably, the police become increasingly isolated and ever more aggressive, arrogant and resentful. The cycle tightens and things continue to deteriorate.

The police force was founded to protect honest citizens from criminals. It is our tragedy (and to a large extent theirs too) that those in charge of the police have either forgotten this or been pushed so far away from their professional roots that they are no longer aware of it. Like many large organisations the police have become a self-sufficient bureaucracy which now exists in order to exist. There is no responsible leadership from outside (from politicians) and such leadership as exists within the police force is designed to defend, protect and expand the rights and powers of the force. (Just try making a formal complaint about a policeman and watch as the whole system folds in upon itself, like a hedgehog rolling itself into a protective ball.)

There is no one left in power who cares about the legal rights of the 'people'.

* * *

No society has ever had as many laws as we have.

Since the New Labour Government took over the country it has created (as I write) 661 new criminal offences. By the time you read this there will doubtless be more.

In a way this is hardly surprising. The Labour Government, like most modern governments, consist largely of men and women who, although they may have little or no practical real life experience of the law, were originally trained as lawyers.

Lawyers, not surprisingly, like laws and regulations. They understand laws. That is how they think. You and I might think it would be a good idea to remove one old law for each new one made. Lawyers would regard that as an almost blasphemous thought.

* * *

We may have lots of laws, but few societies have had less justice.

Most of the laws which exist today were created not to protect individuals or communities but to protect the system – the establishment – or to raise money to help sustain the establishment. These days the law always puts society before individuals. Attacking or threatening the 'system' invariably attracts a harsher sentence than rape or battery because the security and sanctity of the system is considered paramount; violence against the individual merely affects the individual. Animal rights protesters who damage laboratory facilities are likely to receive longer prison sentences than people who commit murder.

The law was originally introduced to protect individuals but both the courts and the police seem to have forgotten this.

* * *

In October 2003 the courts in the UK ruled that evidence obtained from prisoners or witnesses who have been tortured is valid. It doesn't matter whether the prisoners or witnesses have been tortured in the UK, in prisons run by the Americans, or elsewhere in the world – the evidence will always be valid.

The witnesses who are tortured need not have been charged with any offence (let alone tried and found guilty of anything).

Using the attack which took place in America on the 11th of September 2001 as an excuse, the British Government has given itself the right to put people in prison without telling them why, charging them with any offence or allowing them legal representation.

Is that really the society we are expected to defend?

Is it even worth defending?

How can ordinary people be expected to respect the legal system in the UK when the courts announce (apparently without shame or embarrassment) that they will accept evidence which has been obtained through torture?

I would remind you that we are not talking here about Chile or

China. We are talking about Britain. The birthplace of Shakespeare and Churchill. The birthplace of cricket, muffins, and cream teas and the concept of 'fair play'.

Britain, the nation of the Duke of Wellington and Admiral Horatio Nelson, now officially tortures people who haven't been charged with a crime (let alone convicted) in order to obtain 'evidence' which can then be used to arrest other innocent people.

We presumably now have official torturers. Are they civil servants? Do they get paid a fee or a salary? Are they eligible for promotion? What pension rights does a torturer have in New Labour's glorious Britain?

This is what Tony Blair has done to our country. He has learned well, too well, from the Americans. No wonder Blair did not complain too loudly about the Americans keeping innocent Britons in the concentration camp at Guantanamo Bay.

* * *

Powerful lobby groups representing criminals of all types have given offenders significantly greater rights than victims. It has become politically incorrect to worry about victims and politically correct to show concern for those who commit crimes. In the UK today there are around 20 organisations providing care, support and sympathy for victims but there are over 400 organisations (many of them receiving taxpayers' funds) providing care, support and sympathy for criminals.

A teenager gang leader who was jailed for terrorising his community, and banned from the district where he had terrified residents was, on his release, put into a hotel room which was equipped with en suite facilities and satellite television. The youth had 26 separate convictions for stealing cars, trespassing and other offences. The police said they thought the youth had committed many more offences but that witnesses were too scared to give statements. Publicly hired counsellors were said to be working with the youth to address his specific needs. (Maybe room service wasn't up to scratch.)

When another convicted criminal failed to keep to a curfew he had been given by a court the curfew was repealed. The court did this on the grounds that the criminal 'clearly found it difficult to stick to'.

* * *

BEFORE IT GETS BETTER

Our politicians lie about everything. They do it routinely, regularly and repeatedly. They call it 'spin' as though that makes it OK. But it isn't 'spin'. And it isn't OK.

For example, the Home Office has produced statistics purporting to show (and reported in the media as showing) that the reconviction rate of young offenders fell by 22% between 1997 and 2000. (The first three years of Blair's reign.)

Now, people who saw these statistics probably found them difficult to believe. We all know darned well that our streets are more dangerous than ever. In many parts of the country it is impossible to leave a car on the street and expect to find it there, undamaged, upon your return. Millions of people – particularly the elderly and the infirm – no longer dare to leave their homes after dark.

When we see the Government telling us that things are getting better, but in our hearts we know that things are getting worse, we lose faith in our own judgement. We wonder if perhaps it's just us. Maybe we live in a bad area. Maybe we have had unfortunate experiences. And that, of course, is precisely what the Government wants. Despite our scepticism most of us tend to believe what we read and we tend to believe what the Government says. When what we hear doesn't match what we see we tend to lose heart and faith in our own judgement. 'What can I do about it anyway?' we ask ourselves, turning our faces to the wall.

The real truth is that the statistics are just lies.

New Labour politicians have decided that they will judge the Home Office according to the Government's own pre-defined definitions.

'The Home Office's success in its fight against crime will be judged on outcomes which have been defined in agreement with the Treasury,' begins the Government's statistical paper showing that crime by young people is going down.

Just how do they do this? How do they prove that it's sunny and it's Saturday when in reality we all know that it's wet and it's Thursday?

Easy.

Here's how they did this one.

The official statistics exclude young people who have been sentenced to imprisonment.

Huh?

Quite.

The sleight of hand might be convincing but the Government's claim that crime was falling is a lie. In 1997, the year that Blair came to power there were 46,300 children aged between 10 and 17 sentenced for indictable offences. By 2002, after five years of fiddling the figures, the number of indictable offences committed by criminals aged between 10 and 17 had still gone up to 49,200.

That, however, isn't the only piece of trickery.

The Government's figures seem to prove that the best way to deal with young criminals is to tell them off. You don't stick them into a cell (an expensive way of getting young voters off the streets). You give them a damned good ticking off. Well, a bit of a reprimand. And when you do this they are far less likely to be naughty again.

How one earth does the Home Office prove this?

Again, it's easy.

They have made sure that the police catch loads of young people doing things which aren't very naughty at all (crossing the road when the lights are red, playing a radio loudly, defacing posters of Tory politicians) and then tell them off. (Obviously defacing posters of New Labour politicians would merit a long prison sentence.)

These kids were never hardened criminals and the chances are that they would never have done anything bad again. And when the police don't catch them doing anything else naughty the Government can state that their 'ticking off policy' has worked wonders.

You don't have to think about this long to realise that it is absolute cobblers. Taken to its logical conclusion it means that the very best way to deal with offenders will be to do nothing at all. If the mildest punishment works best then no punishment will probably work better than a mild punishment. Indeed, logically, the best remedy is probably not to punish kids for committing crimes but to reward them.

And that would be daft, wouldn't it?

Er, well no, actually.

That, believe it or not, is exactly what the Government is now doing.

One policeman recently told me that a young criminal he'd arrested had subsequently boasted to him that his punishment consisted of attending a supervised surfing outing once a week. More serious offenders are sent abroad. Young burglars, for example, may be forced to spend a month scuba-diving off the Great Barrier Reef. (This is not a joke.)

How long will it be before criminals commit extra crimes so that they can be sent to the Caribbean rather than being given a fortnight surfing in Cornwall?

* * *

Many crimes are committed by drug addicts and there is much sympathy among professional 'sympathisers' for drug addicts who mug and burgle in order to pay for their habits.

The professional sympathisers seem unaware that in due course, and as a direct result of the trauma they have endured, many victims become addicted to far more dangerous and addictive drugs than the drugs the criminals choose to take. Heroin and cocaine are not very addictive at all (they are, for example, far less addictive than tobacco or alcohol and aren't in the same league as many prescription drugs – particularly benzodiazepine tranquillisers).

Drugs are not the cause of the crime in our world. Drugs – alcohol, tobacco, cannabis, heroin, glue or whatever – are merely a symptom of the disaffection so many people feel. The sympathy and support drug addicts receive often encourages their addictions. Their victims must suffer the consequences of the crimes committed by drug addicts without either support or sympathy.

* * *

Having created a criminal-friendly environment in which criminals know that their chances of being caught are exceedingly slim – and that even if they are caught the chances of their being punished are slimmer – New Labour now plans to let persistent petty criminals escape prosecution if they write letters of apology.

Unbelievably, vandals, thieves and people guilty of assault can escape with a caution if they are prepared to say sorry to their victims. The Government has said that it may also allow criminals accused of robbery, burglary and violent attacks to take advantage of this new scheme. There are no plans to have a limit on the number of apologies a criminal may make. (There is, of course, no way to check that an apology is genuinely meant.)

The Government is introducing this scheme to help 'cut' crime figures and this it will certainly do.

Only a Government Minister with 24 hour police protection could have possibly thought up such a scheme.

When he first heard about this particular piece of nonsense a friend announced he was planning to catch a train to London, after first stuffing a sheaf of photocopied apologies in his pocket, to thump every New Labour Minister he could find.

This scheme is stark raving bonkers, of course. I don't know whether it came from the EU or is something Blunkett thought up in the bath but the end result will inevitably be another dramatic rise in real crime. The scheme won't help the victims of crime. And it won't help the criminals. (Constant forgiveness destroys the soul.) But it will help the Government.

Incidentally, this utterly potty scheme does illustrate another problem New Labour politicians have got: their inability to think consistently.

This new legislation depends entirely on trusting criminals to apologise in good faith.

But at about the same time as they were announcing this piece of Alice in Wonderland lunacy, New Labour announced plans to arrest adults who befriended children with the intention of abusing them.

You can see where they're going with this, of course. It's a vote winning ploy designed to appeal to readers of *The Sun* who would like to see all paedophiles hung, drawn and quartered before being sent down for life.

But how, pray, will the authorities know (let alone prove) the intentions of adults who befriend children? I predict that this absurd new law will simply make it quite impossible for any adult to speak to any unrelated child without being hauled away by the New Labour Gestapo. We have already created a society in which it is quite impossible for a passing stranger innocently to stop and push a child on a park swing. It is already no longer possible for an adult to buy a passing child a bag of sweets or an ice cream. How many adults would dare stop to help a child who was lost in the park or in a store? I have a strong suspicion that in some instances when paedophiles kill their victims it is because they know that the punishment for molesting a child will be as great as the punishment for killing one. If you push people too hard they will kill because it doesn't matter to them. Anyone who works with choirboys, scouts, guides, or youngsters wanting to be coached in sport, music or anything else is exposing themselves to an absurd and unacceptable risk. How can the male adult who coaches a boys football team possibly prove that his intentions were wholesome? He can't. And so, in our new 'guilty until proved innocent' society, the courts will undoubtedly find him guilty and lock him up. It is typical of the current Government that they should put a huge amount of effort into an utterly impractical piece of legislation designed not to protect children but to win votes (and, at the same time remove freedom) while they steadfastly ignore the abuse of the mentally ill and the elderly. (There are no votes to be won by protecting either of these groups.)

* * *

New politically correct legislation means that citizens are no longer allowed to protect themselves or their homes. If you catch a burglar in your house and lock him in the bathroom you are likely to be arrested for kidnapping. Catch a burglar and accidentally bruise him and you'll find yourself facing charges of assault. Leave garden tools carelessly lying around and if a burglar trips up in your garden he'll sue you. A burglar who ripped his clothes climbing over a gate and smashing his way through a window sued the householder for damages.

The police are, with increasing hysteria, demanding that if the public want to stop crime they themselves should do more. This illustrates, better than anything, their complete failure to understand the mood of the country. Millions of citizens would love to be able to arrest troublemakers, vandals, muggers and other criminals but they know that if they do it is they, and not the criminal, who will be arrested. (It seems relevant to point out that in a police or fascist state it is always rare for the people to go to the aid of the police.)

♦ A father spent 17 years turning a muddy a pond into a picturesque idyll. He planted flowers and put fish into the pond. When he spotted a group of boys throwing rubbish into his pool he caught three of them and told them to remove the rubbish from the water. The following evening, at 11 pm, the pond owner was arrested by eight policemen. He and his son were subsequently sentenced to 80 hours community service, electronically tagged for four months, given a criminal record and told to pay £519 each in costs. The boys were not punished. One was given counselling to help him over the upset.

♦ A businessman who stood up to two youths who were vandalising his home was arrested after he reported the incident. The youths were not arrested.

♦ A disabled pensioner who defended himself against a gang of youths was cautioned by police when he reported the incident. The police told him that he could face assault charges. The police made no attempt to catch the criminals and didn't even ask for their descriptions but they did warn the disabled pensioner that if any of the gang made a complaint they would arrest him.

♦ A woman who caught three boys vandalising her garden centre was about to call the police when the boys pleaded with her not to do so. The woman unwisely agreed to let the boys mend the hedge they had damaged getting into the nursery. As a result the woman was arrested and spent a day in police cells. She then had a seven month ordeal waiting for her case to reach court. In the end she was bound over to keep the peace for 12 months. The woman complained that she had endured thefts, burglaries and smashed windows but often had a hard time getting the police to respond.

A senior policeman recently attacked the public for not making more citizen's arrests. Is he mad?

It seems that these days whenever anyone does make a citizen's arrest he is arrested – and then usually hit with a civil lawsuit for damages. No one in their right mind would tackle a burglar or go to the help of a policeman in trouble. The police have only themselves to blame for this sad state of affairs. The police seem to have lost the plot. They seem unable to understand what the public does and does not consider to be a crime. The police did themselves no good at all when they arrested a man who had been collecting and selling balls which golfers had hit into a lake in the middle of a golf course. The golfers happily bought back the balls they'd lost. They didn't care. Where was the crime? Where was the victim? Where was the criminal?

* * *

The fact that crime is now commonplace, and that members of the public are nervous about trying to interfere, has encouraged even ordinary citizens to adopt a topsy-turvey view of the world. After an elderly woman was badly beaten up in her bedroom by a burglar a woman on local radio expressed (with apparent sincerity) the view that the woman was responsible for her own beating because she had left her bedroom window open.

And after a burglary in my neighbourhood (when a burglar tried to get into eight homes, stole from two and stole from two cars) a neighbour told me, as though being helpful, that he had seen a strange man climbing a fence into our garden at 7.30 pm the previous evening. He chose to keep this information to himself until 20 hours later. Such is public responsibility and community spirit these days.

* * *

The Government claims that crime is falling but if you want to be a spoilsport all you have to do is to look at the real crime figures and the real, unspun, figures for recidivism. These, you will probably not be surprised to hear, show that crime and recidivism are both rocketing.

Your eyes have not deceived you. The politicians have.

New Labour constantly claim to be tough on crime (and the causes of crime) but in fact they are pitifully weak on both. The crime figures show that (despite constant massaging) there are more crimes now than ever before. When a friend reported that she'd been mugged an officer gave her a reference number of 544. "Is that the number of local muggings this week?" she asked, horrified. "Oh no," came the reply. "That's the number so far today."

The number of street robberies in England and Wales rose faster during Tony Blair's first term than crime rose anywhere else in Europe. Muggings rose by 92% between 1997 and 2001. Robberies went up three times as fast as the average in other EU countries and the UK figures, unlike the figures elsewhere, cleverly exclude shoplifting, crime against children and crime against businesses.

New Labour has constantly promised more police. But the number of policemen on the streets has fallen and the number of police employed is now lower than almost anywhere else in Europe.

New Labour say this isn't true, of course. They say they have recruited millions of policemen and that there are policemen now standing on every street corner. Unfortunately these, like the doctors they claim to have recruited, are invisible to the normal eye. Things aren't helped by the fact that in Britain we have more policemen involved in speed camera management than any other country in the galaxy. The authorities do not seem to realise that the increase in the amount of violence on our streets is connected to the fact that most policemen are now so busy tending to speed cameras that they no longer have time even to drive around commercial or residential areas. Most children have probably never seen a policeman walking and may, indeed, be unaware that policemen do have legs.

A crime involving a gun now takes place every hour in Britain – a country which was, until just a few years, almost free of guns. The figures show serious recorded crime going up and up like dot com share prices during the Internet boom. The figures for violence, assault, possession of weapons, murder, wounding, criminal damage and sexual offences are all going up rapidly.

And since thousands of victims no longer bother to report crimes (thousands more can't find a police station open or get through to anyone to whom they can report a crime) the real figures are undoubtedly far, far worse than the ones we think are real.

* * *

Why have crime rates soared so fast and so high?

A few decades ago most criminals had a real and understandable motive. Lust, greed, jealousy – the reasons for violence may not have been excusable but they were at least explicable.

If you picked your friends carefully, avoided angry scenes at home and stayed away from notorious trouble spots you could pretty much rely on keeping violence out of your life. Mindless, motiveless crimes were rare. The frail, the weak, the innocent, the poor and the elderly could walk freely through our towns and cities.

Not any more.

Today we live in an awful, frightening world and life, for millions of gentle, law abiding citizens has become a living nightmare. I doubt if anyone doesn't know, or know of, someone who has been the victim of a senseless, wicked crime. Why? What is going on?

An increasing number of violent crimes are committed for their own sake – for kicks rather than for rewards. Many of those who commit these motiveless crimes come from comfortable backgrounds. The crimes aren't committed because of poverty, hunger or real needs: they are, instead, a result of a lack of personal responsibility and discipline: they are a result of a lack of compassion.

Today's criminals seem to be inspired by boredom and frustration as much as lust or greed. Today's criminals are the pampered and cossetted children of the welfare society. They have been cared for and looked after and they have learned to regard security as their right. They take but they do not give – they don't know how to give. They expect everything and offer nothing.

Even worse we have created a society in which violence is glorified. Television shows endless programmes teaching children the power of the gun, the knife and the fist. By the age of twelve children have seen thousands of murders committed in their own living room. We ban sex from our screens but welcome violence into our homes. Popular soaps such as Eastenders (broadcast on the BBC with licence payers' money) seem to me to concentrate on violence to the exclusion of almost everything else.

Professional footballers, (whose predecessors used to take their position as role models seriously), kick and punch on the pitch without any thought for the example they are setting to young spectators. Off the pitch footballers drink, brawl and visit nightclubs to find girls to gang-bang.

Newspapers and magazines report all this ugly decadence with great glee; filling their pages with pictures of half-dressed women with their silicone enhanced breasts dangling out of their underwear.

We have created a world in which the future holds so little hope that thousands of teenagers simply do not care what happens to them. Millions of young people have given up all ambition and all hope. They know that they don't stand a chance of getting decent jobs. They know they can't change the corruption which exists in high places. They know that they are doomed to spend their lives being pushed around, being hassled and being patronised. The Government lies, banks steal and doctors cheat. Is it any wonder that young people simply don't care about anything or anyone?

The boredom and dissatisfaction of these new criminals is deeply ingrained. Many of those who roam our streets looking for excitement are full of suppressed anger; they are looking for trouble because they are frightened and their lives are devoid of challenge. They are so alienated from the world in which they live that they don't care whether they live or die. Their lives are so empty of purpose that threatening to deny them life is no longer an effective punishment. The police cannot control the new rebels because none of the weapons in their armoury are relevant.

Why Everything is Going to Get Worse

***

Law abiding citizens of Britain feel alienated from the police, the courts, the Home Office and the entire British legal system. They feel alienated for a number of reasons.

The authorities have consistently failed to do anything to halt the rise in crime in Britain. The authorities don't bother much with preventing burglaries or catching the perpetrators and so crime rates go up and up. According to Home Office figures the police recorded 889,000 break-ins during 2003 but only 26,300 offenders were convicted and of these just 13,350 were jailed. That means that 1.5% of burglars go to prison and 98.5% go free. (This is, of course, one of the reasons why insurance premiums have rocketed recently). Law-abiding citizens don't feel safe on the streets. Indeed, they don't even feel safe in their own homes. Criminals know that if they are caught they will suffer little if they have attacked the householder, or even killed him or her. There is a positive incentive for criminals to be violent.

The anger and resentment felt by ordinary citizens is enhanced by the widespread feeling that those in authority (themselves invariably safeguarded by permanent police protection) simply do not understand the anger and feeling of betrayal which most ordinary citizens feel at the way their lives and property are left without protection. Even traditionally quiet country towns have, in recent years, become increasingly unpleasant and, indeed, dangerous. Millions of people now no longer venture out of their homes after dark because they know that there will be gangs of belligerent youths strutting through most built-up areas. There will not, of course, be any patrolling police officers to be seen.

When a woman, living alone, awoke to hear burglars plotting to break into her secluded home in the middle of the night she telephoned the police for help. She was told to call the local environmental health department (which would undoubtedly have had an answering machine taking calls) if the intruders were being noisy and disturbing her sleep. (I'm not making this up.) Roused to fury she let her tiny pet terrier into the garden. The dog bit one of the crooks. When the woman rang the police and told them this they warned her that she could be arrested for injuring the burglar.

When the burglars had finally retreated the woman lay awake waiting for the police to call. They never came. She was probably lucky. They might have arrested her.

We would perhaps all benefit if judges and politicians lost their police protection and were exposed to the same dangers as the rest of us. If a few more judges were burgled and mugged and a few politicians arrived home to find the TV set missing then our streets and our world might become safer.

Do these people realise that citizens who have been burgled peer through the windows at the slightest noise, become obsessed with locks and daren't go downstairs at night? I know people, sane, sensible people, who now keep all their most treasured possessions in their bedroom when they go to bed at night. They double lock the bedroom door and they don't open it again until it's light.

The Government now use the police to oppress the public and to suppress debate and opposition to government policies. In the last few years the police have been given extraordinary new powers. Using money laundering, illegal drug trafficking and, most recently, terrorism as an excuse the Government has, in a very short period of time, introduced an almost endless series of bills which have taken many long established freedoms away from ordinary citizens and given extraordinarily draconian powers to the police. A growing number of people admit that they are now more frightened of the police than they are of criminals. Tony Blair's New Labour Government is tougher on protestors and demonstrators than any other Government ever has been. And things are going to get much, much worse. New legislation is being introduced which will make it illegal for anyone to travel to a demonstration ever again in Britain. (I have personal experience of this legislation for I have already been stopped from travelling on a public highway because I was travelling to a planned demonstration.)

The standard police excuse for failing to put down their mugs of tea and do something is that they are woefully under-manned. But there are always plenty of policemen for persecuting politically inconvenient demonstrators.

The law has itself become a tyrant. The Labour Government (which has, to the astonishment of many, turned out to be far more right wing and repressive than any Conservative Government) has given the police powers (granted, inevitably, under the convenient catch-all excuse of 'anti-terrorism legislation') of random stop and search. Those who dare to attend demonstrations (against almost anything) seem particularly likely to have their collars (and everything else) felt.

This happened to me in Oxford, when heading for the railway station after giving a lecture.

I was stopped, made to get out of the car in which I was travelling and detained and searched. My belongings were spread out on the pavement in the suburbs of Oxford and I missed my train.

My crime?

Travelling as a passenger in a car and intending to catch a train.

The police claimed that the 'occupants of the vehicle had been seen acting suspiciously'. The search record for me says that they were looking for 'implements for commission of crime'. The search record for the car says that they were searching for 'weapons'. (The police did not seem to be armed when they stopped the car in which I was travelling. Something which would, it seems to me, have been commonplace precaution for police officers stopping a vehicle suspected of carrying weapons.)

The order to search us came, the police said, from one of their 'command posts'. (This is significant because what subsequently happened was clearly not occurring at the whim of one or two policemen in a patrol car.)

The police van which stopped me contained nine police officers. These were quickly joined by another two officers, in an unmarked police car. One of the officers in this car carried a video camera. The camera was used to film me from every possible angle. (Not by accident I had a tape recorder and a camera with me. I photographed and taped the entire proceedings and kept my mobile telephone switched through to the editorial offices of a national newspaper. I recommend this course of action to anyone who is stopped by the police.)

Eleven police officers were not considered enough and a third car, carrying an additional two officers was also called.

So, there we all were, me and thirteen police officers, on a Saturday afternoon in Oxford.

The four vehicles were parked on a narrow road which has double yellow lines down both edges. Three cars were parked on one side of the road. One car was parked on the other side of the road. There was, inevitably, great inconvenience to passing motorists. All had to slow down. Many, wound down their windows to stare at us. I was forced to empty out my pockets and my bag and I was searched by a policeman. My belongings were lain out on the pavement. Even an apple I had been eating was handled by one of the policemen who was conducting the search. Maybe they thought it could be a hand grenade in disguise. Maybe apples are now officially regarded as dangerous weapons. Maybe the fact that it was organic was considered a legal hazard.

In a way the whole thing was a farce. One officer spent some time examining my telescopic umbrella in silent wonderment. He peered at it like a savage looking at some piece of mysterious Western technology. When another studied the personal alarm which I carry to protect myself against street criminals I eventually took it off him and pulled out the pin which set it off. I'm delighted to say that it startled him. I don't think he'd ever seen anything like it before.

Eventually, they let me go – although they insisted on following the car to the railway station. I was not overwhelmed with apologies for my time being wasted or for the fact that I missed my train.

Goodbye Freedom. Hello Police State.

On a previous occasion I travelled to Oxfordshire to speak at a rally drawing attention to the Labour government's failure to fulfil its pre-election promises to ban hunting, halt badger killing and set up a Royal Commission to investigate the value of animal experiments.

I didn't get to speak.

The Government banned the meeting and stopped me travelling.

I took the Chief Constable to court for failing to give advance notice of an exclusion ban which prevented me travelling to the site of a planned demonstration. The police didn't announce the ban until demonstrators were already arriving in the area. At best this was discourteous. At worst it was intended to annoy, aggravate and waste time and money. I was not particularly surprised when the judge threw out my case.

What has happened to our right to protest?

What has happened to our right to travel about freely?

What has happened to our freedom to speak out about issues which we care about passionately and deeply?

Of course the Government doesn't just disapprove of protests about animal abuses. Protests about China, America, the war against Iraq and many other things seem to attract disapproval, heavy policing and, on many occasions, either a ban or a commitment to heavy-handed policing designed to intimidate would-be protestors.

While Government ministers race by in a cavalcade of expensive black limousines (rather like Russian ministers in the 1970s) demonstrators have their flags and banners confiscated and find themselves in the back of a police van.

During an unwanted and unpopular visit by the Chinese president Jiang Zemin to London in October 1999, demonstrators were forcibly removed from places where the Chinese president might see them. Their banners were seized. Blair declared (as compensation for this suppression of public protest) that he had raised human rights issues with the Chinese president. However, several years later Clare Short, a former Cabinet Minister, admitted that she had been at the meeting between Blair and Zemin and that Blair had done no such thing.

The New Labour Government is constantly bringing in new laws to make protesting and demonstrating more difficult.

(The one group of people who seem to be able to protest without any risk of attracting political or police disapproval are those campaigning on behalf of hunting. In the autumn of 2003 thousands of pro-hunters signed a petition claiming that if a law was passed outlawing hunting with dogs they would ignore it and carry on hunting. If pro-animal campaigners had arrogantly announced their intention to break the law I rather suspect that the authorities might have used its various new legal powers to charge the protestors with conspiracy. At least one magistrate stated openly that he would not find anyone guilty of a hunting offence – I wonder if he treated anti-hunt protestors with equal kindness. I wonder how the authorities would respond if an anti-hunting magistrate (were there to be one) announced his intention to find all hunt saboteurs not guilty.)

There are always plenty of policeman available when politically inconvenient protests need to be squashed.

When a group of protestors burnt a bonfire with effigies of welfare scroungers, campaigners called upon the police to use anti-race discrimination legislation and arrest those involved. No one bothered to explain (or even wonder) which racial group might be represented by welfare scroungers. Indeed, I would not be surprised to find out that welfare scroungers had, indeed, become a race of their own – entitled to the full protection of the law.

BEFORE IT GETS BETTER

* * *

There is a general feeling that the Government and the police are obsessed with pursuing middle-class, law abiding motorists – an easy source of revenue for the Government and targets who are unlikely to shoot, fight or complain for the police. This is no misconception. In 2002 British courts sent 10,178 burglars and 15,039 motorists to gaol. The vast majority of the motorists gaoled had been convicted on minor offences and this seems to be more evidence that the authorities do seem to prefer tackling law abiding motorists – who are likely to pay their fines without protest – than tearaway criminals who are likely to be difficult to 'process'.

* * *

Criticising the police, or daring to comment on their methods, can be a dangerous business these days. When a businesswoman stood up for motorists at a public meeting she was subsequently branded a racist though some found it a little difficult to understand why accusing the police of hounding drivers could in any way have the 'sinister racist undertones' of which the police later complained.

Motorists complain about absurd and unfair parking restrictions, bizarrely and illogically situated bollards, chicanes and speed humps (all of which add to congestion and increase the danger on the roads) but nothing illustrates the divide between the way the police operate and the way the public (their employers) want them to operate better than the speed camera, widely promoted as being used to prevent road accidents but now generally accepted as being used primarily as a way to tax motorists for using roads.

The Chief Constable of Durham has said that there is nowhere in his area where he believes a fixed camera would help save lives or prevent serious injury. The accident rate in Durham is 30% lower than the national average. The Chief Constable of South Yorkshire has blamed speed cameras for wrecking the police force's relationship with drivers. The Commissioner of the Metropolitan Police has said that he doesn't approve of the use of speed cameras as money-making devices. And the police chief who was responsible for introducing speed cameras to the UK has called for their growth to be stalled and has admitted that all three of his children now have speeding convictions.

WHY EVERYTHING IS GOING TO GET WORSE

Enormous numbers of policemen are now, it seems, fully occupied operating and looking after speed cameras. The Government has recruited the enthusiastic support of police forces by giving them a 'cut' of the take. The result is that a huge proportion of the policemen available to prevent crime and protect citizens are now occupied spending their time sitting on or behind motorway bridges catching speeding motorists. (The police now take speed cameras so seriously that motorists have been arrested for making rude gestures at them.)

Over 40 police forces have already joined the Government scheme which enables policemen to keep some of the revenue obtained from fines. The number of forces applying to join this bizarre 'cash for cameras' scheme is rising rapidly. Chasing criminals costs money and, as far as the police and society are concerned, offer little. On the other hand, chasing motorists (or, better still, merely taking photographs of them) can be an extremely profitable business.

Perhaps as a result of the fact that the police can now make money out of arresting motorists many complaints are made that speed cameras are positioned not to stop accidents but in order to make money. For example, one favourite trick is to put a speed camera at the end of a stretch of roadworks on a motorway, where the speed limit changes from 50 m.p.h. to 70 m.p.h. The camera will be situated between the end of the roadworks and the start of the derestricted zone. The idea is that motorists, seeing that the roadworks are finishing will speed up and get caught by the speed camera. On one occasion when a camera was mistakenly put *after* the derestricted area had started more than 2,500 motorists were each fined £60 (and given three points on their licences) for exceeding 50 mph in a 70 mph zone. The authorities which had put the speed camera in the wrong place said that they had no intention of telling motorists that they had been wrongly fined. It was, they said, up to motorists to appeal against their convictions.

The speed camera industry is so profitable that three quarters of the revenue raised this way is simply used to buy and erect more cameras. Speed cameras have become one of Britain's most successful, self-sustaining growth industries. Both police and local authorities set secret targets for the number of drivers they intend to trap. (If the cameras were there to prevent speeding there could surely be no targets.) Speed limits are altered and suddenly lowered to increase the number of motorists being caught.

BEFORE IT GETS BETTER

Burglaries, muggings and vandalism rise inexorably. The police are so incompetent that conviction rates fall. Crime is so commonplace that, despite the fact that numerous criminals are allowed to walk free, prisons become ever more crowded. The only success the police have is in prosecuting (or should that be persecuting) motorists.

Anger is also caused by the fact that more and more police forces are illegally parking speed camera vans on pavements and grass verges (often causing great danger to pedestrians and motorists). One camera parked illegally caught 7,000 motorists in ten weeks and generated £420,000 in revenue. The police invariably remain totally unconcerned about the problems for citizens who are inconvenienced, or whose lives are endangered, by these illegal cash machines.

Another dangerous trick is to vary the speed limits on a motorway. On some roads it is almost impossible (and certainly extremely dangerous) to try to stick to all the changing speed limits. The speed limit will change from 40 mph to 60 mph to 50 mph to 70 mph to 40 mph all within a few miles. Motorists who do not suddenly brake (and risk causing a pile-up behind them) are likely to be caught by speed cameras. Changing speed limits every few miles creates queues and tiredness and results in massive extra costs for motorists. (Apart from the amount of time that is lost many modern cars tend to use up far more petrol when travelling at low speeds.)

The authorities invariably claim that speed cameras save lives and prevent accidents. This is a myth. It is generally agreed by experts that speed cameras don't deter drivers from speeding, are entirely unsuccessful at saving lives and may well cause accidents. Speed cameras are a dangerous distraction which make accidents more likely. Instead of keeping their eyes on the road motorists are constantly looking out for speed cameras – and then braking suddenly when they think they see one. In Essex, for example, one of the few studies done of speed cameras showed that the number of deaths and serious injuries within 500 metres of a camera rose by 15%.

In the autumn of 2003 the RAC said about speed cameras: 'They are not saving lives. They are an abuse of our civil liberties, a serious nuisance and a waste of money.' The RAC said that the police obsession with speed cameras meant that there were few patrols out on the roads to catch drunk, drugged and potentially lethal drivers in defective and uninsured cars.

The number of serious serial traffic offenders is constantly rising. One traffic offender who has been to court for driving while disqualified no less than 30 times is now officially disqualified from driving until December 3001.

The RAC also pointed out that most accidents are caused by young, male drivers but that it is middle-aged professionals who are most commonly caught by speed cameras as they head for work. Many motorists are now losing their jobs because they have lost their licences after convictions for speeding. It is difficult to see how this helps anyone. The police seem to have forgotten that they exist to protect the public – not to harass them, alienate them and make their daily life intolerable.

When a couple were attacked by knife wielding thugs they dialled 999 and called the police. It took the police five hours to arrive. But in the same town three police officers found time to conduct random inspections of motor cars parked at residents' homes. After a 30 minute search of one car the policemen found that the man's car had an empty windscreen fluid reservoir and a loose battery connection. The man, who had been watching television when the police arrived, was served with a £60 fixed penalty fine and a three point endorsement. It is difficult to know how the police knew he wasn't planning to check his water squirter level before using his car. It is even more difficult to understand how the police found time to wander around doing spot checks on innocent motorists when they claim they are too busy to provide householders with a basic level of protection.

In 2003 it was estimated that there were around 6,000 speed cameras in the UK – more than in any other country – with the number rising rapidly. Each camera costs about £30,000 to buy. When New Labour came to power around 200,000 motorists a year received fixed penalties for speeding. By 2002 there were around nearly two million fines handed out and this was almost doubling annually. By the middle of 2003 one in six motorists had at least three points on their licences as a result of speeding convictions. In the same period the number of warnings handed to the drivers of dangerous or un-roadworthy vehicles halved.

'If you are a law abiding driver with a licence, insurance and an MOT and you commit a minor offence such as parking illegally you'll be issued with a fixed penalty ticket because these are processed at a central office,' admitted one serving policeman. 'But if you don't bother taking a driving test or insurance and commit a more serious offence such as driving without due care and attention you'll get off scot-free as the police station is too busy to deal with you ... Only last week I stopped a known criminal driving an unregistered car on a provisional licence with no MOT or insurance. But we had to let him go with a warning as the offences he was committing were too serious to issue a fixed penalty ticket.'

Persecuting motorists may provide short-term funds for the Government and for police forces but it is creating a serious and probably permanent rift in the relationship between the public and the police. Dozens of speed cameras have been defaced, painted, burned, toppled, axed, driven into and shot at by angry motorists. One was even destroyed by a home-made bomb.

Motorists would probably complain less if the police did more to protect them and their property while on the roads. When vandals did £10,000 worth of damage to my car the police wouldn't even bother to look at the damage or take a statement from me. The car had been parked outside a local town hall, just a few yards from a police station, when the damage was done.

However, when I was a GP I was taken to court (and fined) for driving with my hazard flashers switched on when driving to a patient whose wife thought he was having a heart attack. The traffic was busy and I thought it a sensible idea. Unfortunately, a policeman saw my car and chased after me. I have always wondered if he could have been annoyed by the fact that he couldn't catch me and have always hoped that he never has a heart attack and has to wait too long for a doctor to arrive.

* * *

Things are made worse by the fact that the people employed by society to uphold and administer the law on behalf of the ordinary people too often seem to take advantage of their positions to abuse their powers. The interpretation of the law is so often at the discretion of those who are paid to uphold it that those who have been hired by society become the law itself.

Many people now believe that there is one law for 'us' and one law for 'them'. Thousands of policemen speed but are not prosecuted. A policeman who was charged with speeding was allowed to avoid prosecution by claiming that he couldn't remember who was driving his car at the time. So many innocent citizens have been killed by recklessly driven police cars that at least one police force has now sensibly banned police chases.

A hungry man waiting to take part in a police identity parade stole a cheese sandwich from a policeman's lunch box. When spotted and caught the sandwich thief was locked in a cell for over eight hours, arrested and taken to court where he was given a six month conditional discharge and ordered to pay £25. I suspect that if a member of the public had had a sandwich stolen (and the police could be persuaded to take action) the thief would have been given counselling and the owner of the sandwich arrested for causing an offence by putting temptation in the way of a hungry man. In theory all stolen sandwiches should result in a prosecution, a conviction and a punishment. The problem here is that I can't help wondering if this case got special treatment because the owner of the sandwich happened to be a policeman.

It is impossible to keep track of the number of occasions when the police are guilty of shooting or beating up innocent people. But on these occasions no one in the police force ever seems to be held responsible. When riot police attacked a group of peaceful football fans the attackers could not be prosecuted because their superiors were 'unable to name them'. The police paid out around £100,000 of taxpayers' money in compensation. If policemen had to pay such damages out of their wages or their pension fund they might be a little more careful about whom they beat up.

There is a growing fear that the police now fabricate evidence and fit up innocent people (particularly if they are poor, uneducated and not too bright) in order to get convictions. The word most people think of when the police are mentioned is now 'suspicion'. A few years ago it would have been 'trust'.

Judges, who seem to be completely out of touch with the real world and who are I suspect the only group of people in the country who believe that a policeman's word is worth anything, believe anything and everything any policeman tells them and are happy to accept a policeman's word in court on the grounds that policemen would never commit perjury. It seems that there is no end to judicial naivety.

It isn't just the police who seem to get away with blue murder. Politicians sometimes seem to get favourable treatment too.

After a much publicised incident when Deputy Prime Minister John

Prescott lashed out at a voter the authorities let him off without so much as a binding over to keep the peace or a couple of hours community service. 'That's just John,' said the Prime Minister, explaining his deputy's attack on an ordinary citizen with his usual sickly grin.

I wonder if the police would have been so forgiving if old Mrs Smith had said the same thing after her son John had punched someone in the street? Would I escape scot-free if I punched John Prescott?

When Labour Home Secretary Jack Straw's car was caught speeding at over 100 mph on a motorway the politician's driver escaped any censure on the grounds that the Home Secretary had been in a rush to get to a meeting.

When a man was arrested under anti-terrorism laws another Labour Home Secretary, David Blunkett, publicly announced that the man arrested 'posed a very real threat to the life and liberty of our country' and stated that the security services believed that he had connections with al-Queda groups.

When lawyers warned that the Home Secretary's remarks could jeopardise the man's chances of a fair trial the Attorney General brushed aside the complaint and said that Blunkett's remarks did not 'create a substantial risk of serious prejudice to any proceedings'. Personally, if I was the defendant I would think that any sort of prejudice might be unwelcome. And I certainly believe that if you or I had made widely-publicised judgmental remarks about a man who had been arrested but not yet brought to court we would have found ourselves in court.

After a local village burnt an effigy of a gipsy at its annual Guy Fawkes night celebration twelve people were arrested for 'racial' crimes. But when Jack Straw MP described gipsies as people 'who think that it's perfectly OK to cause mayhem in an area, to go burgling, thieving and breaking into vehicles, causing all kinds of trouble' he was not arrested. The difference? The twelve villagers were ordinary folk. Jack Straw MP was Home Secretary at the time.

Too often society allows officers of the courts to abuse their power to satisfy their own personal prejudices, grievances and ambitions. In return society's structure is protected by the people who benefit from its patronage. It is the worst sort of symbiotic relationship.

As the oppression of individuals continues, lawlessness (and disrespect for the law) grows among officials and those in power.

Millions of voters now believe, probably with justification, that police officers will manufacture evidence when they find it difficult to obtain a conviction – particularly in a high profile case where the public pressure to find a suspect is greater than their ability to do so. Brutality, arrogance, corruption and hypocrisy have all damaged public faith in the law but the only response from society has been to create new laws to outlaw disapproval. Society's primary interest is to protect itself and society is not concerned with justice, freedom or equality since those are values which are appreciated only by individuals. Society is concerned with progress and power and its own survival.

* * *

There is anger and confusion about the fact that there aren't any policemen on our streets any more. This is something that confuses and bewilders most ordinary citizens.

Why don't policemen patrol our towns and villages on foot any more? When policemen are spotted they are invariably cocooned in their expensive motor cars; usually parked behind motorway bridges. Occasionally, a pair of officers may be spotted strutting around a local town, wearing bullet proof vests and harassing street traders and buskers. Their car will be parked nearby, invariably abandoned illegally and causing a dangerous obstruction to traffic and pedestrians alike.

Throughout the rest of Europe it is common to see policemen patrolling cities, towns and villages on foot. In France policemen can even be seen patrolling on bicycles and rollerblades. When was the last time a policeman walked or pedalled past your home?

When the Government was asked why there are not more policemen on the street the (almost unbelievable) response was that this would 'frighten people unnecessarily.'

Eventually responding to criticisms that there are never any policemen on our streets the British Government announced that it plans to introduce 'civil enforcement officers'. These new officials will be there not to help but to fine motorists for parking badly or offending any of the many new laws constantly being introduced. They will have a financial incentive to fine as many motorists as possible.

The politicians and senior police officers sometimes seem to be living in a different world to the rest of us. In a way, of course, they are. They don't have to worry about muggers and burglars because their homes are constantly guarded.

After an elderly citizen was murdered in broad daylight millions of angry citizens clamoured for more police patrols. A high ranking policeman responded by going on television and angrily blaming the public for not caring enough.

* * *

There is growing concern at the way British lawyers are adopting the ambulance chasing habits of their American counterparts. Most people now realise that there is no point in expecting lawyers to campaign for justice because they are too busy making money out of the system; using greedy citizens to help them suck money out of our corporate and public institutions. The system seems designed to ensure that the litigation will only stop when the lawyers have got all the money. In America three out of every ten people have already been sued (or are about to be sued).

My wife, the Welsh Princess, tripped and dived gracefully onto the pavement during a recent shopping expedition. She ruined a pair of tights and hurt her leg quite badly. It wasn't difficult to find a cause for the fall. The pavement where she fell was quite uneven.

'The pavement isn't our responsibility, you know,' said a worried looking shopkeeper. He had come hurrying out of his shop when he had seen my wife take a tumble.

I was busy providing the appropriate medically approved support, but I paused and looked up, puzzled.

'You have to sue the council,' he said. 'Not me.'

I frowned. 'Why would we want to sue anyone?'

The shopkeeper glanced in my wife's direction and then looked back at me. He seemed puzzled. I suddenly realised that he automatically expected us to sue someone.

'I wasn't looking properly,' said the Welsh Princess. 'It was my fault.'

Sadly, I suspect that is a phrase which we won't be hearing much of in the future.

The shopkeeper's reaction was understandable. These days growing numbers of people are learning to regard every accident as a potential lawsuit.

This is of course one of those terrible, destructive American habits.

Remember the woman who won a million because she spilt a cup of hot coffee on herself and got scalded?

And the burglar who won massive damages after falling through a skylight?

And the would-be-suicide who threw himself under a train, survived and won damages from the train company?

And the woman who sued a gun company because her husband shot himself with one of their products?

All are American examples of lawsuit madness. The latest fad is for fat Americans to sue food manufacturers for making them fat. (Haven't any of these people ever heard of the word 'responsibility'? Do the lawyers involved realise that if they win these lawsuits – and there are a number of them pending – they will have 'legalised' the right of individuals to hand over just about every aspect of their own lives to others?)

Now the madness has come to Britain. Common sense is now rarer than snow in Tahiti. When a surgeon removed both of a patient's legs by mistake the patient received a modest cash settlement in damages. The surgeon was allowed to carry on unpunished. Since the doctor's insurance company paid all the costs of the lawsuit the doctor suffered only some embarrassment and, perhaps, remorse. But when a company boss innocently complimented a female employee on her dress she sued him for sexual harassment and received a vast sum in damages. Her boss was publicly censored and then demoted. Compare and contrast, as schoolteachers used to say, back in the days when schools were encouraged to teach the English language to their pupils. Everyone to whom something awful happens wants compensation, though it is difficult to see what the compensation is for. The parents of children who are murdered receive compensation from taxpayers. Why? It is right that society should apprehend and punish the murderer. But why should taxpayers be fined? Parents whose children's organs were removed without consent were given compensation. Why? It is proper that the offenders (those who removed the organs) should be punished. But why should taxpayers be fined? What is the money for?

Who do you think pays for all this nonsensical litigation?

It's certainly not the insurance companies.

It's you and I.

Those wretched companies which advertise for customers in newspapers and on TV encourage the assumption that whatever happens there is always someone to blame – and to sue.

They have helped create a world in which dissatisfaction leads to blame; we are taught that when something goes wrong we should always look for someone else to take responsibility; we are taught, by the lawyers, that when we are disappointed in some way we should expect a financial payout. Out there, somewhere, there will be an organisation, a department, a company or an individual with money in the bank. And even if the lawsuit is frivolous most victims of legal harassment (and it is, so often, the defendants who are the real victims) will settle in order to avoid a lengthy and expensive trial. The defendant will know that the plaintiff's costs, however vast they may become, will be carried by his or her lawyer, working for a share of the profits. The ambulance chasing lawyers who are involved in this sort of legal chicanery get rich because when they win they can win (literally) billions. Innocent defendants know that they have a choice: they either spend years (and all the money they can raise) fighting the case or else they settle out of court.

The really sad thing about all this is that dissatisfaction can be (and always used to be) a trigger to creativeness.

Edwin Land invented the Polaroid Instant camera after his three-year-old daughter wanted to know why she couldn't see a photograph as soon as it was taken. He didn't sue the camera maker or the film developer. Walt Disney created Disneyland after taking his two young daughters to a disappointingly tawdry local amusement park. The park was operated by surly employees and full of bored parents and unhappy children. Instead of suing the park owner Disney created something positive out of his miserable experience. When an American family had a miserable time at a roadside motel near Washington the father of the family founded the Holiday Inns hotel chain instead of consulting a lawyer.

Today, however, instead of using the grain of sand as an irritant to create a pearl we expect the grain of sand to produce a lawsuit. All over Britain local community events have had to be cancelled because of the threat of litigation. Trees are being chopped down and children's playgrounds closed because councils are frightened of being sued.

There are nearly one million lawyers working in the USA; that's more than one for every ten businesses. All those lawyers have to do something for a living (they can't all go into politics) and so Americans are encouraged to sue each other all the time. Not long ago an American passenger sued an airline for serving free peanuts.

Naturally, most litigants do not yet realise (and probably never will) that the only people to get really rich from litigation are the lawyers. At least one lawyer is reputed to have made more than a billion dollars out of the settlement made with the big tobacco companies.

Invariably, the litigants who take action (the smokers, the people injured by prescription drugs, the individuals who claim money as a result of accidents at work or in the street) receive neither justice nor much money. The people who really make the big money out of all this litigation are the lawyers.

Adopting the American method of allowing lawyers to share in the proceeds has further led to a serious deterioration in our system of justice and a wider deterioration in the quality of life in Britain.

Insurance policy premiums have rocketed as insurance companies claw back the money they are having to pay out. Many small businessmen have gone bust because they cannot afford the premiums they've been expected to pay. Public services have deteriorated still further as central and local governments are forced to spend an increasing amount of money and time fighting or settling legal battles brought by people who see a small piece of misfortune as an opportunity to get rich quick.

Naturally, many people have sought to get rich quickly without having to undergo the pain and inconvenience of an accident. Others have found ways to find someone else to blame for an accident for which they were responsible. For example, one man received a payout of £238,000 in compensation from his local Council after claiming that he had broken his ankle in a pot hole. (How much would he have got if he had been really seriously injured I wonder?)

Claims of this type are now big business. Council officials in Liverpool set aside £5.3 million of rate payers money to cover potential payouts to people who sued after claiming that they had tripped on uneven pavements. In the year 2000 Liverpool Council received 2,200 claims from people who had tripped over in what are called 'highway related incidents'; people wanting compensation for injuries caused by uneven pavements and kerbstones. In 2001 it was 4,000. In 2002 it was 6,000 and rising fast. Other cities have similar bills. Council officials reckon 80% of claims are false. One man was in prison on the date when he claimed he had fallen. Another apparently files a claim every year in time for Christmas. One entire family claimed they had been hurt tripping over the same stretch of pavement. One council spokesman said: 'A lot of these claims are down to the very aggressive sales tactics used by ambulance chasing insurance companies offering people no win no fee lawsuits. Many people think they can put in claims because they have nothing to lose.'

There seems no end to the imagination of those bringing lawsuits.

Just before Christmas 2003 it was announced that a postman was suing a university lecturer for posting too many letters. The postman claimed that he had pulled a back muscle after lifting a sackful of journals the lecturer had posted. The lecturer had put the mail into a standard red pillar box. The postman's claim was being funded by his trade union.

A schoolteacher who damaged knee ligaments after slipping on a chip outside a school canteen was awarded £55,000. Thousands of employees who have, often through their own carelessness, had a minor accident, have sued an employer who has provided them with secure employment for much of their lives. The sums of money won are often derisory after the lawyers have taken their share but the relationships between employees and employers have been permanently destroyed. Large companies, which have their own in-house lawyers can cope with litigation of this kind. But people running small businesses invariably find such litigation devastating.

The end result, of course, is that the people who really do have a right to complain lose out.

They lose out because, however honest their claim, they will be treated as liars and cheats by insurance company lawyers who are desperate to minimise their clients' losses.

But perhaps the worst result of all this is the fact that government departments, local councils and many large corporations have become extremely defensive when dealing with complaints.

It has long been acknowledged, in both public and private service that if you make a mistake you risk damaging the trust between your organisation and your 'customers'. The best way to repair this loss of trust has always been to listen and, where appropriate, to apologise; to put things right as quickly as possible, keeping the complainant fully informed.

Do this, so the argument always went, and you would be able to repair the trust between you and the complainant; you might, indeed, make that sense of trust stronger than ever, in the same way that when damaged skin heals a scar is eventually produced which will be tougher than ever. Fail to listen and to act on complaints, went the argument, and all trust will eventually be lost.

These days no one dares listen to complaints any more; they are terrified of the legal consequences. An apology is seen as a blank cheque for a lawsuit.

Nowadays, instead of responding to a complaint with a genuine attempt to understand the complainant's point of view, and to make sure that the same thing doesn't happen again, the department or company receiving the complaint will defend their employee at all costs. They do this because it's what their lawyers tell them to do. Accepting a complaint and dealing with it sympathetically is simply too risky; it is too likely to result in a lawsuit.

The end result is, to give just one example, that there is now virtually no point in complaining about anything that happens in an NHS hospital.

I used to encourage patients to complain when things went wrong. It was, I thought, the only way to improve the way the NHS works. (And, the aggrieved patient who complains will suffer far less frustration and stress if they know that someone has listened to – and acted on – their complaint.)

But when things go wrong in the NHS today the professionals working for the complaints system seem to take the side of the employee rather than the patient. The patient goes away aggrieved, disappointed and resentful. The image and reputation of the hospital and the NHS are damaged. And, worst of all, the offence which caused the complaint is likely to be repeated time and time again.

* * *

The truth is that the Government doesn't want us to feel safe. They want us to feel on edge. It suits their purpose for us to feel insecure and frightened. And it doesn't matter to them personally that crime rates are soaring. They, like judges and other members of the establishment, have police guards. No one will ever be able to burgle or mug Tony Blair. His children are safe. And, in the end, the crime figures don't matter to the politicians because they can lie their way out of trouble – by pretending that crime is less prevalent than it actually is.

* * *

Advice To Help You Protect Yourself And Your Family

You can no longer rely on the police to protect you or your family. There is no doubt that this is wrong. You have been let down by society. But until things change you must do everything you can to protect yourself, your loved ones and your property. The tips which follow should help.

1. The first place burglars look when searching a house is the master bedroom. That is the last place where you should hide anything valuable or private to you. Here are some good hiding places:
   - inside rolled-up window blinds
   - under the insulation in the attic
   - inside a dog kennel
   - in the bottom of the cat litter bag
   - in a box of sanitary towels or tampons
   - inside an old TV set abandoned in your garage
   - inside old junk mail envelopes

2. Don't trust policemen. They lie, they fabricate evidence and they frame innocent people. Do not assume that policemen can be trusted and never, ever assume that you have nothing to worry about because you are innocent. Many people have learned to regret such naivety.

3. The law used to provide us with guidance for our behaviour. No more. Today's laws have nothing whatsoever to do with justice or decency. Do not expect justice and you will not be disappointed. If you wish to live an honest, honourable and decent life then you should decide upon, and then keep, your own ethical principles. Behave towards others as you would like them to behave towards you and you will not go far wrong.

4. Think carefully before trying to arrest a criminal because if you do this there is a risk that you will end up being arrested yourself.

5. Never answer the door unless you know who is there – and what they want. Just as car hijacking has replaced ordinary car theft (it is easier to hijack a car than it is to try and overcome the sophisticated car lock) so house hijacking has now become the method of choice among young thugs. They ring your doorbell and then, when you open up, they burst in. Very few chains will keep out a determined shoulder charge. It is safer to keep the door closed.

6. Never allow strangers into your home unless you have to. If you must let them in, don't let them wander around alone. If you have to hire a workman stay with him. One innocent houseowner who allowed a traveller into his house to use the phone found himself facing three car loads of policemen just two hours later. The traveller had noticed a number of drugs on a cabinet in the hallway. When he left the house, after making his call, he stopped again and telephoned the police. He explained that he thought he had just been into the house of a drug dealer. It took the doctor who owned the house several hours to convince the police that he was innocent and to get rid of them from his home. It took him several months to deal with the complaint that his drug supplies had not been locked away from strangers. In the end he felt lucky not to have been struck off the medical register. Don't let strangers into your house unless you really need them there.

7. Random violence has escalated in recent years. It has now been estimated that around 99% of us will be exposed to or be a victim of a violent crime. Here are some tips to help you minimise your chances of being a victim:

   • When travelling at home or abroad carry a dummy wallet (aka a mugger's wallet). Put in a few low denomination notes and old bits of plastic that look like credit cards. If a mugger demands your wallet this is the one you will give him.

   • When walking in a town or city area make sure that you walk tall. Swing your arms. Don't walk in alleyways or drive in bad neighbourhoods at night.

   • When approaching your car after you have parked it look underneath to make sure that no one is hiding there. Check out other nearby vehicles. If when you get back to your car you find that a large van is parked next to the driver's side door of your car, and you can't be sure it's empty, get into your car from the passenger door. Before getting into your car look inside and check there is no one hiding in it. Check the back seat, and the area behind the front seats. When you get into your car the first thing you should do is to lock the doors. Drive away quickly.

   • Try to avoid parking in multi-storey car parks – especially at night.

   • I really hate to say this but don't be sympathetic to strangers

100

who seem in need of help. Ted Bundy, the infamous American serial killer, was well-educated and good-looking. His modus operandi was to ask strangers for help.

There is more information about how to avoid being mugged in my book *People Watching*.

8. Put a 'Beware of the dog' sign on your gate. (Bizarrely it is legally dangerous to have one of these signs if you really do have a dog because if someone is bitten by your dog they could argue that your sign indicated that you knew the dog to be dangerous and should have kept it locked up.) Throw a rubber bone and a couple of balls onto the lawn to add colour to your sign.

9. If someone tries to hijack your car, get out of it. Scream, run away or faint. Fainting is good. Go limp and fall on the ground. (But pick a spot where you won't be run over.)

10. Remember that customs and immigration inspectors can do whatever they like. Once you walk into their catchment area all your human rights disappear. If they ask to see something, let them see it. Don't argue. When they say 'This is nothing to worry about' they mean 'You are trouble'. When one is very nice to you he is trying to trick you.

11. If you get arrested for speeding (or any other minor traffic offence) be polite and respectful. Admit your guilt and offer no excuse. Do not get into an argument about the value of speed cameras. The policeman may be so astonished that he lets you off with a warning.

12. My friend Oscar says that in a life and death situation the fastest way to get help is to call the fire brigade. He says that if you are alone in the house and you suspect that burglars are either already in the house, or are about to get in, you should call the fire brigade as well as the police. Naturally, I do *not* recommend that you follow Oscar's advice. His advice is illegal and you will get into trouble if you follow it.

13. I wouldn't rely on the Government if a member of my family was kidnapped or arrested abroad. I would go straight to the media and ignore the Government's plea for silence. Government officials would, I suspect, want me to stay quiet because that would make their life easier. Remember: neither your Government nor any of

its employees care about what happens to you or any member of your family. British Embassy staff in foreign countries are paid to look after Britons abroad but they often give the impression of hating travellers whom they regard as a nuisance, getting in the way of their comfortable, workless days. Don't rely upon the Government for anything because it will always let you down.

14. If you are put on jury service remember that a jury has the power to ignore the law when it considers that the law is wrong. If you believe that the accused acted properly and morally (and that the law is being an ass) find the accused not guilty.

15. Without beliefs and integrity we are nothing. But in our world many values have disappeared so we need to find our own. Do not blindly accept all of society's rules. Accept the rules you approve of. You have a right and a responsibility to rely on your own conclusions. Integrity means matching your actions to your moral beliefs and being prepared to change if you are proved wrong. It is your duty to act with the courage of your convictions. This requires two things: courage and convictions. Don't allow society's servants to convince you that what you are doing is right when in your heart you know it is wrong.

Chapter 4
The Sickening Health Service

Back in the middle ages people were reluctant to go into hospital. They knew that they were unlikely to get out alive. Those patients who survived the incompetent ministrations of doctors and nurses were likely to die of infections contracted on the ward.

Things didn't get much better until well into the last century when the discovery of anaesthetics, antiseptics and antibiotics gradually meant that patients going into hospital had a reasonable chance of benefiting from the experience.

But the good days are now over.

Modern medicine has again become a major hazard. We're pretty much back where we started. Doctors are again one of the most significant causes of death and ill health. Today, they're up there alongside heart disease and cancer as Britain's three biggest killers. And patients who survive the incompetent ministrations of doctors and nurses are once again likely to die of infections contracted on the ward.

The NHS is moribund. Preventative medicine is in as bad a way as curative medicine.

* * *

Today's doctors and nurses should carry a health hazard warning

103

stamped on their foreheads. Each hospital should have a health warning notice hung over its entrance. If you rely on the NHS to look after you then you will be putting your health – and your life – at risk. At least one in three of the patients who die in NHS hospitals die unnecessarily.

* * *

The NHS is appallingly unfair.

The NHS was founded to ensure that everyone got equal care – regardless of wealth but there have always been inequalities. Some areas have better hospitals than others. It's called a 'National' Health Service but your chances of surviving have always depended on where you live. The way the NHS is run has always been divisive and grossly unequal. Back in the early 1970s I remember presenting a television programme pointing out that patients in different parts of the country were getting different levels of care. I had a huge map on a blackboard to illustrate my argument. In late 2003, thirty years later, I watched a television presenter illustrate variations in the so-called National Health Service with the aid of a huge map. The only thing that had changed was the fact that, thanks to new technology, the map appeared on the screen rather than being pinned to a blackboard.

The variations don't just involve hospitals.

One of Tony Blair's early promises was that everyone in the UK would have access to an NHS dentist. When a dentist in Carmarthen, Wales announced that he was taking on 300 more NHS patients, there were queues of over 600 people. People had driven for hours to try and join the practice and started queuing at 11.30 pm on Sunday night. Many were in tears when they were turned away. Similar scenes have occurred elsewhere in Britain. The NHS dental service will soon be of little more than historical interest.

* * *

Both the number of nurses working in the NHS and the number of beds available for patients have been falling steadily for years. (There are now more administrators than nurses or beds in NHS hospitals. There are now three times as many hospital beds per potential patient in Germany as there are in Britain.)

New Labour promised to produce more doctors and nurses but they have failed. Every time they have failed to meet their own targets they have simply changed the targets. Eventually a BMA spokesman admitted: 'It is difficult to untangle the figures because the targets keep shifting'.

Here are some examples of the sort of health care provided in Britain in the 21st century:

- A schoolboy who lived two miles from a major hospital was taken on a 100 mile round trip to have his broken wrist set. He was turned away by three hospitals and spent more than nine hours in agony.

- A woman of 93 who was dumped at the wrong address by an ambulance crew tried to walk home. She fell and broke both hips and was found lying in her garden. (The woman had been dropped at a house five miles from her own home. She had told the ambulance crew that she didn't live where they were dumping her but they claim they just thought she was 'confused'.)

- A young man who waited eight hours for treatment in an NHS hospital casualty department died. The hospital later admitted that he could have been saved if staff had acted a little more speedily.

- A 51-year-old woman was forced to sleep in a wheelchair for 15 months because anonymous bureaucrats working for a hospital trust decided that it was too dangerous for nurses to lift her into bed. The woman the nurses couldn't or wouldn't lift weighed just eight stone.

- A consultant surgeon admitted that he had been told by administrators to operate on non-urgent patients before dealing with patients with cancer. The order came so that the hospital would meet Government waiting list targets. The surgeon was told to deal with the non-urgent patients (including one requiring surgery on a scar and one waiting for breast augmentation) so that they would not have waited more than twelve months.

- Relatives of a World War II veteran were told he would have to wait until someone died before funding could be found to offer him a place in a care home. The council took five months to complete their assessment of his needs, though they didn't explain why it should take so long to assess someone. While the council completed its assessment and highly paid bureaucrats shuffled papers, ordered coffee and biscuits and arranged more meetings the elderly ex-soldier wandered the streets at night in his slippers searching for his wife who had died five years earlier.

♦ Two surgeons who removed a patient's only healthy kidney did so after one of them had put X-rays the wrong way round before the operation. Neither surgeon had checked the patient's notes or records or the consent form. The surgeons were suspended for twelve months.

♦ When five bureaucrats visited a woman at home (to assess her care requirements) she fell onto the floor at their feet while trying to show them round. When she begged them to help her up they all stood and stared at her either because they didn't know how to help someone up off the floor or because they felt it was beneath them. Perhaps they couldn't find anywhere to put their clipboards. All five were, after all, bureaucrats; they weren't in the actually-really-helping-someone business.

♦ A black woman had a foot amputated in an NHS hospital. She was told that if she wanted a black artificial foot (as opposed to a white one) she would have to pay extra. Black false feet cost more than white ones and the hospital employee said the hospital would only provide her with a white one. What sort of person makes a decision like this? What are people like this doing working for a hospital or in any sort of caring industry?

♦ A 75-year-old woman who was found dead in her home had been waiting for an ambulance for five hours. A relative who had telephoned the local hospital had been assured that the patient had already been admitted. The woman's GP had diagnosed pneumonia and ordered an ambulance. Five hours later, when the ambulance finally puttered up to the door, paramedics found the woman, who was alone, collapsed on the bathroom floor. When I was a GP it was common practice to wait with the patient until the ambulance arrived. But, I guess, this probably isn't possible in a world where ambulances take five hours to complete emergency calls.

♦ A woman of 92 with a broken leg lay on a pavement for more than an hour waiting for an ambulance. The hospital to which she was eventually taken was a few hundred yards away.

It is hardly surprising that asylum seekers from Turkey and countries even further East now choose to go back home if they fall ill – because the medical care they receive there is better than it is in Britain. (After receiving the required medical treatment they return to the UK, with its far superior cash payment benefits system.)

How can any of these things happen in a so-called 'civilised' society? How did Britain's health care system – once the envy of the world – become so bad that even asylum seekers regard it as unacceptable? Do none of the overpaid dross running the NHS these days have any understanding of the word 'responsibility'? Do they not appreciate that in return for a fat salary, a huge pension and the wherewithal to pay for expensive suits, private school fees, five-bedroomed houses and smart two litre limousines they are supposed to show a little accountability? As far as I know none of the NHS staff involved in the by no means exceptional list of incidents above was fired or offered to resign. If I ran the NHS I'd have had every single one of the quarter-witted nincompoops responsible transported to America. If they want to behave like Americans they can damned well live there.

* * *

Today's NHS bureaucrats are poikilothermic creatures; untouched by pain and suffering. They seem to have succeeded in divorcing themselves from the idea that they are employed to look after sick people. There is plenty of money for pot plants, fitted carpets and conferences in exotic locations. But wards have to stay shut because there isn't enough money to hire nurses. There is, however, plenty of money for bureaucrats to design forms for nurses to fill in. Recruitment companies supplying nurses to the NHS now have to provide 27 pieces of paperwork for each nurse. They also have to show that each nurse has had extra training in rescuing patients from burning hospitals. It would, perhaps, be more useful if all nurses had to show that they had been trained in how to care for patients being looked after in hospitals that weren't burning. Since New Labour took power the NHS has recruited managers at three times the rate at which it has recruited doctors and nurses. There has been a 59% rise in the number of NHS bureaucrats since 1997. Many managers now earn more than top doctors.

Changing a light bulb costs a small fortune in administrative costs and it can take so long to persuade five administrators to send along one electrician that I've known nurses take in their own light bulbs and surreptitiously change them themselves. It is so much quicker and easier than filling in all the necessary forms.

The excessive expenditure on bureaucrats means that there are problems in community care too. Long-stay hospitals are closed because it is considered politically incorrect to provide long-term accommodation for the long-term ill.

* * *

Care homes and nursing homes for the elderly and infirm are closing fast. Red tape means that in Britain today a dozen such homes are closing every week. No one in the NHS seems to have had the wit to explain to the red tape wielding bureaucrats that every time a care home closes another dozen beds in an NHS hospital become blocked. And NHS waiting lists go up yet again.

We can blame the administrators for failing to administer the NHS properly but we must also blame the politicians for giving them the power they are now abusing. New Labour's response has been to introduce new regulations forcing builders to put a bedroom with an en-suite bathroom on the ground floor of every new house. They have admitted they are doing this so that in the future more sick people can be looked after at home – by relatives.

* * *

Although the politicians and the administrators waste money and resources, and have undoubtedly weakened the health service, it isn't their fault that doctors and hospitals now do more harm than good.

The main reason that orthodox medicine has become a menace to patients is that the medical establishment has sold itself – body and soul – to the drug industry. Sadly, too many doctors have given up caring for their patients; they have their snouts stuck so firmly in the trough that they cannot see what is going on around them. Perhaps they don't want to see.

In my first book (*The Medicine Men*) which was published in 1975, I complained that medicine was no longer a 'profession' because doctors had become a marketing arm for the pharmaceutical industry. It was considered outrageous then. The medical establishment declared me persona not at all grata. But I doubt if any doctor would bother to dispute it these days. It isn't difficult to find examples of the way doctors follow drug company instructions without the sort of critical assessment that you might reasonably expect from qualified professionals.

If you're naive and innocent you probably imagine that when a doctor decides to prescribe a drug for you he selects a product which independent research has shown to be most effective for your condition. Ho bloody ho. He doesn't.

Most doctors probably wouldn't know what to do with independent research if they had it delivered on a plate.

Doctors, once a responsible and respectable group of men and women, have sold their souls for an endless supply of free meals, free pens and free golf balls. They prescribe what the drug companies tell them to prescribe; even though, when it comes to honest and reliable advertising the drug companies come a long way after second-hand car salesmen.

One in six patients in hospital today are there because they have been made ill by doctors. Most of those people are in hospital because they were injured by drugs or vaccines. This would not be so terrible if drugs always saved lives or did what they are supposed to do. But most prescription drugs don't do any good at all for the people who take them. More than 90% of drugs work in less than half of the people who take them. This makes the downside risk unacceptable. Sadly, drug companies have bought up much of the medical establishment; and do their best to stifle the truth. And most doctors are too gutless to stand up for their own profession or, more importantly, their patients.

Over a quarter of a century ago, when I had just qualified as a doctor, I edited a medical journal for a while. I had just published my book *The Medicine Men* attacking drug companies and their links to the medical establishment. I was in a room one day when the publisher asked two drug company executives how he could persuade them to advertise in the journal. The senior drug company executive looked at me. 'Fire him!' he said. The publisher duly did just that.

***

Much of the stuff doctors prescribe has never been shown to be either safe or effective.

For example, antidepressant prescriptions issued by GPs in the UK more than doubled between 1975 and 1998. By 1998 GPs were writing out 23.4 million prescriptions a year for these drugs. But this increase happened despite the fact that there had been very few clinical trials dealing with the drug treatment of depression in general practice. Most clinical trials of these drugs were conducted on patients in a hospital environment and did not, therefore, relate to patients at home.

It is quite likely that much antidepressant prescribing is pointless and unnecessarily dangerous and expensive. Indeed, one of the few studies which have been done found that antidepressants were no better than sugar pills.

The fact is, of course, that most people's problems simply can't be solved with drugs. Most people who are feeling miserable or unhappy (more accurate terms than 'depression' for 99 out of 100 patients) will only get better if they are given money or a holiday or both.

(As an aside, could there possibly be a link between the increased incidence of cot death and the vast numbers of women now taking psychotropic drugs of one kind or another? Many of these drugs are excreted in breast milk and the infants of women who take the drugs during pregnancy would undoubtedly have the drugs in their bloodstreams.)

Doctors hand out drugs for two reasons: firstly, most areas have a waiting list of over a year if a patient wants to see a real life person to talk about their problems and secondly, the drug companies have promoted their antidepressant products very effectively. They did so because too many patients had become wary of benzodiazepine tranquillisers such as Valium, Librium and Ativan. Doctors don't know what else to do and so they hand out pills. It's rather pathetic but I'm afraid it's what happens. (Twenty years ago, when benzodiazepine prescribing was being brought under control as a result of one of my early campaigns, I forecast that the drug companies would encourage doctors to prescribe more anti-depressant drugs, and that doctors would comply.)

The drug companies benefit because they make huge profits. The medical establishment benefits because doctors can stuff their patients' mouths with antidepressants and stop them complaining. And society as a whole benefits because people think they are being treated, shut up and don't see what a mess the politicians are making of everything.

BEFORE IT GETS BETTER

* * *

When Andy Warhol was shot and thought to be dying, he was put into an ambulance. A friend got into the ambulance with him. 'If we sound the siren, it'll cost five dollars extra,' said the ambulance driver.

This happened, of course, in America. But since New Labour politicians are great fans of all things American it will, presumably, not be long before this is also the British way.

* * *

When taxes rise the Government claims that the extra money is needed for the NHS. Pfui. Money won't cure what's wrong with the NHS. In today's NHS the emphasis is on 'profit' rather than 'cure' or 'care'.

The NHS has become a bureaucratic monster. Most hospitals are awash with cash but far too much of the money goes on administration. The whole caring philosophy has been forgotten. Who would have dreamt, just a generation ago, that hospitals would one day charge patients or visitors a big fee just to park their cars? Overpaid hospital staff get guaranteed, free car parking spaces. The patients have to pay. Nothing better illustrates the fact that in today's NHS the administrators are the most important people in the hospitals.

The NHS is riddled with corruption, dishonesty, laziness and contempt for patients. It becomes clearer each day that the organisation is run not for the sake of the 'patients' (the electors who pay for it) but for the convenience of the state employees who run it.

Courtesy and respect are simply rather old-fashioned words which have little relevance today. When I worked as a doctor I used to call male patients either Mr or 'Sir'. Today only the administrators get called 'Sir'. The patients are all called by their first name.

Most of the extra money raised by increased taxation is simply spent on hiring more administrators or giving pay rises to the ones we've already got. (In 2003 health service bosses got pay rises of up to 30% while nurses got just 3.2%.) Patients don't benefit at all.

Extra layers of administration mean that basic running costs rocket while the quality of care steadily but remorselessly deteriorates. I would argue that because of this the more money the NHS gets the worse it becomes.

More than 60% of NHS employees are bureaucrats. Things are getting worse by the week. Doctors and nurses are minority employees in today's NHS.

Most of the administrators working in hospitals have no idea of the fear patients feel when they go into hospital – at least not until they themselves need help, when they usually demand (and get) special treatment.

In additional to a Ministry, the health service is run by over 750 boards, committees, executive councils, local health authorities and quangos. Administration within the NHS is a sick joke. It's hardly surprising that doctors and nurses are demoralised and that patients are treated as if they were all a nuisance. Like other huge state industries the NHS has forgotten that it exists to serve. The system has a bureaucratic life of its own and patients are regarded as troublesome outsiders. Doctors and nurses who care simply leave or take retirement as soon as they can.

* * *

The Government doesn't much care about any of this. They know that they won't have to worry about the NHS for long. If Britain joins the euro the NHS will have to be closed down.

That's not a prediction. It's what the European Central Bank has told the Government. I expect the Government meant to mention it but forgot.

* * *

The NHS is hooked on waiting lists. Neither consultants nor administrators can give them up. However, if I ran the NHS I could get rid of all waiting lists with one simple administrative change that would take about 30 seconds to complete. Within weeks waiting lists would disappear. Patients (and voters) would welcome the change that is necessary.

The idea of patients having to wait for essential, and possibly life-saving treatment, is something we've got used to. But Britain is the only country in the world where patients routinely have to wait for weeks, months or even years for essential treatment. Patients and doctors in other countries don't even understand the concept of a waiting list.

Waiting lists were originally an invention of part-time NHS

consultants who wanted to boost their earnings from private patients. They kept their NHS lists long to encourage patients to pay for treatment.

I first revealed this scandal in 1986.

I was attacked rather viciously by doctors at the time but no one has bothered to deny the truth of this for many years. Thousands of hospital consultants have for years been 'hooked' on the extra income they receive from private patients.

All that was bad enough.

But things have got worse and NHS hospitals have themselves become dependent on the extra income they receive from private patients. They need the cash desperate patients pay for investigations and treatment in order to pay the hugely inflated salary bill for administrators and managers.

Private care in the UK is flourishing because health care in the NHS is so poor. The UK has the most unreliable, most unfair, most unjust health service around. Patients fall between two stools – NHS and private care. Doctors get rich. Patients die.

Hospitals can make money out of private patients because even full-time salaried NHS hospital consultants (the ones who have signed contracts promising to work full-time for the NHS rather than to share their working lives between NHS and private patients) are allowed to charge NHS patients for private treatment – and to pocket the money they make.

Since they don't have private consulting rooms or private hospital facilities available they are, of course, allowed to use NHS facilities, NHS equipment and NHS staff. They are even allowed to use NHS secretaries, NHS stationery and NHS stamps to deal with the paperwork (such as sending out appointments and bills).

NHS hospitals charge private patients the same fees as private hospitals, though they provide a much more basic service. (The precise fees vary from doctor to doctor and hospital to hospital. Both doctors and hospitals know that patients are usually too frightened to shop around to find the 'best buy'.) A study of 540 NHS prices showed that the average difference between the lowest and highest NHS surgery price is 1,570 %. A cataract operation in an NHS hospital will cost on average £1,055 but could cost as little as £270 or as much as £2,918. How on earth can this be? (For comparison a cataract operation at an up-market private clinic might cost around £1,800.) Some NHS hospitals charge £2,080 for a hip replacement operation. Others will charge £8,150. (The top price I could find for a private clinic was £8,000.)

Patients are still trusting. And they are a captive market. Consultants working in NHS hospitals invariably charge the same massive fees as genuinely private consultants – but they don't bother with the smiles, the handshakes, the comforting words or the expensive suits. They know that they're not selling 'special care'. They're flogging a chance to be seen this week instead of next year. They're selling a chance to be treated before it's too late. They're flogging a chance to stay alive. You don't have to tart things up when you're selling life itself.

The full-time NHS consultants, and the administrators running these official 'private NHS clinics' don't bother with expensive magazines, cups of tea and smiling receptionists. Neither doctors nor hospitals pretend to be offering anything more than a chance to be seen more speedily.

Greedy consultants are getting rich, preying on patients who are struggling to stay alive in the wreckage of the NHS.

The way it all works in practice is alarmingly simple.

A patient who needs to have a scan to find out whether their pain is caused by a developing cancer may be told by his or her GP that there is, say, a one year waiting list. But if the patient is prepared to pay for the scan then it can be done within a week. The staff, the equipment and the venue remain the same. There is no welcoming cup of tea for relatives and friends. No obsequious consultant in a pin-striped suit. No explanations, no welcome and none of the perks that patients have traditionally paid for when buying private treatment. 'Private patients' sit alongside the standard (second-class) NHS patients on hard chairs and wait to be called. The only difference is that the patient gets a diagnosis before it's too late and pays the hospital around £500 for the scan and the radiologist between £150 and £200 to send a letter reporting the results. Hospitals and consultants are unashamedly flogging off places higher up the waiting list; naturally, if there wasn't a waiting list they wouldn't have anything to sell.

One reader of mine paid £90 to an NHS consultant for a standard five minute consultation. She had to pay the NHS hospital another £60 for the use of their grubby facilities. What did she get out of it? She jumped the waiting list.

Another reader had to pay £180 to a consultant who reported on a scan. The consultant hadn't even been there when the scan was done. The NHS hospital then sent a bill for another £250. Once again the hospital was simply selling a place higher up its waiting list. When NHS hospitals do this they are effectively selling the right to life.

The final irony is that much of the equipment (for example, most of the scanners) in NHS hospitals was bought with money raised by local patients. So patients who contributed to the fund to buy a scanner for their local hospital are now being told to pay huge fees to use it.

Most patients are so scared of what is happening that they don't even ask how much the bill is going to be. They are perfect marks for unscrupulous doctors.

'If patients don't ask I don't tell them how much it will cost,' boasted one consultant to me. 'If they want to know how much the bill will be it's up to them to ask.' Doctors are simply taking advantage of the fact that the vast majority of patients never dream of asking the doctor how much a consultation, a test or an operation is going to cost. They are not accustomed to paying and don't even think of the cost. Patients brought up on the NHS and the idea of free health care as a right, are easy fodder for greedy consultants. Patients forget, if they ever knew, that private medicine has the same underlying purpose as public houses and brothels: to make a profit. Patients who visit a doctor are worried – they (and their relatives and friends) have things other than money on their minds. Patients know that they have to be treated. They are vulnerable and easy pickings for greedy doctors. They trust the doctor not to rip them off. It is only later that they discover that their trust has been misplaced.

* * *

The modern NHS consultant has the best of both worlds. He combines a stable income with an excellent pension, sick pay cover and all the other perks of government employment, with the ability to earn additional money through 'private patients'. He doesn't even have to hire a consulting room or secretary. He doesn't have to go out and find the private patients. The NHS finds them for him.

Doctors have become as greedy and grasping as a bunch of Arthur Daleys. They snatch every penny they can from frightened and desperate patients and their frightened and desperate relatives. And for doctors and hospitals there is a bonus: NHS patients who are seen as 'private' patients cannot use the NHS complaints machinery. The patient may have been seen in an NHS building by a salaried NHS doctor using NHS equipment and dictating his report to an NHS secretary using NHS notepaper but if the patient has agreed to hand over money to jump the queue the hospital won't accept any complaint about itself or a doctor. Patients who pay to jump the queue lose all their rights and safeguards. (Not, to be honest, that the NHS complaints machinery is worth a used syringe. The machine seems to me designed to protect the staff rather than the patients.)

When the money runs out the patients simply go back into the NHS system and waits for the next instalment of their treatment.

* * *

If all this sounds too bad to be true you can check it out for yourself in minutes. Pick a speciality (any speciality). Ring your nearest large NHS hospital and ask to speak to a secretary working for a consultant in that speciality. Name an operation or an investigation and ask how long the waiting list is. Then ask how long you'd have to wait if you paid for private care. Hospital managers don't try to hide what is happening. They brazenly admit that they're flogging places on the waiting list.

If waiting lists were to disappear NHS hospitals (and NHS consultants) would lose this nice little earner. Many NHS hospitals would go bust and a lot of NHS consultants would have to sell the second BMW and the chalet in Switzerland.

The real irony is that now that the NHS is dependent upon providing private treatment the whole NHS has a vested interest in producing a poor service: it is the only way the NHS can still pay the administrators their fat salaries.

* * *

Last year, 300,000 people paid privately so that they could jump the NHS waiting list. Heaven knows how many paid privately for X-rays and scans. It's impossible to say how much we are talking about but this is undoubtedly a multi-billion pound a year scam.

The NHS offers a two-tier service. Money doesn't buy better care. But it buys faster care. And that's crucial. The modern NHS is flourishing by taking advantage of the fact that some patients can afford to pay (or will find the money by selling the car or re-mortgaging the house). In today's NHS this new way of doing things means that if you're poor and cannot afford to 'buy' a higher place on the waiting list your chances of surviving your illness are dramatically reduced.

Yet, this horrifying scandal could be stopped within minutes.

Waiting lists could be permanently eradicated. And countless lives saved.

The Government simply has to tell NHS managers to stop charging patients. And all hospital consultants must be told to choose between the full-time NHS work (meaning just that: full-time NHS work and no private patients) and private practice.

Politicians are frightened that if they confront hospital consultants they will leave the NHS. This is simply a sign that politicians don't understand doctors. Hospital consultants may grumble but they won't quit the NHS. If the NHS becomes one-tier again then there will be no need for waiting lists. And without waiting lists the demand for private care will collapse. There will still be patients who want a hospital room with two TV sets, a fax machine and a private phone. They'll use private hospitals. But there won't be enough private work for NHS doctors to quit in large numbers.

NHS hospitals would be short of cash for a while but there are more managers (many of them very highly paid) than there are nurses or beds in today's NHS and surely even a politician can work out where to make the necessary cuts.

* * *

GPs are becoming increasingly disillusioned as they struggle to deal with a corrupt hospital service which now exists to serve doctors and bureaucrats rather than patients.

General practitioners are now so thoroughly fed up that many are taking early retirement and those remaining have just negotiated new contracts under which they will be able to opt out of all-night working and 24 hour responsibility for their patients' health – two responsibilities which have always been two cornerstones of the GP's role (the other two cornerstones, independence and trust disappeared years ago).

Even without the need to accept 24 hour responsibility doctors are quitting in thousands and the shortage of GPs in England and Wales is rocketing. In some urban communities there simply aren't any GPs any more. The NHS is short of 3,000 GPs. A few years ago patients used to have to wait a day or two to see the doctor of their choice. Today patients have to wait a day or two to see any doctor.

Britain has a dire hospital service and a grotesque shortage of dentists and GPs. But there are plenty of administrators.

* * *

The NHS is a massive, overstaffed bureaucratic organisation which is badly run (actually, it isn't really run at all) and which has lost sight of its purpose: caring for patients. Morale is low too. The only surprise is that just when everyone working in the NHS thinks morale has reached rock bottom things get even worse.

But the NHS could be taken out of intensive care and put well on the road to recovery in a week if the politicians would take the action that is needed.

This is what they should do:

♦ Close the Department of Health in London. This massive but entirely useless organisation is a white elephant which adds nothing but confusion to health care – and kills far more people than it cures. The Government should sell the posh offices, fire the overpaid staff and use the money to build more hospitals and hire more nurses.

♦ Fire at least two out of three administrators.

♦ Inform drug companies that the NHS will cut the prices paid for drugs by a third. Britain pays higher drug prices than any other country. The NHS drug bill is soaring – as are international drug company profits. Soft politicians are allowing the drug multinationals to bleed the NHS dry. This simple move will liberate billions for patient care.

♦ Force doctors to incorporate the best aspects of alternative care into the NHS. Heart disease can be cured without drugs – as can many cancers. Alternative cures are often cheaper and safer as well as being more effective. The drug industry wants to get rid of the competition from safe and natural therapies because these cannot be patented and the profits are too small. (Plus natural therapies tend to keep people healthy and help prevent illness and that simply isn't good for business.)

♦ Begin a massive health education programme designed to teach

118

people the facts about healthy living. Most people don't realise it but at least 8 out of 10 cancers can be prevented. Most cases of heart disease can be prevented too.

♦ Publish details of hospital and doctor success and failure rates. This would enable patients to vote with their feet (arms, legs, gall bladders, tonsils etc.).

♦ Improve hospital food. Astonishingly, 40% of adults on hospital wards are suffering from malnutrition because they have been fed so badly. The food in hospitals is often inedible. Chefs and dieticians need to be retrained.

♦ Train nurses properly. A few years ago leading nurses decided that they as a profession would gain more respect if they had more academic qualifications. It was decided that the only way a nurse should get a promotion or a salary increase would be to move into management. So all the best nurses stopped dealing with patients and started pushing bits of paper around a desk instead. These two developments have destroyed nursing as a caring profession. Today there are too many nurses who regard themselves as too important to do any practical caring; feeding patients is just too demeaning for someone with letters after their name. Academic training means that instead of describing a patient as 'unconscious' nurses now say that the patient has 'an altered state of consciousness'. Too many nurses have become 'jobsworths', unwilling, unhelpful and far too self-important. For decades I have been screaming that we need to bring back matrons, ward sisters (and ward clerks to deal with the paperwork). I firmly believe that hospitals went into terminal decline when old-fashioned matrons were phased out and replaced by battalions of uncaring bureaucrats. And we desperately need to get rid of the rules which make it impossible for a consultant or a senior nurse to discipline – or even admonish – a nurse who makes a stupid, careless or thoughtless mistake. 'You can't shout at anyone,' said one frustrated doctor. 'If you do, they'll sue you.' The NHS has acquired a no-blame culture. Staff can never be blamed for anything; they have to be nurtured. Just try making a formal complaint about any NHS employee and you will see what I mean. (Curiously, doctors seem to be the exception. One consultant was allegedly suspended from work for taking an extra helping of croutons with his soup in the hospital canteen. Another doctor remained suspended on full pay for eleven years.) No one gives a damn for the poor patients who are being maltreated. In the end the really bad nurses are usually promoted to management positions, to keep them away from patients. New Labour has set up 31 separate health watchdogs and quangos employing nearly 20,000 highly paid administrators but it is estimated that over 1.4 million people are injured or killed by preventable errors in the NHS.

♦ The NHS needs a fair, patient-oriented complaints scheme. At the moment there is little likelihood that a patient complaining will receive an apology and, thanks to mollycoddling legislation which is designed to protect the bad and the mad as well as the incompetent, virtually no chance that the member of staff responsible will be admonished or fired. Despite their remarkable capacity to offend doctors, nurses and patients while, at the same time, losing vast amounts of taxpayers' money bureaucrats remain as unregulated as urine therapists. All staff should be reminded daily that patients are entitled to privacy and dignity.

♦ Stop trying to provide care for optional medical treatments on the NHS. For example, IVF treatment is not life-saving and should not be provided free of charge as long as patients who are dying remain untreated. A recent study concluded that women who have multiple births after IVF treatment are far more likely to become depressed than single birth mothers and far more likely to require intense care from health services (inevitably reducing still further the availability of medical help for those whose lives really depend upon it). Why do we need state aided IVF when thousands of children remain unadopted? Britain has the worst cancer care record in Europe. But we have free IVF for everyone who asks. The two are not unconnected. This is madness. It is an outrage that patients are given sex change operations or breast enlargement operations or fertility treatment on the NHS when patients are dying because the NHS cannot provide basic diagnostic or treatment facilities. Providing infertility clinics on the NHS at the moment is like putting go-faster stripes on a car without an engine. Similarly, it is an outrage that so many women now demand (and expect) elective Caesarian sections simply because it is more convenient (or less painful) to have a baby delivered that way. (The problem of 'fashionable' Caesarian sections, regarded as new by the media, has been simmering for at least 30 years.)

✱ ✱ ✱

Whole armies of bureaucrats are now employed to protect us and help maintain our 'health and safety'. Councils employ these people by the thousand. Most of them sit in offices, creating new rules, making life impossible for people in the catering industry, but doing nothing to improve conditions. But, despite the bureaucrats, our health and safety has never before been so much under threat.

When a national newspaper conducted an investigation it found that almost half the ice cubes served in pubs and bars in Britain were contaminated with bugs. Of 104 samples collected 46 failed one or more of three tests for bacteria. The samples were tested for the presence of E.Coli and other coliform bacteria – the sort normally found on the hands of people who don't wash properly after visiting the lavatory. The contaminants had got into the ice either because the bar staff hadn't washed their hands properly when serving customers or because they hadn't washed their hands properly before cleaning the ice making machine. A survey of sandwiches showed that there was hardly a sandwich being sold in Britain that wasn't contaminated with similar bugs – all through sheer dirty habits.

Actually, to be fair, our hygiene habits in the home have gone haywire too. Our topsy-turvy habits mean that children grow up failing to develop immunity to common bugs and becoming vulnerable to many different types of allergy – including asthma.

The UK spends almost as much on household cleaning products as the whole of Eastern Europe but we suffer far more from allergies. One in three Britons now suffer from hay fever and asthma affects one in eight. There are alleged to be 3.7 million asthma suffers living in the UK. (As I have pointed out in other books this figure is artificially high. Encouraged by drug companies, doctors now diagnose everyone who ever wheezes as 'asthmatic'.)

Why? What on earth is going on?

One problem is that our *real* standards of personal hygiene have fallen to an abysmally low level. People have simply stopped washing their hands properly. Mothers are particularly guilty and nappies are the commonest cause of household infection. The immune system of a baby is ineffective against gut infections so babies are more likely to pass on dangerous infections than adults. It isn't the baby which needs protecting from the world but the world which needs protecting from babies. A study done in the North West of England showed that only half of all mothers bothered to wash their hands after changing their babies nappies. As a result, half the door handles in their homes harboured faecal viruses. The most common reservoirs of infection are toilet bowls, washing-up bowls, dishcloths, sponges, scouring pads, face-cloths, nailbrushes and toothbrushes. Plastic chopping boards are also a source of infection. (It was shown long ago that bacteria grew more slowly on wooden chopping boards than on plastic chopping boards because wood contains hundreds of natural compounds which have evolved over the years to fight bugs.)

Antibiotic resistance means that good home hygiene is crucial for survival. But although soap and water are the best way of keeping yourself and your home clean most people now rely on products which have been impregnated with antibacterials.

Too much of the wrong sort of hygiene has wiped out bugs which protect us from allergies. Sealed windows, central heating and air-conditioning all provide a perfect environment for dust mites and for circulating bugs.

A hundred years ago the infant mortality rate in the UK was higher than it is in Africa now. (Two million children die every year in undeveloped countries simply because they and their parents do not have soap and water to wash their hands.) It was only when the Victorians built new sewage pipes and fresh water supplies, piped into every home, that infant mortality levels fell.

But, just as doctors and nurses have forgotten about basic hygiene since they have had antibiotics to rely on, so most people have become sloppy at home because they have access to antibacterial products.

Supermarkets sell a whole range of products – even clothing – which have been impregnated with antibacterials. This is grossly irresponsible. These products help to create superbugs and kill off the harmless bacteria which help to keep the environment healthy. One common active ingredient in antibacterial products is now turning up in mother's breast milk.

What we ignore is that some exposure to the right sort of dirt and germs is essential for teaching our immune systems how to operate effectively. When Germany was reunified doctors in the more affluent West were amazed to find that although standards of hygiene and health care were much lower in the East, children who lived there were much less likely to suffer from asthma. As health standards in the East have risen so has the incidence of asthma. In Ireland gypsy children who live in what most people would regard as 'rough' conditions have half the level of asthma as the rest of the population. Children who spend a lot of their time with animals are far less likely to develop allergy problems.

* * *

The MRSA superbug (methicillin resistant staphylococcus aureus) is a serious problem in hospitals. It kills 5,000 patients a year and costs the NHS at least £1 billion annually. The bug infects patients weakened by illness or surgery and spreads rapidly throughout their bodies causing organ failure.

The bug is common because doctors have overprescribed antibiotics and because hygiene practices in hospitals are pitiful. Doctors and nurses simply don't bother to wash their hands.

The bug used to be found only in hospitals but it is now rife in public places. A survey which involved taking 31 swabs in public places in central London found five positive sites: including on the button of a pedestrian crossing, on the floor of a changing room in a clothes store and on the button of the handdryer in a public lavatory.

The MRSA bug will survive for 30 minutes on any surface and the evidence suggests that public places are being constantly reinfected. The bug can be carried in the nose or fingers for an indefinite period. The most dangerous places are the ones which are in constant use. Door handles and buttons of any kind are now a very real health hazard.

The superbug problem has been introduced into the outside world by patients, doctors, nurses and orderlies who came out of hospital without washing their hands.

I first wrote about this problem 30 years ago, in my very first book. It was pretty obvious then that antibiotic-resistant bugs were going to become a serious problem, thanks to the affection of doctors for over-prescribing antibiotics, the enthusiasm of farmers for giving antibiotics to animals in order to increase meat production and lax attitudes towards hygiene in hospitals. (Doctors and nurses have become sloppy because they have learned to rely too much on antibiotics.)

* * *

Hygiene standards aren't helped by the fact that there are more administrators than nurses in our hospitals. This means that the nurses who are working are constantly rushing around. The Government's response to this growing problem has been to hire more administrators to make sure that doctors and nurses wash their hands.

You couldn't make it up, could you?

* * *

The primary problem with health prevention at the moment is that it is organised for the benefit of corporations rather than patients.

A perfect example of this is to look at what is happening in developing countries.

In developing countries life expectancy at birth is around 50. In 'developed' countries life expectancy at birth is 77. The difference is largely due to deaths among under fives. And children under five usually die because they have been drinking contaminated drinking water. It is now generally agreed (by those who have no vested interest) that advances in longevity in developed countries are due not to expensive drugs but to the availability of (relatively) clean water supplies and to the presence of facilities for removing sewage.

But in underdeveloped countries the representatives of developed countries still recommend the building of high-tech hospitals *before* they recommend providing clean water and sewage facilities.

This is done because it is easier to make profits out of building hospitals and supplying drugs than it is to make money out of showing people how to provide themselves with sewage facilities and clean drinking water.

Instead of making sure that children have access to clean drinking water we persuade developing countries to build transplant units. And we persuade mothers to use powdered milk instead of breast milk when feeding their children. 'It is the way we do things,' we tell them. And, wanting to be like us, they do as we tell them. Of course the powdered milk has to be made up with contaminated water so even more children die.

Politicians, international conglomerates and the medical establishment are to blame. But we let them do it. And so we are to blame too.

When our leaders behave so shabbily among the poor and sick of the undeveloped world is it really any surprise that at home they 'promote' drugs and surgery for everything, and deny the efficacy of simple and safe forms of prevention and treatment? What is the point of preventing heart disease when you can sell a cure? What is the point in treating heart disease with a system which costs nothing to implement when, instead, you can treat heart disease with an operation which will provide wealth for surgeons, nurses, administrators and hospitals?

Fatty foods, tobacco and alcohol may all be legal. But they are major killers – responsible for millions of deaths. It is ironic that marijuana (which seems to have some medicinal qualities) should be illegal when such deadly substances can be promoted and sold so freely.

* * *

The NHS doesn't need more money. It needs basic restructuring and rethinking. No one has really 'run' the NHS for decades. It has become a monster, a disorganised shambles with no discernible structure and no really effective leadership. When there is a power vacuum managers and administrators divide the power among them – and create rules and regulations which serve their own purpose, rather than the purpose of the institution or the people the institution was created to serve. The NHS (the lifeless, leviathan institution itself) has taken control. The system is now run to sustain the system.

* * *

Advice To Help You Stay Healthy (And Survive Britain's Healthcare System)

1. Do everything you can to ensure that you stay as healthy as possible in the future. Do not rely on being able to obtain skilled and reliable medical help. The quality of health care has been sliding steadily for decades and the quantity of available care has also been diminishing. Obtaining health care is likely to be increasingly difficult and expensive. To preserve your health you must carefully watch what you eat, lose any excess weight and avoid tobacco smoke (taken directly or indirectly) whenever possible. The biggest killers (and disablers) in the developed world (cancer, heart disease and

stroke) are strongly related to lifestyle. You can dramatically – and fairly easily – reduce your chances of suffering from any of these three big killers by watching what you eat, by taking modest, regular exercise (such as walking) and by increasing your resistance to and your exposure to unwanted stress. By keeping your weight under control you will minimise your chances of developing diabetes or arthritis – two disorders which cause much immobility and disablement. As golfer Gary Player says: 'If you look after your body it could last you a lifetime.'

2. Remember that doctors and hospitals are now a major cause of illness and death. One in six patients in hospital are there because they have been made ill by a doctor.

3. Make whatever financial arrangements you can to ensure that you can afford to buy whatever professional help you may need in the future. I suggest that you do not rely on state funded schemes such as the NHS in Britain. Nor am I enthusiastic about privately funded health insurance schemes. The policies available are incomprehensibly complicated and it is difficult to work out which type of policy is best. The small print exclusions mean that many patients suddenly find that when they need help it isn't there. Older patients find themselves excluded by rising premiums. Healthy, careful, fit people who look after themselves lose out if they pay into an insurance policy because they will be helping to pay for the extra risks incurred by smokers, red meat eaters and others who take no care of their own health and who will, therefore, be far more likely to need expensive medical attention. Remember that if you are paying into a health insurance scheme you are also paying for expensive administrative, management and marketing costs. Some private insurers won't pay for alternative therapies – even when those therapies might be safer, cheaper and more effective than orthodox therapies. If you are worried about how you'll cope if you aren't able to work then my own preference is for an ordinary sickness policy which simply pays out cash when you can't work; insurance that will pay you a fixed cash sum every week or month. Most of the insurance companies which offer this type of cover will charge less if you buy a policy which only pays out after a fixed period of, say, 4, 8 or 12 weeks of illness. But I would supplement

126

that, and plan for the future, simply by investing the money I would have paid for private health insurance and keeping it as a 'private' and 'personal' health nest egg. Think how much you could save in a few years by investing the sort of money private health insurers require in premiums.

4. If you travel abroad a good deal take out an annual travel insurance policy.

5. Remember that you can mix orthodox and alternative medical treatments. But do make sure that everyone treating you knows exactly what is going on. And make sure that all the health professionals you visit are properly trained and qualified.

6. If you want private medical treatment arrange for it to be provided in a private hospital and not in an NHS hospital. Some private hospitals are better equipped, better staffed and cheaper than NHS hospitals. NHS staff are sometimes rude and resentful when treating patients who are paying for private treatment. And, if there is time, don't be afraid to shop around. There is no correlation between cost and quality. Some of the most expensive consultants are the most incompetent.

7. You can mix and match private and NHS care. Some hospital consultants will tell you that you can't do this. They are lying. You can. It's your NHS and you paid for it.

8. Don't bother to complain if you have problems with the NHS. It annoys me a great deal to have to say this but if you try complaining about anyone working for the NHS you will wear yourself out before you get any action. If patients were of one race then NHS staff would be accused of institutional racism. As anyone who has tried to use it will probably confirm, the NHS complaints procedure is (like most official complaints procedures in the UK) a sick joke, designed to protect the staff from criticism and the hospital from lawsuits.

9. If you are ill make sure you learn as much as you can about your condition. Don't just hand yourself over to doctors and nurses. Visit your library or bookshop and borrow or buy as many books dealing with your illness as you can find. Get hold of a copy of *Help!* which contains addresses, telephone numbers, fax numbers

and e-mail addresses for a huge number of patients' organisations dealing with specific disorders. The directory can be purchased from G Text, Freepost NWW6775, Blackpool FY4 3GA, UK. I also suggest that you contact the World Research Foundation, World Research Building, 41 Bell Rock Plaza, Sedona, AZ 86351, USA and ask them to send you a list of the research packets they can supply.

10. Don't trust anyone who calls patients 'clients' or 'customers'.

11. If you want to see your GP urgently and are told that there is a two week waiting list just tell the receptionist that you must be seen at home. They will suddenly find you an appointment for today.

12. Plan to spend the final third of your life in a fairly self-contained environment – and well within your means. State pensions, already small, are likely to become increasingly derisory. I have absolutely no desire to offer a scary scenario for the future but I owe it to you to be realistic and I believe that all the social evidence suggests that our society is going to become increasingly violent. For over a decade I have been warning that thefts and muggings are going to become commoner and commoner. Since it is also likely to become increasingly difficult to find electricians, plumbers, carpenters, decorators and other tradesmen you might be wise either to learn how to deal with these problems yourself or to choose accommodation which is unlikely to require constant, complicated maintenance.

13. You should also be constantly aware that many of the chronically disabling illnesses of the 21st century are caused by drug therapy.

    For example, I wonder how many people know that tinnitus – that desperately depressing constant ringing of the ears which causes so much distress and ruins so many lives – is frequently a side effect of anti-depressant therapy? A reader who was put on anti-depressants and who subsequently complained of tinnitus was assured by nine highly qualified experts that her tinnitus could not possibly have been caused by the drug she was taking. Because the tinnitus was making her more depressed they increased the dose of the drug. The tinnitus got worse. The experts seemed surprised that when she stopped the drug the tinnitus went away and the depression lifted.

Most doctors prescribe far too many different drugs and as a result they have no idea what side effects are associated with the drugs they are handing out. You should remember Coleman's First Law of Modern Medicine: 'If you develop new symptoms while being treated for any medical condition the chances are that the new symptoms are caused by the treatment you are receiving.' One in six patients in hospital are there because they have been made ill by doctors. The reason is simple. Few doctors know Coleman's First Law of Modern Medicine. You should never forget it. It will be a vital weapon in your self-defence armoury in the years ahead.

14. Many people still trust their doctor (just about) but sadly that trust is often misapplied. Remember that most doctors would love to give up and do something else for a living (if they could only find something else that paid as well). Many now regard the patient as the enemy. The old doctor patient relationship (which was first damaged when appointment systems were introduced into general practice) has now been damaged beyond repair. Today, doctors have to be treated with the same degree of caution as you might treat a plumber or a car mechanic or estate agent. For example, when the doctor says you need a vaccination can you trust him? Or is he simply trying to make money by selling you something you don't really need? (Remember that these days doctors often receive bonus payments if they can persuade enough of their patients to be vaccinated.)

15. To protect yourself against the MRSA superbug try not to touch buttons and handles in public places. If you must do so then make sure you clean your hands afterwards. Use a piece of tissue to cover your hand if you can when handling items (such as buttons and handles) which you think may be infected. The simple hygiene rules you were taught as a child are no longer good enough. Don't wash your hands in public places – use 'wet wipes' instead. In addition you should do what you can to ensure that you keep yourself healthy by building up a strong immune system. (There is advice on this in my book *Superbody*.)

16. Wherever you live make sure you know the name, address and telephone number of the nearest hospital which has an open casualty department.

17. If a doctor insists on vaccinating you or a member of your family get him to sign a short letter accepting responsibility for whatever short, medium or long-term problems may ensue. Write down details of what vaccination was given, when it was given and by whom. Also make a note of the vaccine name, manufacturer and batch number.

18. Sadly, you can no longer expect your doctor to treat what you tell him with total confidence. Traditionally, doctors have always regarded patient confidentiality as inviolable. 'You cannot be a bit confidential, any more than a woman can be a bit pregnant,' said one elderly GP. But for years social workers, policemen and bureaucrats have been chipping away at the inviolability – annoyed that doctors dared to keep secrets from them. Now the confidentiality has gone. Britain's New Labour Government has introduced new legislation forcing GPs to share information about their patients with 'relevant public bodies'. 'GPs are probably the most reluctant partners of all the professions in terms of sharing information. They tend to refuse to cooperate,' moaned one Minister, seemingly unaware of the fact that information ought to be treated as confidential not out of spite or commercial need but simply out of respect for patients, a need for trust and something old-fashioned called 'medical ethics'.

19. We all like to clear our desks of problems. This is never again going to be possible. The chaos, the uncertainty and the problems are never going to end. In addition to the big problems which have always beset mankind we have to face a constant dribble of frustrations and annoyances. It is not surprising that stress-related diseases continue to rise in both number and severity. We all tend to underestimate the number of unforeseen crises we will encounter in our daily lives. And we definitely underestimate the time those problems will take to clear up. If you assume that every small problem you face is going to take ten times as long to solve as you think it merits then only occasionally will you be pleasantly surprised. We all have a box inside us which fills up every day with small moments of anger and frustration. It is hardly surprising that rage is now commonplace on the roads, in shops, in airports and elsewhere. Our personal anger box is kept so full that the slightest thing can

result in an overflow or rage. The only answer is to make regular, deliberate attempts to chill out – to escape from the world and the problems which beset you.

20. It has for many years seemed to me that hotels often provide better accommodation, better service and better value than many nursing homes and care homes. It usually costs far less to live in a good hotel than it costs to live in a poor nursing home. The reason? Simple. Nursing homes have to comply with absurd regulations and tons of unnecessary paperwork. Your hard earned savings are being used to keep bureaucrats happy. Hotels provide fresh linen and towels every day and give customers free soap and shampoo. Many have a pool, gymnasium, lounge, bar and choice of restaurants. They usually have a night porter and room service. They apologise if things are faulty and provide good breakfasts. Mixing with people of different ages is far healthier too. And it's easy (and fun) for friends and family to come and stay. If you get bored you can simply move to another hotel for a few months.

21. We have many worries and many choices to make and we tend to put the same effort into dealing with the small choices as we do into dealing with the big decisions. This is, of course, a mistake. When making small decisions (which shirt to wear, which film to see) try to let instinct take over. Make a quick decision and stick to it. Keep your 'worrypower' for the big problems.

Chapter 5
Education, Education, Education

Despite New Labour's constant promises about 'education, education, education' the general quality of education is continuing to fall. Millions of adults in the UK are functionally illiterate and a recent survey showed that one in four British adults cannot calculate the change they should get from £2 after buying three items. According to figures from the Department of Education itself a significant number of adults think that 10% of £300 is less than £25.

Research done by the Financial Services Authority shows that one in four people with a pension policy do not realise that a high proportion of their money is likely to be invested in the stock market.

You don't have to look far to find evidence of falling standards. I visited a bookshop recently where signs advertised 'Stationary' and 'Quizes books'. If even bookshops are managed by illiterates the future looks bleak. (At least the bookshop contained some books. Several local authorities in Britain have recently commissioned expensive new libraries and then forgotten to order any books. Officials at one authority were probably close to embarrassment when local dignitaries turned up to the opening of a new public library which did not contain a single book.)

When a group of 16-year-old school children (allegedly the brightest of their age group in modern British schools) were given an 11 plus examination from the 1950s most of them failed miserably. Over two thirds of today's top pupils failed a simple English grammar test which had been designed for 11-year-olds half a century ago. The students, seemingly unembarrassed by their failure, complained that they had not been taught English grammar, punctuation or spelling and clearly regarded these basic building bricks of communication as unnecessary and rather beneath them. Around a quarter of these 16-year-old students went on to get grade A results in their public examinations. Around 95% of them passed their examinations. These, remember were 16-year-old students and the papers from the 1950s which they had taken (and done so badly at) were designed for 11-year-olds.

* * *

'Many Brits are stupid and uneducated; one in five adults is practically illiterate or have problems counting money in their purses.'
STERN MAGAZINE (GERMANY)

* * *

The New Labour Government has poured huge amounts of taxpayers' money into education – and has failed miserably to improve the quality of our schools. The annual spending on education has gone up 25% since New Labour took over in 1997. In that same period teacher vacancies have doubled, class sizes have risen and truancy has risen by 22%. (Naturally, there are still one or two good schools. The houses within the catchment areas for those good schools go up in value dramatically as parents try to ensure that their children get a decent education. Somehow, New Labour politicians such as the privately-educated Tony Blair seem to manage to find a way to send their children to these good schools).

* * *

Modern educationalists seem determined to throw aside centuries of wisdom about education. Formal English and maths lessons could soon disappear from British schools in order to stop bored teenagers from "dropping out". In future teenagers will be allowed to sit courses in 'communications' and 'numeracy'. (No one in the Government has yet bothered to explain how students who cannot speak or write English can study or practise 'communications'.)

133

The Government has also abandoned the principles of 'right and wrong' and now prefer teachers and others to offer support and sympathy to the perpetrator rather than to the victim.

Bizarrely, they have also decided that competition is bad for children. The new philosophy is that all children should be rewarded regardless of effort or achievement. At one point the Blair Government even talked (quite seriously) of banning musical chairs on the grounds that the game isn't fair since the fastest, toughest children win. Personally, I would have thought that that made musical chairs an excellent training for life. The NHS is a deathly shambles, the country is at permanent war, crime rates are rocketing, our drinking water is undrinkable and the Government is worried about musical chairs.

Sports days have been banned on the grounds that sports which involve winners and losers are, rather than being a relatively gentle introduction to the way life works, politically unacceptable. This absurd piece of political correctness has enabled the authorities to instruct schools to sell off their unwanted playing fields so that they can purchase text books and pay teachers' salaries. (Conveniently, local councils have abandoned their usual reticence and given planning permission for builders to erect large numbers of houses on the former playing fields) Naturally, the Government, which specialises in avoiding responsibility, blames the current epidemic of obesity among the young entirely on the food industry and sees no link between childhood obesity and the fact that children are now officially encouraged to sit around watching television and playing computer games.

Is it surprising that we now have a world in which school leavers expect a BMW and a loft apartment as a right? Many young adults cannot understand the relationship between effort and reward and don't recognise the relationship between responsibility and authority. Having been deprived of any moral training whatsoever they are brought up to think only of material and sensual pleasures (naturally, this means that they are constantly frustrated) and to be addicted to pleasure. The rich of any era could have told them that having things too easy means that you have nothing to look forward to and can never enjoy the pleasures of working towards, and reaching, a goal.

It isn't just the unemployed and the beggars from abroad who want a free ride and an easy life. I read a news story the other day about a 22-year-old graduate who is working as a management consultant.

Before It Gets Better

She earns £35,000 a year and was complaining that she couldn't afford to buy the house she wanted. Put aside the question of what the hell a 22-year-old graduate can possibly know about running a company and you will still be left with the observation that most people cannot afford the house they want. That's why they work hard and save. And it's why they dream. 'I know what I want but I can't afford it,' moaned the 22-year-old management consultant. 'And I don't want to live somewhere that is not convenient for work,' she added.

Well, of course not, dear. Would a free suite at The Ritz be acceptable while you move yourself up the management consultancy ladder?

* * *

Things are going to get worse, for several reasons.

1. The New Labour Government seems determined to run schools without teachers at all. New laws mean that only the head teacher of a school needs to be qualified. The other 'teachers' need only be adults who have the ability to turn up on a fairly regular basis. Some teachers contributed to this situation by signing up to a deal which was, theoretically, designed to shift the administrative burden from teachers to school support staff (unqualified adults who can be hired for far less money than qualified teachers). I suspect teachers missed a trick here. Perhaps they trusted the Government. A leaked paper from the Department of Education and Skills suggests that the Government intends to take advantage of the agreement which allows it to run schools without teachers. And why shouldn't they? For at least two thirds of the time they're now running the health service without doctors.

2. The Government will not, it seems, be happy until every child in the country goes to university. Everyone, regardless of skills, interests or aptitude must be educated to the same level. (The universities all have their corporate sponsors and will turn out neat, uniform, politically correct acolytes of the corporate dogma. Very few so-called academics these days do not have bank accounts enhanced by fees, share options, bonuses, expenses and other financial inducements. In some disciplines, in some universities, it is nigh on impossible to find an academic whose integrity and independence have not been compromised.)

Naturally, if all school leavers are going to attend university and the emphasis will in future be on quantity rather than quality, standards will have to fall still further.

Why Everything is going to get worse

When a reporter from a national newspaper applied to five universities they all offered him a place. The reporter filled in official university application forms with a false name ('Mickey Mouse'), a false address, false qualifications, false references, horrendous spelling errors and 'a string of obvious clues, such as writing in my personal statement that it was time to wake up and smell the cheese'. He was, nevertheless, accepted to study (among other things) for degrees in human resource management, recreation management, communication of technology and for a combined degree in American studies and tourism and leisure.

Students today prefer what is known in educational circles as the 'soft option'. The most popular degree course in Britain today is 'design studies' (whatever that is). Other popular courses include 'beverage studies' and 'media studies'. More students going to university in 2003 chose 'design studies' than chose to study 'English' and 'mathematics' added together. Employers have little respect for these degrees and there are, inevitably, far too many graduates for the number of jobs available. (Just how big is the market for students with degrees in 'beverage studies'? There is something surreal about the fact that Britain desperately needs dentists but is awash with graduates who know how to brew beer.)

When a British college graduate, who had completed a course in media studies, was found guilty of indecent exposure after exposing her breasts in a bar in Faliraki, she said: 'Everyone of my age walks along in their own little bubble hoping no one will bump into them and pop it and that the real world doesn't intrude too soon.'

The media studies graduate, who was working as a public relations officer, didn't know the name of the President of the USA and said she had forgotten the name of the British Prime Minister. She said she didn't read newspapers or watch the news, preferring MTV and reality TV.

For students, the downside to the Government's plan to send every school leaver to University is considerable. First, since the country cannot possibly be expected to pay for every school leaver to attend university the fees will have to be paid by parents or, ultimately, by the students themselves who will, if they ever find employment, have their university fees automatically deducted from their wages. Second, a degree will be of little or no practical value in the job marketplace. When everyone has one a degree loses its value.

There is an upside but that is enjoyed not by students but by politicians.

The upside is that with students spending three or more years at college the unemployment figures (and the money the Government must pay out in unemployment benefit) will fall.

The downside for the wider community is that the world is going to be cluttered with media studies graduates but disastrously short of plumbers, carpenters and electricians. No one with a degree in media studies, beauty and hair management or human resource control wants to earn a living repairing leaks or installing central heating systems. The result is that plumbers, carpenters, plasterers, electricians, bricklayers and other craftsmen are already becoming the new aristocracy; so rare and so much in demand that they will be able to charge phenomenal fees for their services. Workmen of all varieties will become increasingly arrogant as they realise that the competition for their services is increasing.

If you think about it you will, I think, agree that it is not unreasonable to say that you can blame New Labour when you can't get a plumber. Most of the young men (and women) who might have made good plumbers now have degrees in media studies and are claiming unemployment benefit and looking for glamorous jobs in television. The few plumbers in existence are so well-paid that they are already paying top rate tax and can't be bothered to train more staff because of the unbearable quantities of red tape which New Labour has introduced. When next you struggle to find a plumber remember that it is Tony Blair's fault that there are no plumbers.

The Government's absurd determination to send every child to university is wrecking the balance in every community in Britain. Not everyone wants to lead an intellectual life. It would make far greater sense to send only the most intellectually gifted children to university. Such a scheme would mean that every intellectually gifted child could be educated free of charge.

But such a logical path does not appeal to the Government. They claim that expanding the number of students going to university will accelerate economic growth. This theory is based on the argument that everyone who has a university education will earn more money than the people who don't have a university education.

There is, of course, a flaw in this rather primitive argument. The flaw is that if everyone (or virtually everyone) has a university education who will do the less well-paid, mundane jobs? And will there be enough well-paid jobs to go around?

The truth (as observed in a study done by economists at Warwick University) is that not all students earn more when they graduate than they would have earned without a university education. In fact the research shows that students with arts degrees actually reduce their earning ability. There simply isn't enough demand for all the students qualifying with degrees in art history or media studies. When more than 50% of young people go to university not all the graduates can be chiefs, but the chiefs don't want to hire graduates as Indians. Students suffer a triple whammy: they spend three years without pay at university, they accumulate massive debts and then, when they graduate, they can't find jobs.

There is another flaw, too.

Do students who earn a great deal of money really contribute to the economy?

One of the most popular university courses is law. Students know that lawyers are well-paid and so they want to become solicitors or barristers. In 1950 there were 17,000 solicitors in Britain. In 2002 there were 89,000. And the number of qualified solicitors is still rising fast.

Does anyone really believe that increasing the number of solicitors has a positive impact on the economy? Or do all those extra lawyers simply mean more litigation and more transaction costs?

It is hardly surprising that a survey involving employers showed that 53% already believe that the UK is producing too many graduates and 60% believe that increasing the number of graduates produced is reducing the quality.

I don't believe that the Government doesn't know all this. The real truth, I fear, is that the Government wants to increase the number of young people undergoing further education for one simple reason: it reduces the unemployment figures and means millions of young people are a burden on their parents rather than on the Government.

3. Political correctness and political acceptability are now playing a crucial role in British classrooms. Political acceptability means that children are routinely taught how wonderful the EU is. Political correctness means that millions of pounds (£155 million in 2003) are spent on paying for bilingual classroom assistants so that children whose parents are not British or of British origin, and whose first language is not English, don't have to bother learning English at all.

4. Schools are now graded not according to how good they are but according to how much they have improved. This means that a school which was abysmal but which has improved a little bit and become simply terrible will be given a higher ranking than a school which started off as excellent and has remained excellent. This is both absurd and unfair. It means that if a school improves its basic literacy levels from 10% to 12% it will be put higher on the list than a school which has simply maintained a basic literacy level of 100%. Only a politically correct New Labour politician could possibly think up a scheme so clearly lacking in common sense and so destined to make good and caring teachers feel frustrated and disheartened. The scheme is particularly unfair because the pay levels and bonuses awarded to schoolteachers are handed out according to these grading lists.

All things considered is it any wonder that a growing number of New Labour politicians, although publicly supporting state schools, are now choosing to send their own children to public schools?

* * *

'The only things worth learning are the things you learn after you know it all.'
HARRY TRUMAN

* * *

The failure of the system to teach children properly will continue to be disguised by making examinations easier and easier. Students are now allowed to download essays from the Internet. Officially this is not regarded as plagiarism or cheating. Teachers agree (and even politicians do not bother to dispute) that the examination pass rate (which has been rising steadily for two decades) will soon reach 100% – at which point there will clearly be little point in wasting money holding examinations. It will be simpler to post certificates to everyone who wants one.

The primary purpose of the system remains the same as it always has been (to teach obedience and to discourage originality and invention) but the quality of the education provided as a trade off continues to deteriorate rapidly.

The Government cheats on crime figures and hospital waiting list figures, so why should we be surprised that they cheat over examination figures?

Chapter 6
The Propaganda Business

A democracy needs information but a fascist dictatorship needs propaganda.

It is hardly surprising, therefore, that the British people (like the American people) are now fed almost exclusively on propaganda, rather than supplied with information. Never before has it been so difficult to find the truth. Never before has the media lied so consistently and so thoroughly in defence of the establishment. Never before have journalists betrayed their readers quite so comprehensively. One major survey showed that most people believe that the media is generally inaccurate and that editors and journalists cover up their mistakes rather than admitting them. Two thirds of the population no longer believe what they see, hear or read.

And yet knowledge-based industries are flourishing. Mass market newspapers may be struggling but magazines are being launched so quickly that it is difficult to keep up. And, of course, the Internet contains untold sites which are allegedly dedicated to the dissemination of information. However, the knowledge provided by the media these days is too often suspect and the information unreliable. Ignorance, now probably more widespread than at any time for a century, is created and then sustained by the media. Through newspapers, magazines, radio and television we have access to more information than ever before, but much of the information available to us is worthless. We are drowning in a sea of information but it is increasingly difficult to differentiate between the good and the bad. Most TV programmes, radio programmes, newspapers and magazines are merely vehicles for promotional material or Government propaganda. When the Government has any good news to report they announce it several times believing, accurately, that the media will print the same news twice, three times or, indeed, as many times as they are given it.

Modern publications and broadcasters don't take a moral or ethical stance but prefer instead to follow a commercial or politically expedient line. Western readers were, for example, told a lot about SARS – a disease threatening China, the Chinese economy and visitors to China – but they were told very little about the threat posed by the West Nile Virus, (a major threat to tourists in the USA and possibly an even bigger hazard than SARS). The American and British media don't mind building up scare stories which will harm China but they aren't so keen on stories which might harm the USA.

All history is prejudiced and biased and is written by people who have a perspective, but facts (the building blocks upon which opinions and historical judgements are built) should be treated with great respect. They are not.

It is no coincidence that many modern journalists and editors spend a good deal of their time being flattered and entertained by politicians. (The entertaining is done at public expense; the flattery comes free.) Every contentious issue has lobbyists – whether it is the tobacco industry, banks, governments, drug companies or the medical profession. All employ professional lobbyists. Very few journalists have the faintest idea how to differentiate between what they are being told and what is the truth. Most are susceptible to spin and lazy enough to print the nonsense they are fed. Sometimes the spin is so fast that it takes your breath away.

At one point, when it was announced that American investigators had decided that Iraq did not have weapons of mass destruction, the New Labour Government in Britain announced that this provided conclusive and incontrovertible evidence in support of the war. It was like something out of Alice in Wonderland. The claims varied almost daily. At one point Blair claimed that the Iraqis had factories making weapons of mass destruction. When even his spin-doctors realised that it would be difficult to hide whole factories, the Prime Minister said that the Iraqis had wanted to make weapons and had had plans to do so. Since he had not withdrawn the claim that the Iraqis had weapons which they could deploy in 45 minutes he was presumably claiming that the Iraqis were somehow able to design, test, build, deploy and fire weapons of mass destruction within 45 minutes.

A leaked memo from a chemical industry lobbyist in the USA recommended fighting increased regulation in California by hiring an 'attack dog' public relations firm to spy on industry opponents, arrange protests and recruit conservative talk show hosts. Some of Britain's most trenchant commentators on medical and scientific issues are regular recipients of handsome cheques from the industries on which they comment.

The big issues are regularly ignored by all sections of the media. Time and time again important stories are suppressed, either because they threaten big industry, or because they might upset advertisers, or because the editors who make the decisions don't understand them or because they are simply considered 'too scary'. For example, in the early 1980s I prepared a report showing that Britain's water supplies were contaminated with prescription drug residues. That, like dozens of other significant stories, was quietly suppressed and only really surfaced after I wrote about it in a book. I was once fired from a newspaper for the heinous crime of 'making people think'.

A poll taken by the British Foreign Office showed that 25% of Britons didn't know that Britain was already a member of the European Union. Astonishingly, seven per cent of Britons thought the USA was an EU member.

In Germany, a poll found that 31% of the public had never even heard of the European Commission.

The misinformation is so widespread that it is hardly surprising that millions of people end up believing the lies.

Half of all Americans think (quite wrongly) that Iraqis were on the planes used in the 11/9 attack. By the end of 2003 nearly half of all Americans believed that weapons of mass destruction had been found in Iraq (none had). One in four Americans thought that Saddam had used chemical and biological warfare on 'coalition' troops (he hadn't). And a quarter of Americans were so self-deluded that they believed that world public opinion supported the USA invasion of Iraq (it didn't).

The American media fed their couch potato audience the astonishing story of a young woman soldier who was allegedly rescued from an Iraqi hospital after being seriously injured during a battle in which she had been fighting to the death. According to the American media, Navy Special Operations forces rescued the woman despite being fired upon both going in and coming out of the hospital where she was being held. Two months later the same American media admitted that the soldier 'may not have been shot and stabbed', 'may not have fought like Rambo' and 'was not mistreated at an Iraqi hospital'. The papers also admitted that 'her heroic rescuers did not fight their way up the hospital halls' and that 'the hospital staff may have been eager to hand her over'.

Well, anyone can get a couple of facts wrong.

Another version of the story is that the young woman, whose wounds were not battle related, had been given special medical care by Iraqi hospital staff. An Iraqi nurse sang her to sleep at night and the young American was given extra juice and cookies at bedtime. The Iraqi hospital staff had already tried to turn over their patient to the American authorities and were waiting for them when they finally turned up.

It seems to me that the Iraqis come well out of this. The American military, who presumably made up the lies, come out looking predictably tawdry and the American press come out looking – well, much as we expect the American press to look.

* * *

Why is there so much ignorance? Is it an accident? Or is there a reason?

Well, as always, to find the answer all we have to do is ask a simple question: who benefits?

The answer, of course, is that the people who benefit are the people who have the power: international corporations and governments.

* * *

If journalists had asked themselves who benefited from the heavy promotion of the Atkins Diet (which I first criticised in 1982) they would have realised that the diet gave a tremendous boost to the meat industry. They might also have known that since meat is known to cause cancer a diet which is based on a high meat intake can hardly be good for anyone.

I have been writing about health issues for well over a quarter of a century and I am appalled by the abysmal quality of medical reporting in today's press. Many of the stories aren't original at all, but were first run five, ten or even twenty years ago. Much of what now passes for news is no more than commercial propaganda, fed to journalists by drug companies or by researchers trying to build up their reputations so that they can demand bigger grants. Stories are often presented in an absurd way – seemingly designed either to terrify the life out of readers or to offer them slick answers. For example, when a study in the USA showed that forearm fractures among young people have increased by 42% since the 1970s one national British newspaper carried the story under the headline 'Bones risk to children who don't drink milk'. Nowhere in the story was there any evidence substantiating this headline. There are many possible reasons for the increase in forearm fractures (the popularity of skateboarding and rollerblades for a start).

Hardly any so-called 'medical journalists' have any medical qualifications; few seem capable of assessing a clinical research paper; fewer still seem to realise that it is only possible to judge the quality of medical research when you know who paid for it. Few seem aware that they are now reprinting stories which were either proved or disproved a decade or more ago.

* * *

Today, lying and distorting the news is perfectly legal.

On St. Valentine's Day 2003, a Florida Appeals court ruled that it is not illegal for a media organisation to lie, conceal information or to distort the news.

A journalist had sued an American TV company alleging that she had been pressured to broadcast information which she knew to be false. The lawyers acting on behalf of the TV station argued that the First Amendment gives broadcasters the right to lie or deliberately distort news reports on the public airwaves. The appeals court in Florida decided that the TV station was right; there is no law against distorting the news.

* * *

During the last decade or so Britons have learnt to cope with real life by escaping from it.

They do this in a number of ways. Some take dangerous drugs such as antidepressants and tranquillisers or recreational drugs such as heroin, cocaine and marijuana. Lots drink too much. Some have taken to spiritualism, playing computer games, gambling or going clubbing without any knickers on. Some go to football matches and attack the opposing team's supporters. Some save up all their money and visit Greek islands where they drink themselves senseless and then have sex with strangers.

Most simply stay at home and watch the telly.

The average adult in this country watches between four and five hours of television a day. The average five to nine-year-old spends between two and a half and three hours television a day. Older children and young teenagers watch more. When small children aged between four and six years old were asked to say which they liked best – television or daddy – around half voted for television. Millions of people who don't give a damn about wars (illegal or otherwise) or changes to our constitution would demonstrate naked in the snowy streets if the Government or the EU dared interfere with *Coronation Street* or *Eastenders.*

Five hours a day is 35 hours a week and nearly 2,000 hours a year. Watching television has, for many, become a full-time job. If that's the average, then there must be millions of people in Britain who spend more time watching television than they spend working. (In America the average adult watches television for a mind numbing seven hours a day.) Many of the programmes are explicit and exploitative shows in which contestants are humiliated and in which loutish behaviour is encouraged. Is it any surprise that 84% of British mothers now report that their children regularly have temper tantrums? That, after all, is what they learn from constant watching of football and reality TV shows (starring what patronising middle-class producers call ' real people' – though why ill-educated exhibitionists should be thus described seems beyond me and what is 'real' about these programmes is even more beyond me.)

Watching TV for five hours a day is like giving away a third of your waking life to someone else.

Nero was accused of fiddling while Rome burned. At least he did something creative. Today's free citizen spends around five hours a day watching television and no longer believes that he can make a difference.

* * *

Anyone who doubts that violence on television breeds violence on our streets (a philosophy which I have been fervently arguing for considerably more than two decades) might try to explain why the pattern of gun crime in the UK has changed and is now more and more like that in America. A decade or two ago shootings in Britain were usually confined to fairly well planned bank robberies. Today, shootings are often random and careless as half-witted robbers carry out clumsy unplanned attacks on convenience stores.

* * *

Most worrying of all, perhaps, is the fact that many of the so-called experts who now appear on television do so because they are paid to do so by the company or pressure group which is paying them. Television companies have discovered that they no longer have to pay fees to get experts to appear on their programmes. The experts will be provided free of charge – with the expert's fee paid for by the group for which he is working. It is rare these days to see an independent expert on British television. If you see anyone described as an expert on TV (or hear one on the radio) you should ask yourself who stands to gain by his or her appearance. Moreover, television is even worse than the press for intrusion and sensationalism. Many of those working in television are driven by vanity and personal ambition rather than any determination to expose wrongdoing or tell the truth. The magic box is dominated by self important, intellectually deprived presenters with £60 haircuts and 50p brains. Salacious and hypocritical but rarely courageous or original they have turned a potentially powerful medium into a tool of our fascist state.

* * *

The Government is safe as long as the voters are more concerned with soapland than with reality. The electors sit slumped in front of their nightly five hours of watered down, two dimensional entertainment because they are too frightened to speak up; they are convinced that they cannot make a difference. They may occasionally still feel anger, frustration, alienation and bewilderment. But they dare not speak out for they fear for their own safety. They know that unemployment – and worse – beckons for those who stand up and speak out.

* * *

The first television sets were built as cupboards, just as commodes were disguised as chairs. No one wanted to admit that they had a TV set in their living room any more than their ancestors wanted a commode parked next to the Adam fireplace. Maybe we should combine these two thoughts and make TV sets disguised as commodes. Both, after all, are full of pretty much the same sort of stuff.

* * *

Publicity and fame are now utterly divorced from talent or achievement and seem to be sought after for their own sake. Many programme makers simply take advantage of the apparently ubiquitous yearning for fame at any price, apparently unconcerned by the fact that the sensational nature of most of the programmes means that the protagonists must spend the rest of their lives learning to live with the notoriety they have achieved and coming to terms with the fact that, as yet, fame by itself does not necessarily lead to great wealth. Below, I've given some examples of modern British television programmes. Note that some of these programmes appeared on the publicly funded BBC.

1. Television game show contestants had to urinate while answering questions.

2. One man had both ears and a nipple pierced on television in order to win a car. He then had to watch as the car he had just won was vandalised by two youths armed with baseball bats who were encouraged by the game show host. The two vandals gave a very good demonstration of how to vandalise a car. When they had spray-painted the car and smashed off the wing mirrors the game show host dismissed them, telling the laughing live audience not to laugh so much and to remember that their cars were parked outside the studio.

3. Two teenagers were shown live having sex. Another show involved sticking a contestant to the ceiling to see how long it was before he fell off.

4. A reality TV show was devised in which couples in long-term relationships were encouraged to prove how far they would go for cash. In the final two couples had to have sex with each other's partners live on TV.

5. A healthy young American shut himself in a plastic box and starved himself for 44 days. Afterwards he was taken (in an ambulance) to a hospital to see if there had been any lasting damage to his health. The person involved claimed he performed the stunt because he was fascinated by death, didn't like life and wanted to allow people to watch him suffer.

6. Ordinary people taking part in a so-called reality programme are shown using the lavatory.

7. Cameras are allowed into a hospital and a reporter is permitted to accompany doctors and nurses treating patients. (This must inevitably affect the quality of treatment provided.) On one programme a patient being filmed in a casualty department asked a doctor: 'Am I dying?' The doctor replied: 'I hope not. I don't think so.'

8. A girl in a bikini asked passers-by to lick an ice cream cone fixed in her cleavage.

9. A naked man earned money by being slapped with a fish

10. Documentaries are regularly shown in which young people (usually on holiday) get drunk, take off all their clothes and have sex with complete strangers.

11. A televised pop music talent show contest included a youth who had spent six months in a detention centre after assault and theft (he had been involved in the brutal mugging of a man who was left for dead – an offence which a court somewhere regarded as worth just six months punishment). When the youth failed to win the competition he complained that it was because of his criminal past. Moaning that it wasn't fair he said: 'there are lots of people on TV with criminal records'.

* * *

The organisation Reporters Without Borders publishes an annual list ranking press freedom in different countries. The organisation asks journalists, researchers, jurists and human rights activists to fill in a questionnaire evaluating respect for press freedom in individual countries. British journalists and editors should be embarrassed to know that the UK came 27th in the latest list. (American journalists and editors have no right to crow: the USA came 31st.)

The only bright spot in all this gloom is the fact that less than one in five people trust the press (or journalists) in Britain to tell them the truth – three quarters of the population say that they positively do *not* trust anything they read in the press. Journalists are alongside politicians at the bottom of the 'trust' poll – way below scientists, business leaders, trade unions, estate agents and the police. (This distrust is not confined to the UK. It is universal.)

Since it has become impossible for the ordinary reader to differentiate between the useful and the useless, all information provided by the various branches of the mass media is now worthless. If you can't tell which is good and which is bad then all information is unreliable and therefore of no value whatsoever.

Those of us who want the truth have to learn to read between the lines and, every time we hear something, ask ourselves who benefits from this 'news'. In this roundabout way (and by also relying on more reliable sources, such as independently published newsletters and books) it is possible to get much nearer to the truth.

* * *

My own faith in the independence and courage of the British press took a considerable battering in the spring of 2003 when America and Britain began their illegal, immoral and unpopular invasion of Iraq.

At the time I was writing a weekly column for a Sunday tabloid newspaper called *The People*. (It is of some small significance that I was one of the highest paid columnists in the country). I wrote a piece pointing out that a war which is illegal and immoral before it starts remains illegal and immoral after it has begun. The article I wrote was intended to encourage, and to provide comfort to, those who opposed the war and were being made to feel guilty for this by Government propaganda accusing those who opposed the war of a lack of patriotism and of disloyalty to British troops.

The editor refused to print my column and so I resigned. Subsequently, the paper did not even have the courage to defend this outrageous piece of censorship. (Presumably, even they realised that it was indefensible.) Instead, the paper claimed that I was asked not to mention the war because of the amount of war news elsewhere in the paper. That was a piece of spin of which New Labour itself would have been proud.

Although I was, I believe, the only columnist to resign on a matter of principle over the war, the book in which I described precisely what had happened (*People Push Bottles Up Peaceniks*) was ignored by most media correspondents, possibly because they found the idea of a principle being executed at financial cost rather scary, possibly because none of them could find the courage to criticise the editor of another newspaper. Maybe they didn't think censorship worthy of discussion. Maybe their own newspapers had secrets which they feared might be exposed.

In retrospect, it turns out that the editors of *The People* may have misjudged their readers. In the six months after I had left, after publicising what the editors had done and predicting that the circulation would dive, the circulation of *The People* fell by 14%. This was, during that period, the largest decline of any national newspaper. I found it a cheering sign; suggesting that editors who betray their readers can expect to pay the price.

Chapter 7

Disappearing Morality And The Twin Curses Of Political Correctness And Multiculturalism

Britain is suffering from a lack of moral leadership.

Everywhere we look we see nothing but greed.

Politicians are in politics not for what they can put in but for what they can get out. Business leaders are, generally speaking, as dishonest as they are greedy. And they are very, very greedy. Most don't give a fig for their customers, their shareholders or their employees. Investors are fleeced by crooked advisors. (The UK has been described as 'Europe's fraud capital'.) Big organisations have 'mission statements' but they no longer have values and most employees neither know nor care what their company actually does. In commerce, as in politics, the word scandal doesn't mean much any more. When did you last hear of a company boss (or politician) resigning in shame? When did you last see a company boss (or politician) blushing with embarrassment?

* * *

One of the unnoticed ironies of our modern society is that although political correctness is rampant, moral values have all but disappeared.

More and more people who disliked her at the time now think fondly of the 'Margaret Thatcher days' and of her Victorian values. At least there were values. There was something to agree with or to oppose. With New Labour there are no values, no principles and no passion. Being in Government is, for them, an end in itself. Integrity, decency and respect for parliament and the electors are yesterday's values and alien concepts to Blair's government.

Blair has destroyed trust in politics and in politicians, and in consequence he has damaged what was left of democracy itself. His ability to be out of the country whenever there is trouble suggests that he works on the motto 'when the going gets tough, find somewhere else to go'. He has also ensured that the general quality of politicians entering public life in Britain in the future will remain as low as it is now. Honest people look at modern politicians, see that the only way to get on is to lie, cheat and bully, and choose to do something else with their lives.

There is something rather curious about the fact that the individuals who most actively promote political correctness are also often the people who seem most determined to destroy moral values. Indeed, it seems that political correctness and morality simply cannot survive together. Those who promote political correctness most enthusiastically are usually the same people who criticise those who talk about moral values and dismiss them as 'old-fashioned', 'bigoted' and 'prejudiced'.

Those who advocate political correctness at the expense of morality and solid values should remember that history shows that when a civilisation loses its moral values it won't be long before there is a revolution of some kind. Remember the final days of the Roman Empire, France before Napoleon and the Berlin of the 1930s.

* * *

Political correctness often seems like a bit of a joke.

In order not to cause offence we are told that we have to talk about 'personhole' covers and 'Personchester' and we're informed that prostitutes must in future be referred to as sex workers. Many chains of newsagents sell magazines aimed at homosexuals but won't sell magazines which offer entertainment to heterosexual males. Magazines aimed at heterosexual men are banned or covered up with opaque wrappers whereas magazines for gay men (carrying photographs of naked or semi-naked young men) are displayed quite openly.

The person in charge of a meeting must be referred to not as the 'chairman' but, ludicrously, as the 'chair'. The local dustman is now a 'refuse disposal operative' and I know of one local odd job man who has the words 'Multidisciplinary Task Technician' painted in fairly neat letters on the side of his van. (A second has settled for 'Multidisciplinary Consultant'.) The BBC has for years broadcast a programme called 'Woman's Hour'. Would they ever dream of producing a programme called 'Man's Hour'? There is a BBC Radio Scotland, a BBC Radio Wales and a BBC Radio Northern Ireland. But there is no BBC Radio England.

New laws on domestic violence assume that only women ever get hit (although, in reality, as many men as women are victims of domestic violence). Similarly, many rape organisations ignore male victims (and refuse to offer them counselling). The women's liberation movement has had such an impact on our society that a recent survey showed that 60% of men would, if offered a chance at reincarnation, prefer to come back as women. Just 19% of women would choose to be reincarnated as men.

Political correctness, and its advocates, may often appear silly, but in practice political correctness is no joke. It affects our lives in a number of real – and sometimes dangerous – ways. It has contributed nothing to our way of life, but its self-important proponents have created seemingly endless spiritual devastation.

It is political correctness (combined with the demands of the nanny state and particularly nasty varieties of pseudo-science) which has resulted in thousands of children being forcibly removed from their entirely innocent parents (the Government cold-bloodedly admitted the extent of this problem but cold-heartedly said that it was too late to give the children back to their rightful parents) and hundreds of innocent mothers being convicted of murder and receiving prison terms instead of sympathy when their babies died in their cots.

In some colleges and universities young men must now ask for formal permission if they intend to put a hand on a girl's breast and they must then keep on asking her for permission every time they intend to take the romance a stage further. Any man who fails to follow the proper procedure is liable to find himself accused of rape.

Most of the time political correctness results in decisions and changes which are at best bizarre and at worst downright stupid. People working for large companies are no longer allowed to have a 'personnel department' but must, instead have a 'human resources division'. Where is the sense in that? Would you rather report to a department or be considered a resource? It is difficult to think of a more demeaning phrase.

In 2003 the Scottish Parliament banned traditional Christmas cards for fear that they might be offensive to people of other religions. Officials ruled that the words 'Merry Christmas and a Happy New Year' must not appear on cards sent out by Members of the Scottish Parliament or any staff because the wording was not considered to be 'socially inclusive'. Church officials were banned from advertising a Christmas carol service in case it offended non-Christians.

Just before Christmas 2003 the British Red Cross announced that it had banned Jesus Christ from its shops for fear of offending minority faiths. Red Cross volunteers were banned from creating nativity displays or even hanging up advent calendars if they contained offensive pictures of Mary and Joseph or the Three Wise Men. A spokesman for the Moslem Council of Great Britain said 'This is political correctness gone too far...it is this kind of sentiment that can lead to a backlash against members of minority faiths...'

Another charity banned the sale of cards with a religious theme because its bosses didn't want to offend non-Christian British citizens. However, cards celebrating Christmas with a picture of Father Christmas swigging from a bottle of sherry and pinching a young woman's bottom were considered acceptable, even though these might offend Christians. The Muslims, whom it was said that celebrations of Christmas might offend, said they weren't in the slightest offended by Christmas but in fact found the ban rather patronising and unnecessary.

(Many of the politically correct idiots who were involved in trying to ban Christmas lest the Muslims be offended were the same politically correct idiots who had supported the illegal and immoral bombing of Iraq – and the killing of thousands of innocent Muslims. Incidentally, after killing vast numbers of Iraqi women and children the New Labour Government spent a small fortune sending two feminists to Iraq to promote gender equality and diversity.)

✳ ✳ ✳

Voltaire famously once said: 'I disapprove of what you say, but I will defend to the death your right to say it.'

Today, dissenting views (whether offensive or not) are criminalised.

When an elderly evangelical Christian held up a poster calling for an end to homosexuality, lesbianism and immorality he was convicted of a breach of public order. A group of people who objected to his poster (and who attacked him and threw soil and water over him) were not charged with anything.

Gay policemen who want to attend Britain's annual Gay Pride March are to be allowed to do so while wearing their police uniform. Policemen on duty will escort the march, while gay policemen, in uniform, will be part of the march. Are all policemen now going to be allowed to take part in demonstrations while wearing their uniforms? Or will policemen only be allowed to take part in demonstrations which have been classified as 'politically correct'? If a policeman who is an animal rights supporter wants to take part in an anti-hunting march will he be allowed to do so? (That's a rhetorical question. I think you and I both know the answer.)

* * *

And then there is David Blunkett.

I don't like Blunkett, who seems to me to make Mussolini look like a soft-hearted liberal, and who is possibly the most right wing Home Secretary Britain has ever had. He has taken away our freedom and our security. (And it was Blunkett's Home Office which tried to force wrongly convicted prisoners to hand over huge chunks of their compensation to cover the cost of their food, clothes and lodging in prison.)

I'm sure Blunkett won't mind my being honest about him. He can be extremely undiplomatic himself. When he heard that Dr Harold Shipman had committed suicide in hospital Blunkett's response was to say that he felt like cracking open a bottle of champagne. 'You wake up and you receive a call telling you Shipman has topped himself and you think, is it too early to open a bottle?' he told journalists. This hardly seemed to me to be the sort of tone one would expect from a Home Secretary responsible for the safety of prison inmates. We don't hang prisoners in the UK at the moment and as far as I know we don't encourage them to hang themselves. An offer of resignation might have been more appropriate. Shipman may have been a mass murderer but he did leave a grieving family.

Naturally, I admire Blunkett's ambition and determination (though to be fair, Dr Harold Shipman had both those qualities too) but I can't help suppress my concern at the thought of a blind man taking a leading part in running Britain.

It is politically incorrect to mention Blunkett's blindness (though I do sometimes wonder whether he was made Home Secretary because of it rather than despite it) but Blunkett's blindness does matter and is relevant.

My fear is that Blunkett must rely for information on the people around him. How can he study books, pamphlets and articles which aren't in Braille or selected to be read to him? I often send copies of my books to all MPs. I know from the mail I receive that many of them read the books and benefit from them.

Because he is blind Blunkett must rely on his aides to tell him what is happening and to give him information. He can listen to the radio. But he can't watch the TV. He is denied the opportunity to study body language. He can't look into people's eyes. When he signs official papers someone else has to tell him what he is signing and show him where to sign. He cannot possibly know what he is signing unless the documents are in Braille.

Now that we have a blind Home Secretary, there are plans to introduce blind magistrates too.

If we have blind magistrates why not deaf ones? And dumb ones. Where do we draw the line? The extra cost of providing evidence in different formats will be prohibitive. How can defendants possibly get a fair trial when magistrates cannot possibly examine the evidence thoroughly?

The politically correct argue that anyone must be allowed to do any job – regardless of any handicap or disability.

I disagree. I think there are some jobs that people with handicaps cannot do fairly and independently.

Appointing blind Ministers and magistrates may be politically correct but I think it's as daft as having blind firemen, surgeons or pilots.

Would an advocate of political correctness be prepared to sit in a plane being flown by a blind pilot? Would you allow a blind surgeon or a spastic to operate on your brain? Should doctors suffering from Alzheimer's Disease be allowed to practise? Would the advocates of political correctness sit in a bus driven by someone with an IQ of 60?

The trouble is that no one will dare even to discuss this issue because to do so is politically incorrect.

* * *

Employers and the authorities are so desperately conscious of the new laws introduced to prevent racism that they bend over backwards, sideways and forwards to avoid doing anything that could possibly be construed as having racial overtones. Some minority groups now ruthlessly use the 'prejudice and abuse' argument as a 'get out of jail free' card. ('If you fire me, arrest me or do anything else I don't like I will claim that you are doing whatever you are doing because I am black, homosexual or from Mars.')

Schools are also used to create a politically correct society and it is children who often suffer. In many British schools translators are provided so that non-English speaking children of immigrants can have their lessons translated into their own language. Imagine how this must slow things down for British pupils. In order to avoid giving offence the Government doesn't talk about teaching 'English' any more – it now talks about teaching 'communication skills'.

In Wales there are now many schools where Welsh is taught as a first language (this means that other subjects are taught in Welsh) and English is taught as a second or foreign language. I understand and sympathise with Welsh nationalists who are proud of their history and their heritage but forcing children to learn in Welsh is a form of child abuse. Teaching Welsh as a first language is institutionalised child abuse. Children who grow up with Welsh as a primary language will always be at an educational disadvantage at University or when trying to get a job outside Wales. I would accept the notion that Welsh be offered an optional, additional language in schools. But in my view making Welsh a primary language is done not because it is sensible but because it satisfies the politically correct requirements of a rabid minority who see their Welsh nationalism as more important than providing children with a useful education for a demanding world. The politically correct can be, and often are, both patronising and elitist. (I have a suspicion that the government supports the teaching of Welsh as a first language because this suits the purposes of the EU which intend to break up Britain and turn Wales into a separate EU region.)

One of Britain's longest established lifeboat crews has been saving lives for 158 years. During that time they have saved over 2,000 lives. When they needed a new boat they had to find £800,000 so they decided they would raise £600,000 themselves and ask the National Lottery Community Fund for £200,000. It is difficult to think of a better use for Lottery fund money. But the crew's request for help was turned down because the lifeboat does not help the disadvantaged. Personally, I would have thought that anyone drowning was pretty disadvantaged but the people who dole out Lottery money told the lifeboatmen that they couldn't have money because the people they rescue are 'industry related'. Someone in a dinghy or on an airbed is, apparently, part of the holiday industry. A fisherman is part of the fishing industry. Someone who falls from a ferry is part of the shipping industry. And the lottery apparently doesn't rescue people who are part of any industry – even though by those rules I find it difficult to think of anyone doing anything who isn't part of some sort of industry or other. The unfortunate lifeboat crew, denied Lottery support, should perhaps put a little more effort into saving asylum seekers. Perhaps they would then find themselves drowning in money from the Lottery.

It is political correctness which forces medical schools to accept a high percentage of female students – regardless of their suitability as doctors. It is political correctness which encourages many members of NHS staff to refer to (and think of) patients as 'clients' or 'customers'. This may well be politically correct, but people in pyjamas and nightdresses who are lying in hospital beds still like to think of themselves as patients not customers.

Political correctness can sometimes put ordinary citizens in great and unnecessary danger. There is a tuberculosis (TB) epidemic in the UK, largely as a result of the fact that one in six migrants from the third world are infected with TB. (This epidemic was easy to predict. I published warnings about it many times in the mid 1980s.) When it was suggested that migrants should be screened for TB (for their own good as well as for the benefit of the community) the suggestion was immediately attacked as being unacceptably racist. It is hardly surprising that cases of tuberculosis have risen by 20% in Britain over the last decade.

And political correctness is used to excuse, justify and defend violence. For example, Zionists use political correctness to resist criticism of Israel's activities.

Most Europeans (and most European countries) believe that Israel is the world's greatest threat to world peace. This viewpoint owes a great deal to honest pragmatism and nothing whatsoever to racism. However, Zionists tend to regard any criticism of Israel's policies as signs of anti-semitism. Zionists in the USA see such criticism as a sign that Europe has become anti-semitic. Of course, if only the American Zionists had the sense to see it there is a great deal of difference between concern over Israel's illegal treatment of Palestinians (and America's support for Israel) and anti-semitism. Indeed, the two have nothing whatsoever to do with one another. Perhaps the confusion is deliberate – created in an attempt to embarrass those who criticise Israel's aggressive and illegal activities. To confuse disapproval of Israel with anti-semitism is to deliberately obscure the truth and seems to me to be an example of that peculiar mixture of paranoia and racism which seems so common among Zionists. The real irony is that those accusing Europeans of anti-semitism are often themselves far more worthy of the description since the word 'semitic' refers to both Jews and Arabs and the word anti-semitic refers to someone who is opposed to Arabs as well as Jews. In practice, recent history shows that the Americans are the world's most potent anti-semites. (It would not be difficult to argue that many Jews are pretty anti-semitic too.)

Zionists are too quick to use political correctness, and the anti-semitism 'get out of jail free card' just as an old woman may use her weak heart as a weapon with which to excuse her behaviour and to force those around her to accept everything she wants and to provide her with an endless supply of sympathy.

* * *

The people who rule and administer Britain are totally and irredeemably corrupt. Everything they do is done to further their own interests. And since their own interests are enhanced by the strengthening of the State, the State must be strengthened.

All the aspects of our life which might threaten the power of the State (or further the strength of the individual) must be destroyed.

For example, look at what has happened to marriage.

Traditionally, in return for establishing a stable, committed partnership, married couples were given respectability, security, tax breaks and some legal protection (for example, they couldn't be forced to give evidence against one another). The nation regarded itself as consisting of a host of many such small partnerships. The underlying theory was that communities are based on families and that married couples gave communities stability.

'It is marriage which has given man the best of his freedom, given him his little kingdom of his own within the big kingdom of the state, given him his foothold of independence on which to stand and resist an unjust state' wrote D. H. Lawrence 'Break it and you will have to go back to the overwhelming dominance of the state which existed before the Christian era.'

However, our Government seems determined to destroy the most fundamental building blocks of our society – and they have paid particular attention to those building blocks which benefit individuals and the community rather than the State. New Labour seems determined to make the State all powerful and all knowing. They have done their damnedest to destroy the institution of marriage. Astonishingly, even the judiciary have openly supported the demolition of marriage. Britain's first female law lord held a press conference on her appointment and announced her support for gay marriages and more rights for unmarried partners. (There was a time when judges were supposed to be impartial and leave press conferences to politicians.)

Today, anyone defending marriage is regarded as an intolerant bigot. Feminists and homosexuals have provided the cover for the fascists as they have worked to create a country without marriage, family life or community. As a reward for the support they have received the fascists have made civil partnerships for homosexuals legal.

* * *

We have a multicultural society and we are frequently instructed that this is the only decent way to live.

Why? Why do people come to Britain if they don't admire our nation and our ways? (You and I know that many come for the benefits we hand out. But we have to try and ignore that.) Britons who go to France don't expect the French to start speaking English, playing cricket and serving warm beer. Why is it racist to admire and respect our own nationality but essential to admire and respect the nationality of others? Why is it a 'good thing' to be a Welsh nationalist or a Scottish nationalist but a modern sin to be an English nationalist?

There is absolutely nothing wrong with nationalism. There is nothing wrong with being proud of your country and your heritage. To debase nationalism by dismissing it as racism is both stupid and ultimately dangerous. Multiculturalism has created racism where it never existed and has exacerbated resentment where it was merely smouldering.

The theory of multiculturalism outlaws criticism of the number of immigrants and allows mini versions of other countries to be created in our cities. (The politically incorrect, but entirely accurate, term for these mini versions is 'ghettoes'.) Multiculturalism results in English children being taught Urdu in school. It results in schools having to provide translators so that the increasing numbers of children who don't speak English can study. (Under these circumstances, it is hardly surprising that an increasing number of British children grow up illiterate and innumerate.)

Karl Marx had a dual strategy for destroying capitalism. He believed that if he could debase a nation's currency and its language then capitalism would fall. Our currency was debased years ago when it was separated from the gold standard. The Government now plans to destroy our currency completely and to replace it with the euro. Our language has been debased by falling educational standards and the steady influx of immigrants who insist on speaking only their original language.

Multiculturalism results in the Government printing official forms in a dozen languages and it results in the Government allowing the ritual slaughter of animals. (The feelings and principles of the millions of Britons who find ritual slaughter deeply offensive are ignored. If expressed in public they are dismissed as 'racist' rantings.)

Multiculturalism is responsible for the 'them and us' situation which will lead to violence in the future. Political correctness has done exactly the opposite to what its proponents claimed to want. The very word 'multicultural' stinks. I like lots of cultures. But I don't want or expect or prefer them all mixed up. It is not at all racist to oppose multi-culturalism. Indeed, the essence of multiculturalism (the destruction of individual races and discrimination against members of a particular race) is itself fundamentally racist.

Those who advocate multiculturalism don't simply advocate coexistence – they want us all to mix together, to abandon our individual traditions, to forget our histories and to create a new master race of no race. This is nonsense. I like chocolate ice cream, pizza and tomato soup. But I wouldn't want them all mixed up together. That's the madness of multiculturalism.

Individuals from different races and different cultures tend to get on well together. It is only when those individuals are told that they must forget their personal beliefs, suppress their cultural individuality and subscribe to a bland and tasteless politically correct, multicultural party dogma that the problems really arise.

Multiculturalism is a cause of many of our problems – it creates ghettoes in our towns and cities and it is, like it or not, a major reason why the community spirit has gone out of our life.

How can there be any community spirit when schools allow translators to stand in a classroom so that immigrants don't have to bother learning English?

The famous Norman Tebbit cricket test – now widely derided as racist – seems to me to be perfectly sound. If you claim to be English, and want all the advantages of being English, then should your primary loyalties not be to the England cricket team? A former England cricketer who declared that young Asians brought up in Britain should get behind England at cricket was pilloried by some for making this entirely sensible and laudable observation.

I have been at test matches in England and watched aghast as Britons of Indian or Pakistani origin have booed every success of the England side and cheered every success of the visiting team. This was blatant racism. (But discriminating against the English seems to be a politically acceptable pastime these days. The city of London spent £100,000 of public money celebrating St. Patrick's Day but refused to spend a penny to celebrate St. George's Day.)

The most extreme examples of racism I have ever seen have occurred at matches between India and Pakistan. Others have noticed the same thing. 'Far and away the most racist behaviour I have ever encountered at a sports event came at a cricket match between Pakistan and India at Old Trafford four years ago,' wrote Michael Henderson in *The Spectator*. 'Pakistan won, and the foul-mouthed, sexually-threatening conduct of some of their supporters inside and outside the ground passed without comment. Had the offenders been white, it would have been very different.'

Reversing the trends started by the multiculturalists will be difficult for those who advocate multiculturalism are both blind and humourless.

'What about America?' demanded one multiculturalist, asked to offer one society where multiculturalism worked.

The very fact that anyone can offer America as an example of a successful multicultural society is rather glum proof of the problems we face.

In an interview in the *Financial Times*, Norman Tebbit argued that the reason why it is not safe for young people (or possibly anyone) to walk through central London in the dark is partly because of a 'disintegration of the community spirit'.

This, said a reporter from the *Financial Times*, smacked 'of blatant racism. And, if nothing else, it's a joyless view of the world.'

Huh?

Tebbit's comment was honest and accurate but it was neither racist, nor in itself, joyless. What is truly joyless is the life we are forced to lead in a society which has, for whatever reasons, lost its community spirit.

Much of the beauty and fascination of the human world lies in the diversity of our cultures. We should all respect one another's cultures. But we have to respect our own culture too.

* * *

Where is the moral courage that once exemplified the British? Where is the moral leadership? (Tony Blair constantly reminds us that he is a Christian but I am rather losing track of the wars he's helped to start. Starting a war on the basis of lies seems about as immoral as anyone can get.)

The world is now replete with fraud which is common among bankers, investment advisers, charities, lawyers, doctors, politicians (of course), journalists, estate agents, insurance companies and sportsmen.

Tory sleaze usually involved sex. Labour sleaze is invariably about money. (I much preferred the Tory sleaze – it was far more interesting and it didn't affect me.) Since they came to power New Labour has been constantly accused of accepting money for political favours. ('You give us money and we'll give you a Government contract.') Corporations have been bribing politicians for years in Japan, Germany and USA. Now it's common in the UK too.

I can remember when sportsmen were honourable and when cheating was simply unacceptable. No more. Today, nasty, thuggish footballers get away with violent behaviour and they even get paid for talking and writing about it. Professional cricketers who have presumably never heard the phrase 'that isn't cricket' now cheat openly – fielders claim catches that haven't been caught and batsmen stand their ground when they know they are out. Players abuse one another so much they even have a word to describe it – 'sledging'. How can anyone be surprised when sports fans also behave badly?

* * *

'Whenever business funds are passed to candidates or political parties, the presumption is that a quid pro quo is expected,'
ALVIN TOFFLER

* * *

I am not arguing that Britain is alone in having lost any sense of morality. Other countries are equally corrupt. (Though we have to remember that other countries have different moral values to the ones we have traditionally upheld. A survey in the Ukraine showed that 40% of teenage students think that prostitution is just as desirable a career as being a fashion model, stewardess or interpreter.)

But whereas countries such as France and Italy have at least retained some basic charms there seem, sadly, to be woefully few charms left in Britain. Where are the graces which will save us from our present perfidious Government and administration?

Here are just a few examples of the way that morality is disappearing in Britain.

1. Ethical practices are now illegal.

Caring about animals is not allowed. Feeding the birds used to be a pleasant pastime enjoyed by thousands of kindly folk. Today, anyone who feeds the birds runs the risk of being arrested and ending up in gaol.

The British Government long ago classified animal rights campaigners as terrorists. This was done when, at the end of the Cold War, the security services were looking for a reason to exist. But the 'terrorist' tag has remained, presumably justified because animal lovers are a serious threat to the meat industry, the fur industry and the drug industry (among others).

BEFORE IT GETS BETTER

The World Trade Organisation now insists that free trade must take precedence over animal welfare legislation and that countries cannot ban imports on ethical grounds. So, even if Britain bans cruel practices (such as keeping calves, pigs or hens in small cages) we are obliged by law to allow countries where these practices are accepted to export into our market. Since their costs are lower the unethical producers will thrive.

2. Scientists have sold out

The world is full of scientific experts whose views are valueless because they have been bought and paid for. The scientists seen being interviewed on television often fail to give honest answers to sensible questions because they are receiving a salary, a fee, a grant or a bunch of shares from a commercial company with an interest in the subject.

The food industry has for years been buying up popular spokesmen and women (and the regulatory establishment) and today the rest of the scientific establishment is also a commodity available to the highest bidder. Many well-known pressure groups, campaigning groups and patients' advice groups (which invariably describe themselves as independent) were founded by food or drug companies or have close links with them.

3. Professionals now concentrate on looking after themselves

Thousands of lawyers, doctors and other professionals have all been 'bought' by various industries. Even vets have succumbed to the call of money. One vet admitted to me that he prescribed vast quantities of antibiotics for farmers so that they could give them to their animals as 'growth stimulants'. (For some reason not thoroughly understood animals who are given antibiotics grow faster and can be sold for a better price.) The vet confessed that he knew that what he was doing was grossly irresponsible because it was leading directly to the development of antibiotic resistance among infectious organisms. He admitted that he realised that patients were dying because of the problem of antibiotic resistance. But he excused his behaviour on the grounds that if he didn't do it someone else would.

Another vet told me (in the mid 1990s) that he knew that the Government was destroying sheep which had been infected with the disorder known as mad cow disease after eating contaminated animal feed. The vet refused to confirm this statement in public because he was frightened of losing Government work.

4. Britain has gone on the fiddle

Most people now agree with Mr Bumble and regard the law as an ass. So, naturally, they ignore it when they can. Most people realise that the constant avalanche of irrelevant and inappropriate legislation from the Government and the EU means that it is nigh on impossible to get through a day without breaking a law.

Many ordinary citizens now feel that it is necessary to break the rules in order to survive. They realise that the only relevant rule today is 'Don't get caught'. (There is a second rule: if you do get caught you must whinge about it not being fair and claim that you had a bad childhood and are under a lot of stress. If you can point to your membership of some ethnic or cultural minority that will help too.)

When criminologists at Keele University surveyed 4,500 people aged 25 to 65 and asked them if they had ever committed some of the most common frauds and fiddles they found that even 'respectable' people are now often dishonest. Fiddling insurance claims, claiming unjustified refunds and stealing from work are becoming frighteningly normal.

Two thirds of those who took part in the survey admitted that they had lied or cheated in dealings with shops, restaurants, employers or insurers. Many (who still thought of themselves as honest) claimed that they were motivated by their frustration with rip-off Britain – and were fighting back by doing some of the ripping off themselves.

'We are ripped off by scroungers and ripped off by uncivil servants and ripped off by politicians and big company bosses and pension fund managers,' admitted one elector who confessed to having done some ripping off of his own. 'We're just getting our own back.' Three quarters of the population said that they had been caught out by small print or red tape when they tried to make legitimate claims against insurance companies. Many said that they felt sure they had been charged for bogus repairs by mechanics and other repairmen. (How many people would really know if they needed a new exhaust manifold or rear differential?) Some had found out that they had been sold used parts as new.

Here are some of the ways in which people are cheating:

♦   People admit that if they wanted planning permission (for an extension or alteration to their home) they would (if they could) take advantage of having a contact in planning department in order to make sure that they got their permission.

♦ Many women admit buying a dress for the office Christmas party and returning the dress afterwards – claiming a full refund.

♦ The black market (or 'shadow economy') is growing constantly. At the last count it was estimated to be at least 20% of Gross Domestic Product in Belgium, Italy, Spain and Germany. (It is, of course, impossible to make an accurate estimate of an illegal activity.) People operate in the black market in order to avoid paying tax or (particularly in the UK) in order to retain Government benefits. Naturally, when so many people avoid paying tax there is a shortfall and taxes must go up. When taxes go up more people feel that it is worthwhile going 'underground'.

5. Pretending to be ill

The biggest example of dishonesty is perhaps the way that millions of people now take time off work by pretending to be sick. This habit (known as taking a 'sickie') has become endemic and is particularly prevalent in national and local government offices where the work demands are slight and co-workers are unlikely to complain. The highest incidence of people taking days off sick occurs among: civil servants, teachers, health workers, social workers and police officers. Stress is the favoured illness of choice (having overtaken the once ubiquitous 'bad back') and is preferred because the symptoms are so vague that it is almost impossible to prove that someone is not suffering from it. (The people who suffer most from stress at work are the self employed or the businessmen and businesswomen running their own small businesses and struggling to cope with the red tape produced by the Government and the EU. They, however, are unlikely to be able to take time off work so easily. If they don't work they don't earn.) Many government employees enjoy their days off so much they retire permanently 'sick' in their 40s or 50s. (Again, the contrast with the hard-working self-employed and entrepreneurs is dramatic. Thanks to the way the New Labour Government has destroyed their pensions they are likely to have to work on until their 70s or 80s if, indeed, they can ever save enough to be able to stop work.) Naturally, all government employees who are unable to work through stress are given special stress counselling in addition to the pensions and cash sums they receive in order to ease their pain.

At any one time a quarter of Britain's policemen (and policewomen) are off work 'sick'. An astonishing 70% retire on long-term sick leave. The result is that one third of the budget in some large police forces is now used to pay those on pensions and on long-term sick pay. Many of the State employees who have retired on substantial, index linked pensions then earn extra by doing odd jobs or by turning a hobby into a money making venture. There are, for example, thousands of former civil servants now selling stories, articles and photographs to magazines and newspapers. Since they have their sick pay or pension to live on they are happy to work for small amounts of money. The self-employed professionals in those categories simply cannot compete.

The fakes who have retired early on sick pay are destroying our community and will make life difficult for the genuinely ill. For thousands the disability pension offers a pool winner's lifestyle. They may well have had some emotional or physical discomfort when they were awarded their pay-out and pension but often the pain disappears but the pension does not. The stress and the backache become a memory. But the taxpayer goes on paying out the monthly pension payments. In a just world there would be a twice yearly appraisal. But in our world the pension payments, the holidays and the new cars just keep on coming.

Today, an astonishing 2.4 million Britons of working age are currently claiming long-term incapacity benefit. That figure, which excludes pensioners and people off sick for less than six months, is up by more than 250,000 since New Labour took office and, together with the dramatic increase in the number of civil servants and the growth in the public sector paid for construction industry explains Britain's relatively low unemployment figures. At the beginning of 2004 there were just under 1 million Britons officially unemployed, though that figure doesn't allow for all the unofficially unemployed who were on special schemes designed more to lower the unemployment figures than to provide any realistic training programme.

This problem is a much bigger problem than our ageing population. Pensioners usually claim money from the State for an average of ten years or so. Individuals receiving long-term sickness payments may take money out of the system for 30 or 40 years.

Part of the problem is the fact that doctors (hired to look after the sick) are also given the job of acting as a ticket office for the benefits system. A survey of 300 doctors found that 77% admitted signing 'workers' off just to get rid of them. A survey of 67 doctors, conducted by researchers at Aberdeen University and published in the *British Medical Journal*, found that most doctors tend to hand out sick notes when they are asked to do so. Stress has replaced backache as the disease of choice for individuals who want to be paid for doing nothing. One million of the Britons currently off work through 'ill health' are suffering from 'stress'. The problem for doctors is that stress is a vague disorder and the symptoms are conveniently hard to diagnose. All a patient has to do is say that they are worried, can't sleep, aren't eating properly and don't want to go out much. Tossing in a line about having a nasty boss is the cherry on the cake. (The long-term sickness figures of 2.4 million are, at any one time, supplemented by another 3.5 million workers who are off work for less than six months at a time.)

In parts of South Wales (a country, incidentally, in which most of the people who *are* in work are working for the Government) over 25% of working age men are claiming sickness benefit. This is obviously nothing less than a long-term fraud. The vast majority of these people are off work for alleged stress-related problems or 'depression'.

There is, incidentally, a common conclusion that unemployment leads to depression. This is false. Many of those who are claiming to be 'depressed' do so in order to increase the size of their weekly benefit payment.

(In London's commuter belt, where stress is a significant factor, the number of working age men claiming sickness benefit is below 5% so it isn't difficult to reach the conclusion that four out of five Welshmen claiming sickness benefit are fraudsters.)

Doctors don't have time to work through people's problems with them, to help find a cause or work out what to do, so they just hand over a sick note and some tablets. Around 10% of the patients who get a sick note are probably genuinely ill (and need more help than a bottle of tablets and a sick note). The other 90% are just crooks.

Ironically, it is those on benefits who complain most about the failure of the public services (such as the NHS). They fail to understand that public services (such as the NHS) have failed, at least in part, because far too much public money is being wasted on paying benefits to people who could and should be working. Too much of those who have become parasites fail to understand that a country's wealth comes from its workers.

As the number of fakers and parasites increases so the resentment increases. We all have the same amount of time (today's prime resource) and it is hardly surprising that the people who earn and pay tax are sometimes aggrieved and full of resentment when they rush past the park and see perfectly healthy people on benefits sitting in the sunshine reading a newspaper.

6. The compensation culture

Compensation has taken over from the football pools and the lottery as the way to get rich quick in 21st century Britain. It is a particularly big earner for State employees (and, of course, their lawyers).

For example, the compensation culture now costs the police £330 million a year (around 7% of its total wage bill). One former ex-policeman received nearly £90,000 compensation for the trauma of seeing a woman die after he crashed into her car during a 999 call (policemen cause a tremendous number of accidents – so many, indeed, that one force has stopped its drivers from speeding). The husband of the woman killed by the policeman received £16,000 compensation. A former female police officer was awarded (it is tempting to use the word 'won') an estimated £1,000,000 in a package, after complaining of bullying and sexual and racial harassment. A policewoman who slipped on a banana skin at work claimed £200,000 compensation – though she was already receiving a police pension. (The maximum pay-out for a victim of crime from the criminal injuries compensation authority is £250,000 for paralysis or loss of all four limbs. Someone who is the victim of a gang rape may receive £10,000 and someone who receives moderate brain damage as a result of an assault may receive £15,000.)

There is some irony in that bureaucrats – the people who create most of the stress in our world, and who themselves live largely stress-free working lives – are the ones who most commonly demand compensation and early retirement.

7. Politicians have corrupted the value of information and are themselves corrupt beyond redemption

Blair and the rest of New Labour have corrupted the value of information. Since we are already in information overload Blair has made it impossible to tell which information is good and which isn't. Blair, whose speciality seems to me to be the impersonation of a compassionate man of integrity, seems to believe that if you make stuff up and then repeat it often enough then eventually it will become the 'truth'. Does Tony Blair really believe that he is the honest, straightforward sort of guy he claims to be? Or does he, in his heart, know that he should be selling extended warranties or previously owned vehicles? Blair, who has institutionalised ruthlessness, is a political meringue; frothy and unsubstantial he looks good but has no nutritional value.

New Labour politicians have script writers to produce their speeches and the articles that appear under their names in the national and regional newspapers. To assume that when a politician speaks he is saying what he thinks, or reading his own script, is as naive as thinking that when film stars speak they are saying their own words. I've tried hard to think of a way to describe this and have eventually decided that the most appropriate word is 'deception'.

Since any politician who wishes to compete with New Labour has to play the same game the whole quality of information has been irrevocably changed. If you don't spin (for which read: lie and deceive) then you can't win. Politicians have always lied a bit – but New Labour have made lying the fundamental part of the business of politics. New Labour even claims to have done things they simply haven't done. Their friends in the media print and broadcast these lies and eventually the new lies become old truths. They claimed to have improved the NHS and to have abolished the House of Lords when both are blatant lies. The Labour Government had promised to get rid of the House of Lords and to replace it with something more democratic. It was difficult to argue with that. Why should a group of men who had inherited their title make judgements about our future? But Blair's idea of 'more democratic' was to replace the hereditary peers with a bunch of his chums (led by an old flatmate) in a wholly appointed chamber. Blair trampled on tradition and replaced a long established, if unrepresentative house of independents with a second chamber full of puppets and toadies. The British people were infinitely better off with the original House of Lords. The most surprising thing about Blair's decision to turn the House of Lords into a club for his pals is that the man really does seem to have

171

enough former playmates and flatmates to fill an entire House of Lords. The old-fashioned idea of being born with a silver spoon in your mouth has been replaced by having shared digs with Tony at some stage in your career. The previous version of the House of Lords was cheaper to run too since the new Blair-made 'Lords' are greedier than the old batty ones. Before the reform just 15 peers claimed £30,000 in annual expenses, seven asked for more than £35,000 in annual expenses and none wanted more than £40,000. Immediately after the reform it was revealed that 57 of the Blair-made peers claimed £30,000 in expenses, 23 demanded £35,000 and 11 wanted £40,000. Blair had obviously stocked the House of Lords with experienced freeloaders.

Even after the American Government had admitted that there weren't any weapons of mass destruction in Iraq, Blair continued to insist that there were – obviously hoping that if he continued to plod on with this feeble defence of an indefensible strategy we would, in the end, all get tired and forget about it. Blair's legacy is that we can never go back to honesty; real damage has been done to trust, honesty, morality and the very structure and foundation stones of our society. Blair's legacy is that no one now trusts politicians any more; and until there is some sort of revolution in British politics they won't trust them again. I am proud to say that in 1997 I told a huge crowd in Trafalgar Square that they could not, and should not, trust Tony Blair or New Labour. In the same year I regularly tried to persuade the editors at *The People* (for which I was then writing a column) that I wanted to spell Blair as Bliar not because I didn't know how to spell the Prime Minister's name but because I thought it suited him better. (Telling lies used to be unacceptable for politicians. When former Conservative Minister John Profumo admitted having lied to the House of Commons he immediately resigned. He spent the succeeding decades quietly performing 'good works' in reparation. Today's politicians are committed career professionals. They are in business for themselves rather than their country and seem to regard being able to lie convincingly as one of the essential tools for the job. Integrity and shame are concepts which they do not understand. In comparison to what goes on in parliament today Profumo's sins were microscopic. The former Minister now beams like a beacon of goodness and honesty.)

When New Labour have bad news to put out they do it quietly – looking for days when the newspapers are likely to be busy with other things. (Or looking for days when they have made sure that the newspapers will be busy with other things.) When a Labour spin-doctor was exposed advising a Minister to put out bad news on September 11th 2001 this wasn't exceptional; this was the way New Labour operates.

The same tricks are used all the time.

One easy way to prove that everything is getting better is simply to move the goalposts.

In the case of education the goal mouth is made bigger – examinations are made easier. (Officials have admitted at last that this is exactly what they are doing – on instructions from the politicians.) When you make examinations easier to pass you can announce with great glee that educational standards are improving. Of course, teachers really know that schools are turning out increasing numbers of illiterates.

When the Department of Health tells us that waiting lists and waiting times for hospital treatment are falling we believe them. But, again, they are just lying.

It is now impossible to believe anything the politicians say. There was more truth told in the old USSR than there is in Britain today. When a politician who has needed hospital care claims to have had NHS treatment what he really means is that he had private treatment (in a private ward, with consultants rushing in and out) but didn't pay for it.

The basis of political spin has always been that truth and facts are ultimately of less significance than widely appreciated myths, images and perceived truths. Politicians have always understood that a widely perceived falsehood is more powerful and relevant than a little known truth. They know that history is simply what we remember and what influences our lives (the perception being so much more important than the reality). Unbelieved facts are of far less importance than believable myths. They know that what we believe to be the reality is the reality.

All politicians try to put a brave face on bad news; all present their policies and ideas in the best possible light. That is entirely natural and to be expected. Voters have grown accustomed to this. But what Blair and his colleagues have done in Britain has been to change the rules completely.

We have been led to believe (itself a piece of spin) that spin is somehow harmless; rather clever in a way.

Clever it may be, harmless it certainly is not.

Spin isn't cleverly rearranging the truth; in essence it is simply presenting lies as truth.

To make things worse Blair and his ministers have presented the spin in such a way as to make those rejecting it as unpatriotic or uncaring. They have corrupted the very concept of patriotism by suggesting (with considerable success) that anyone who supports the United Kingdom (or, worse still, England) must be racist. Blair wants us to believe that if we are to be loyal to our country we must be loyal to our Government. This is, of course, a nonsense. It is easy to confuse 'Government' with 'Country'. And it is sometimes difficult to accept that the Government is, today, our country's worst enemy.

Blair and his colleagues have betrayed whatever passions, morals and purposes they may have had simply for personal success. Blair's two main skills seem to be smiling and lying, (though he can, admittedly, manage these either separately or together). Nine out of ten voters say they believe politicians lie. Is it any surprise that more than half of young people say they have no interest in politics?

For Blair an election manifesto is merely a means to get elected; it is not a commitment. Today's politicians don't win elections by being passionate; they win elections simply by knowing how to win elections. Honour is simply a girl's name rather than a concept related to integrity. Few common criminals in Britain are better deserving of punishment than the members of the Blair Government: an array of narcissistic, materialistic politicians, devoid of morality or any understanding of responsibility. Blair, a professional emetic, has damaged Britain permanently; he and his wretched comrades have permanently damaged politics too. New Labour have made lies a fundamental building block of modern government. Making promises is far easier than 'doing', and lying is easier than explaining. Blair, was a man once thought to be of much promise. He is now known to be merely a man of many promises – most of them broken. New Labour practise cronyism and nepotism as though they were members of an imperial family. People are rewarded not for their qualities but because they lived in the right flat or went to the right college. Blair et al have, by handing out jobs to their chums, created a new and sinister breed of professional quango sitters.

* * *

BEFORE IT GETS BETTER

Blair's prime legacy will be in having devalued politics to the point where trust has virtually disappeared. Public life has been devalued so much that most people won't bother to vote. 'What is the point of voting? They all lie. None of them can be trusted. They're all as bad as one another.'

Before he got into power Blair publicly attacked America's state sponsored terrorism, supported unilateral nuclear disarmament, and promised to take the UK out of the EU (on the grounds that it had drained our natural resources, destroyed jobs and taken away Britain's freedom to follow the sort of economic policies the country needs), opposed joining the European Monetary System (the forerunner to the euro) because 'it would put the governor of Germany's Bundesbank in 11 Downing Street' (instead of the Chancellor) and spoke out in favour of mortgage tax relief, promising to retain it. When he became Prime Minister his views changed on all these crucial issues.

On the Falklands War, Blair said: 'If we are faced with an option between compromising and really a full scale war, then I think that realistically we have got to say that we are prepared to compromise.'

This was the same Blair who led Britain into a seemingly endless series of unnecessary, unjustifiable, immoral and illegal wars.

What is Blair in politics for?

It's difficult to avoid the conclusion that Blair is in politics for Blair. He wants a big salary, free accommodation, a chauffeur driven limousine and freebies all around the world.

* * *

Before they were elected in 1997 New Labour made a number of promises on animal issues. They promised to ban hunting (regardless of the House of Lords) and to set up a Royal Commission to investigate vivisection. These promises were merrily abandoned as soon as Blair took office. Principles were abandoned for commercial and political expediency.

There is clear evidence that vivisection, a barbaric and cumbersome process at best, is utterly useless in helping to protect patients. It is of no value to doctors and is used solely because it gives drug companies advantages in marketing their products. Labour reneged on their promise to have a Royal Commission investigate vivisection because they knew that any independent study would be bound to conclude that animal experiments are of absolutely no value to human beings. They knew that such a conclusion would annoy the international drugs industry.

After the people of Cambridge decided they didn't want the University to be allowed to build a new laboratory for animal experiments the Government overruled the wishes of the local people (and the normal democratic process) and gave the university the permission it had requested. Why pretend to have democratic procedures when you just overrule the results when you don't like them? This is fascism.

Despite its pre-1997 animal-friendly promises the Labour Government has proved to be just as unfriendly to animals as any Tory Government. Jack Straw, when Home Secretary, went so far as to describe animal rights campaigners as 'terrorists'.

In late 2003 the Government finally said it would abandon badger killing (done, allegedly, to stop the spread of TB to cattle) because it had realised that this caused more cattle deaths from TB than *not* killing the badgers. I and other experts who had read the evidence had urged this five years earlier. Around 8,000 badgers were killed unnecessarily.

When foot and mouth disease affected farm animals in Britain the Government chose simply to kill all the animals. They killed not just the sick animals but also the healthy animals (in the same sort of way that foresters chop down healthy trees in order to stop a fire spreading).

The killing of several million animals wasn't just entirely unnecessary it was, it seems, illegal. The Government deliberately and callously killed millions of healthy animals – including many which were kept as pets and which would have never entered the 'food chain'.

Tony Blair stated publicly that he was in charge. Why has he not been prosecuted over that illegal slaughter? Why is Blair above the law? Was the mass slaughter simply an attempt to get rid of the animals almost certainly harbouring the 'mad cow disease' virus?

I doubt if any other Prime Minister in history has killed as many perfectly healthy animals for absolutely no reason. Blair, remember, had come to power after promising 'animal friendly' policies.

* * *

Victor Frankl pointed out that 'Everything may be taken from us except the last of the human freedoms – our ability to choose our own attitude in any situation.' Well, Blair and New Labour have done their best to remove that last freedom by severely damaging our ability to choose our own 'attitude'. When you don't know the truth, but are directly led by your leaders to believe what is not true, it becomes exceedingly difficult to know what is right or what you yourself really want.

* * *

Blair wants power, money, status, fame, approval and acclaim. He has all those, but at the moment they are on loan and they come with the job. Blair wants those baubles for himself by right. And he knows that the best way to acquire them is to suck up to the most powerful people in America: the rich, white men who own the oil, the arms industry and the Presidency.

Blair also wants immortality and that he will not have – at least not in the way he had hoped. He will, I suspect, be remembered not as a great man but as an unrelievedly bad man; a liar and a warmonger who unnecessarily and repeatedly led his country to war and betrayed those who put their trust in him. It now seems bizarre to remember that in 1997 Blair pledged his government to a moral foreign policy. Today, with his unceasing thirst for war, he rather reminds me of a film producer who has found a good franchise to exploit. Instead of Rocky 3 this producer gives us Blair's War 3.

* * *

Generally speaking, men (and women) who lie do so because they are afraid of the people they are talking to. Lies always come through fear. Our politicians lie because they are in fear of the electorate. They are in fear of the electorate because they have no other way of earning a living. That is the ultimate irony: our politicians are controlled by the same fear they use to control us.

In the end, the truth is that politicians are frightened to 'do the right thing' because having the power becomes more important than using it. Those with the power become besotted with the trappings of power, forget why they wanted the power in the first place and are so frightened of losing the power they have that they do nothing to change the system whose inadequacies and corruptness may well (in some cases, at least) have been the original spurs which drove them to seek the power they have.

Our politicians are corrupt and self-centred. They do the jobs they do for selfish reasons. The phrase 'public service' no longer applies. They no longer take responsibility for their actions. Morality in Government is now just a memory. In 1982 a man was arrested after climbing into Buckingham Palace. The then home secretary William Whitelaw offered his resignation (it was refused). In 2003 a man entered Windsor Castle and kissed Prince William on both cheeks. This time the home secretary, David Blunkett laughed when reporting the incident to the House of Commons. He did not offer to resign.

* * *

I am not, for an instant, suggesting that immorality in Government is a peculiarly British problem. During the past 10 years 34 out of the 128 cabinet ministers to have served in the French Government have been indicted, mostly for financial crimes. In order to keep himself out of court, French President Chirac has had to rig up an immunity law protecting him from charges that he treated his previous job (as Mayor of Paris) as a source of money for himself, his party and his supporters. In Italy President Silvio Berlusconi has not been free of accusations. And, of course, in the USA corruption seems to be a pre-requisite for virtually any sort of public office.

It is surprising, sometimes, to see the number of politicians who retire early; who, having risen almost to the top, back down again, proclaiming with no one believing a word they say, that they want to spend more time with their families.

Is the truth simply that having touched power, and smelt the air at the top, they realise that they cannot stomach the double dealing, the deceit and the dishonesty that is required? When they reach the pinnacle and shake hands with Dr Faust is the price quite simply too much? Is it simply easier to cash in their political fame for a few well-paid jobs in the city and the media; to sit on the sidelines and regain a little, at least, of their lost integrity?

Is it really any wonder that increasing numbers of relatively decent politicians are walking away from politics and choosing to earn their bread, butter and jam in some other way?

* * *

If you don't live by your own beliefs then you will inevitably (and by default) end up living by someone else's beliefs.

Chapter 8
The Money Game

'Unsure of what they stand for, people increasingly rely on money as the criterion of value. What is more expensive is considered better. What used to be a medium of exchange has usurped the place of fundamental values, reversing the relationship postulated by economic theory. The cult of success has replaced a belief in principles. Society has lost its anchor.'
GEORGE SOROS

* * *

Never before have people worked so hard, been so driven by greed and materialism, and yet been so financially insecure. Never before have so many people faced an uncertain financial future and feared poverty in their old age. Our faith in the honesty of pension providers (whether they be statutory, corporate or private) has never been so low. Our distrust of financial advisors and institutions has never been so low. Never, before New Labour took power, had any government ever done so much to discourage self-reliance and to increase the extent and authority of the Government's own power at the expense of the liberty and freedom of individual citizens. Never has any government done so much to earn the distrust of the electorate (or been held in such widespread contempt).

179

Deceit in politics and business used to be the exception. Now it is the norm. This deceit has an enormous influence on our nation's financial stability.

To give a simple example, for years governments have fiddled the unemployment figures and the inflation figures in a way that would have resulted in prosecutions if they had been running public companies.

The official unemployment figures do not include students (hence the Government's enthusiasm for full-time university and college education) nor do they include the growing number of people (mainly from the public sector) who have taken disability pensions (and who are an even greater drag on society than they would be were they unemployed.) Nor do employment figures allow for the fact that 'new' jobs are often temporary, seasonal, part-time or extremely low paid.

The official inflation figures are laughably inaccurate and are regularly fiddled. Rapidly rising costs, such as rents, house prices and council taxes are deliberately excluded from the figures. Plumbers' charges, gas bills and food bills are excluded from inflation figures because the Government regards them as luxuries. (Necessities, the cost of which are included in the inflation figures, include vodka, manicures and acoustic guitars.)

As if all that wasn't bad enough, investors have to put up with the Government creating new laws and new taxes and changing the rules in such a way that only the Government ever benefits. For the first time in history laws and taxes are being changed retrospectively.

Whenever there is a crisis in public expenditure politicians talk about cutting services and raising taxes. (They never, ever talk about reducing their own bloated salaries or the salaries and perks of their assistants, researchers, spin-doctors and supporting quangos. Politicians these days are like divas – they are seemingly unable to operate without a huge entourage.)

'If you want decent services then you'll have to pay higher taxes,' say the politicians.

And so the decent, law abiding, caring citizens sigh and dig their hands deeper into their pockets. They believe that their society needs a decent health service/reliable railways/proper police force and it never occurs to them that if the Government didn't waste so much money, and wasn't so incompetent and corrupt, they could, and should, already have all these things. It is difficult to estimate just how much money the

Government does waste but the European Central Bank has estimated that the annual wastage figure is around £73 billion. It is worrying to note that the Government takes £450 billion from us in tax and provides us with £250 billion worth of services. Just administrating the tax income presumably takes up the missing £200 billion.

(During the 2003 illegal invasion of Iraq one British Sergeant was ordered to hand his body armour over to another soldier because there was a shortage. As a direct result of this the soldier died. The body armour that would have saved his life while he was fighting for his country would have cost the Government £167.70. That's the price taxpayers paid for each half roll of the wallpaper used to decorate Lord Derry Irvine's Westminster apartments. Blair's New Labour Government spends the taxpayers' money on wallpaper and fripperies, while allowing soldiers to die. Rather reminiscent of France before the Revolution isn't it?)

* * *

'There is no art which the government sooner learns of another than that of draining money from the pockets of the people.'
ADAM SMITH

* * *

Thanks largely to the actions of New Labour and Chancellor Gordon Brown, millions of Britons have abandoned the idea of saving for their old age.

Never before have taxpayers felt so resentful and so frustrated at the failure of central and local governments to provide a reliable, effective infrastructure in return for ever rising taxes. The Government thinks up new ways to tax us and then rewards us not by providing us with better services but by providing us with the one thing we don't want – more government.

New Labour's public spending has for years been growing twice as fast as the economy. Their spending has increased by a third in just six years. Pay rates for public sector workers are rising rapidly and yet, because there has been a dramatic increase in the number of paper shufflers the extra money goes to pay people to do half as much as before.

There are far too many people feeding at the government trough:

the government members, the quango members, the political advisors and the vast numbers of civil servants and absurdly, grandiosely titled politically correct fools employed by local, regional and central government at vast expense to shuffle paper and make life nigh on impossible for people doing real jobs. All these people – who I will refer to as the eunuchs simply because that is a word which best describes their function – constantly give themselves huge pay rises.

(In February 2004 a confidential 195 page report to the Government from the head of its own efficiency review estimated that reforming the civil service could save up to £15 billion a year. The report suggested making 80,000 civil servants redundant. It seemed unlikely that the Government would take much notice of this report since Ministers had already announced that the Government planned to create an additional 360,000 jobs for civil servants between 2003 and 2006.)

An ever increasing percentage of the taxes raised go towards paying the wages, compensation payments, sickness payments and pensions of these greedy, inept and unnecessary servants of the State. They are numbered in their millions and each day their numbers grow as departments of underworked eunuchs are supplemented with legions of assistant eunuchs, supplementary eunuchs and eunuch directorates. There are information eunuchs and advisory eunuchs and eunuchs whose job titles are so absurd that they sound as if they were created by some wild and drunken satirist. The public sector spends two or three times more per employee on 'human resources' than the private sector does. There are several entire industries based on 'regulation'. Even public sector employees are being swamped by the Government's own red tape and demands for paperwork. But attempts to deal with these problems simply result in the creation of extra jobs. When it was pointed out that one quarter of all police time is spent on paperwork the official response was to call for more support officers and 'case managers' (whatever they are) to deal with the bureaucracy. No one in Government seemed to realise that the problem would be best dealt with by getting rid of some of the paperwork.

We sometimes laugh at the eunuchs but in truth they are no laughing matter; they are greedy and malignant. They contribute nothing, sit around getting fat and get in the way.

Next in line in the new pecking order there are the people on benefits. These are the true aristocrats of our time. A hundred years ago aristocrats would spend their days going hunting, playing billiards or croquet and having costume parties. Today's aristocrats sit around watching videos, watching sport on satellite television and tinkering with their cars. Some supplement the unearned income which the State so generously provides with money earned by begging (which involves the tiresome business of sitting in the street looking doleful) while some supplement their unearned income by selling the cars with which they have tinkered or by doing a little plumbing work or slate fixing. For every honest person who needs help there are a dozen who are just parasites; modern, 21st century aristocrats, leeching on society because it's easier than working.

* * *

Judging by New Labour's tax policies it seems clear that owners are now regarded as 'baddies'. But ownership is crucial to our civilisation. Who will repair the house if no one owns it? Will the person renting it repair the damaged roof? Those who oppose ownership don't seem to realise that if no one owns things then no one will care about them or take care of them.

* * *

Governments do not create wealth. Governments create expenses.

* * *

The industrial revolution turned money into a power tool, designed to keep the workers hard at it without needing to be flogged every hour or so.

And thus was born greed. Everyone wanted to have more money so that they could buy more stuff without having to work quite so hard. The children of the industrial revolution started out wanting enough money to have a home with a decent roof and enough food for regular meals. But things have come a long way since then. Today our needs and our wants are blurred by clever advertising; we are encouraged to need more money to pay for double glazing, a second car and a holiday apartment in Spain. We are encouraged to want more money not because we need it but because it is a way of keeping score. At one major American television company a well-known employee has a clause in his contract which guarantees that he will always earn $1 more than any other employee.

It is this unnatural yearning to acquire more for doing as little as possible that has created a society in which millions expect the State to provide them with a living for life, and are happy to use the system not just to enable them to avoid poverty but to enable them to acquire all the trappings of success. It is this same attitude which has made the lottery so successful and it is the same expectation that results in house prices rising inexorably (with worrying dips and terrifying crashes when things get entirely out of hand). Out of greed has been born deceit, distrust and resentment. We're taught to believe that money will solve all our problems. Many people would, perhaps, be surprised to learn that although no one has ever committed suicide because their lottery ticket hasn't won, quite a high percentage of lottery winners do commit suicide. The secret no one dare whisper is that huge wealth can be an unbearable burden; even greater to some than poverty.

* * *

Financial fraud now seems global: corruption is endemic in our financial institutions. Think of a type of financial activity and there has probably been a scandal associated with it in the last year or two. The latest scandals affected foreign exchange trading and mutual funds (the American version of unit trusts) and the problems are now so great that towards the end of 2003 *The Economist* newspaper asked: 'Are there no honest financial markets left in the United States (of America)?'

Making judgements after reading company accounts can be difficult. Company bosses can make even bad results look good by adjusting the way they present them. All they have to do is change the length of time over which plant is depreciated, alter the way that pension commitments are included in the accounts or amend the value of inventories and they can turn a loss making year into a profitable year. Governments have fiddled away like this for years so it is hardly surprising that companies do it too.

(The great government fiddle of all time was, of course, the separation of paper money from any underlying value. In the days when paper money was backed by gold the public knew that the money they handled had some solid value. But, for decades now, governments around the world have operated 'fiat' currencies – printing vast amounts of money with no regard to any underlying value. It is this separation of money from real value that has led to the bankruptcy of America and to the fundamental financial crises which now face the world.)

* * *

Investors have, for years, been encouraged to make investment decisions on the basis of advice given by analysts employed by banks and other institutions. Although the institution employing them may also earn money by offering advice and services to the companies being analysed, it has, in the past, always been argued that analysts are independent and that their views can be trusted. However, it has, during the last few years, become clear that the advice analysts give is often dangerously biased and that analysts are often put under pressure (which they do not resist) to promote shares which they know to be worthless. At the height of the dot.com boom, in March 2000 only 1% of 6,000 stock recommendations were sells. When the market started to collapse analysts continued to encourage small investors to keep buying shares. Many of those who trusted the banks and the analysts lost a fortune.

In July 2002 the FSA revealed that 80% of companies are given a buy or outperform recommendation by their own corporate brokers or advisors. Only 2% are ever given sell recommendations, even when markets are stormy and wise investors should be battening down the hatches. Newspapers usually follow and repeat the advice given by the analysts. (Just as worryingly, it has not been unknown for journalists themselves to buy shares before they are promoted in their newspaper.)

Fund managers are often no more trustworthy than the analysts. Many of those who manage other people's money are in their mid-twenties and paid huge amounts of money. To me the words '25 years old' and 'billions of pounds' really don't go together terribly well. Many of these managers have little or no experience of proper work and since they are young have few or no investments of their own. Most are more concerned with their own financial future than with the profitability of their clients. For example, many fund managers routinely lock in any gains towards the end of the year in order to keep their bonuses safe. This may be good for them but although it may not be overtly or criminally dishonest it totally ignores the long-term interests of the investors. Selling too soon may mean that other gains will be lost. And selling unnecessarily means that unnecessary dealing costs are incurred.

Too few investment managers have their own financial future tied up with their clients. If they did then they might be more careful and more conscientious. This criticism also includes those who manage pension and insurance funds. For example, in 2004 it was predicted that 70% of endowment mortgage holders in Britain would see a shortfall – in other words, the policies they had taken out to pay off their mortgage would not produce enough money and they would be left unable to complete the purchase of their home. This was blamed on falls in the stock market, though to a large extent incompetent investment management must also be blamed. During the period that endowment funds had suffered most (between 1999 and 2002) the bosses of insurance companies had received (or given themselves) pay rises of between 45% and 71%.

In the end it doesn't really matter to the investor whether his money is lost through fraud or through incompetence. Does the pensioner really care whether his savings were stolen by a crook like Robert Maxwell or simply lost by the managers who ran Equitable Life into the ground? (Incidentally, when aggrieved investors wanted lawsuits to be brought against former Equitable Life directors the *Financial Times* wanted to know the point, arguing that the directors were not rich enough to pay back the money that had been lost. The *Financial Times* missed two points. First, revenge may not bring back lost savings but it does provide some slight comfort – especially when those involved seemed to have been unaffected by the financial disaster.) Second, litigation and ruin might, just might, encourage others in charge of investors' money to be a little more careful with it.

* * *

'A broker is someone who invests your money until it's all gone.'
WOODY ALLEN

* * *

It is hardly surprising that house prices keep rising inexorably (in the first six years after New Labour came into power the price of the average British house doubled and by 2004 most young married couples had no chance of ever being able to afford to buy their own home). Investors and would-be-pensioners want to put their heavily taxed savings somewhere where they can find them – and want some reassurance that city tricksters in expensive silk suits won't help themselves to those hard won assets.

Before It Gets Better

The Government, never slow to display economic ignorance, seems to believe that the fact that millions of people are borrowing huge amounts of money to buy residential property is a sign of a booming economy. What they clearly don't understand is that the false profits created by the artificial property bubble are not driving the economy forward in any realistic way. The whole bubble is as absurd as the Dutch tulip bulb fiasco of the 17th century. The boom that is supposed to have kept Britain out of recession has been created by rising property prices and has been sustained by the fact that house owners have been borrowing against the value of their homes and spending that money on fripperies. Still, one should not expect too much from Government Ministers whose own political party is constantly in desperate need of funds.

Most property investors (and these days that includes people living in their own homes, since most home owners now regard their home as an 'investment' as much as a 'sanctuary') think they are getting richer when the value of their home rises. But when the house you're living in goes up in value you don't really become any richer. You have to live somewhere. And when you sell you will have to pay more for your next home. When children leave home they will have to pay more for their first house. Rising house prices redistribute wealth – making the rich richer and the poor poorer – but they don't increase the nation's wealth and in practical terms they don't make much, if any difference, to the wealth of the individual.

* * *

Financial institutions really shouldn't be incompetent at managing money: but they are. The big investors (such as unit trusts, pension funds and so on) have huge advantages over small investors. They pay cheaper commission rates, they have access to company boards, they have access to honest views from their own analysts and they frequently receive information before ordinary investors and yet most still do worse than funds which merely follow a simple (and cheap) 'buy a bit of everything' investment philosophy.

Top professional economists are so bad at economic forecasting that *The Economist* magazine regards a poll of select American economists as 'an excellent contrarian indicator'. At the peak of the Internet boom economists were asked 'Is this a bubble?' They confidently voted 'No.'

(In 1999 the eleven Internet companies floated in London had a combined value of £9.7 billion but, between them, had reported sales totalling just £36 million.) In 2001 they ruled out an American recession (which duly happened). After they predicted that American interest rates would not fall to 1% interest rates proceeded to fall to 1%. In August 2003 they were asked if the dollar would fall to $1.25 against the euro at any time within the next 12 months. All but one said 'No.' Just four months later the dollar had fallen to $1.25. Can professional so-called experts with such an appalling track record really be called 'professional' or 'experts'?

Of the 244 investment funds in the UK all companies sector, over a third seem to track the FTSE 100 nigh on perfectly and yet two thirds of them are marketed as 'actively managed'. In other words the investment companies are charging big fees for 'managing' these funds but are simply buying 'a bit of everything'. Most actively managed UK equity funds have underperformed a good index tracker for the last ten years. Occasionally, one fund manager will have a good year (probably more by luck than judgement). Attracted by his success, thousands of investors will give him their money to look after. And within a year or two they will discover just how big a part luck played in his earlier apparent success. Every now and then the *Financial Times* lists the names of experts whose predicting skills have proved inferior to a small child, a cat randomly choosing figures or stocks picked when a blindfolded player throws darts at a board.

Investment advisers and financial institutions are incompetent and can no longer be trusted. But this isn't terribly surprising when you remember that governments have, for years, been fiddling the figures and 'cooking the books'.

As I've already explained, inflation, for example, is fiddled and the figures provided by governments are nothing less than institutionalised fraud. When inflation seems to be going up too much the Government just changes the way it is measured. They do this so often that no one in the financial world seems to take any notice any more but if anyone else did it, it would be regarded as fraud. (In fact, the way the Government even uses the word 'inflation' is something of a fraud. The word inflation, now invariably taken to mean a rise in prices and a fall in the value of money, was originally designed to refer to an increase in the money supply. But since governments now print money quite freely, and with no reference to any underlying value, the word has conveniently changed its meaning.)

The American Government has a wonderful way of fiddling its own inflation figures. If a new computer has twice the power of one that cost the same a year ago its price is reckoned to have halved. This simple trick can invariably be used to help keep inflation down. Governments benefit from this because so many of the payments they make (pensions for example) are related to the level of inflation. By fiddling the figures the Government steals from its own citizens. But how can you send a government to gaol?

The bottom line is that the Government has created an industry where the innocent can be ripped off with great ease. Although huge amounts of money are spent on 'regulating' banks and other financial institutions (paid for by investors of course) there is no effective regulation of financial service companies.

But then how could investors expect honesty from a Government which boldly stole a major company (Railtrack) from its investor shareholders (many of whom were ex-railway employees who had all their savings invested in 'their' company) and only gave in and handed over some compensation when it realised that the big banks and other lenders would charge it (the Government) more in the future to cover the added risk of lending to a dishonest Government?

* * *

It may seem odd but one of the basic truths about money is that financial institutions really don't give a fig about their customers.

You might imagine that building societies and banks would give their best deals to their best customers. That was the way businesses always used to operate. The small town butcher would keep his best cuts of beef for his best customers. A private hotel would make sure that a good, regular customer always got the best room. But that's not the way banks and other financial institutions operate these days. In fact, the exact opposite is true. These days building societies and banks routinely give their best deals exclusively to new customers. Their existing customers get a rotten deal.

Banks do this because they know that most people are so busy, so stressed and so trusting that they will always take the easy way out. They will accept the rotten interest rate they are receiving, or continue to pay the high mortgage rate they are paying, rather than make the effort to change. This isn't just laziness. Many customers stay with one bank through a misguided sense of loyalty.

The worst thing about all this is that the banks and other institutions don't care if you find out that you've been getting a rotten deal and then change to another bank. They don't even care if you tell everyone you meet just how you got ripped off. They don't care because they know that in the end they will win through inertia and apathy. They are playing a numbers game.

What the banks may not realise (and almost certainly wouldn't care about, even if they did) is that by all this they are encouraging disloyalty and punishing loyalty. What a lesson that is for the community.

(Incidentally, supermarkets and other stores are also responsible for devaluing loyalty. The so-called 'loyalty cards' which many stores issue to their customers offer very little in exchange for customer loyalty but the stores benefit enormously; by analysing the spending habits of their customers they can learn which products to sell to which customers.)

* * *

'Despite its claims to the contrary, the Government pays little heed to private investors, favouring its friends and sponsors in business.'
INVESTORS CHRONICLE, 8.8.03

* * *

Another 21st century truth about money is that company directors tend to benefit at the direct expense of shareholders and customers.

Company bosses are absurdly overpaid when compared to other, lower paid employees. As with so many other problems this one started in the USA where the *average* CEO now makes 411 times the salary of the average employee. In 2003 *top* American CEOs earned (on average) $37.5 million. That was more than 1,000 times the salary of an average worker. In 2003 the board of the New York Stock Exchange agreed to pay its then chairman 'compensation' of $188 million a year.

Most of these highly paid executives had a clause in their contracts which entitled them to a massive pay off if they messed up so badly that they needed to be fired.

Salaries and bonuses running into hundreds of millions of dollars a year are now almost commonplace. One British bank employee was given a £30 million bonus after having had a good year. (Will he have to pay back £30 million if he has a bad year? I rather doubt it.) Bonuses are invariably still paid even when the company makes a loss. A massive 82% of companies offer incentives to directors even if growth falls short of market expectations. On average companies begin to pay their directors performance-related pay when they deliver just a third of the profits growth the markets expect.

American bosses get away with this because they have conned ordinary Americans into thinking that one day they too will be rich. 'Every citizen can grow up to be a millionaire.' That, of course, is nonsense.

Nor are these huge salaries just rewards for men and women who have created great wealth and employment for others. Most of these individuals have not created vast corporations from scratch. Directors of established companies are, at best, bureaucrats, administering the company with the help of professional managers. The average CEO spends most of his time on outside activities and relatively little actually running the company he is responsible for. Corporate bosses are, on the whole, just lucky enough to have the right contacts and to be in the right place at the right time, when the plum jobs were being handed out. The absurd salaries they receive mean that many directors are quite out of touch with reality and the market place. Most have relatively little real responsibility – though, like government employees, they are well-endowed with authority.

British salaries are fast approaching the standard American level of obscenity and absurdity. For example, the boss of Barclays Bank in the UK took home £19,697,000 in a single year. In 2002 the Prudential offered its chief executive an £18 million share option scheme. British directors claim they need to be paid more so that they can have parity with American directors – though they never bother to explain why this should be so. Why do British directors have to be greedy because American directors are greedy? If a British director feels he is worth as much as an American director he is, presumably, free to look for a job in the USA. The excuse that the 'compensation' for directors and executives has to be matched to their counterparts in the USA is more of an excuse than a reasoned explanation. How many UK executives will be employable in Philadelphia and how many would want to go even if they were? Most of the high earning company directors and executives are vastly overpaid; since they are unsuited for proper employment most would, if pushed, happily do their jobs for a tenth of the money and none of the perks.

By 2003 the average British CEO was making 24 times as much as the average worker – that was the widest gap in Europe. In Germany, CEOs were making 15 times as much as the average employee. So if an average worker in a car factory made £15,000 the average boss would be making £225,000.

* * *

The modern capitalist system separates ownership (the shareholders) from the management, and allows the management enormous freedom to take for themselves a disproportionate percentage of the overall profits. Directors (and senior executives) are given bonuses and options to buy shares at ludicrously low prices. These bonuses and options are offered as a reward for having made a profit though when you think about it, it's clear that this is a bit like rewarding a bus driver for picking up passengers. Oddly enough no executive is ever fined or penalised for making a loss.

Throughout the world (but especially in the USA and the UK) company directors give themselves and their friends hugely unwarranted salaries, vast numbers of options (enabling them to buy shares at absurdly low prices), huge bonuses, massive pension payments, rent-free homes, cars, interest-free loans (which sometimes don't even have to be paid back), theatre tickets, perks galore, golden parachutes when they agree to start work or leave, golden hellos when they accept a job and guaranteed pay-outs if they are fired. As if all these weren't enough directors are now giving themselves non-compete fees. When a company sells a subsidiary to a competitor it will agree not to compete in the same market for a period of time. The company which gains from this non-compete clause will pay a fee. But instead of the fee going to the shareholders (who do, after all, own the company and will, therefore, be disadvantaged by the clause) it may go to the directors. One small group of British company directors recently had to admit that they had received over £20 million for guaranteeing not to compete with businesses which the firm had sold to another group. The payments were made without approval from the group's board and went to individual directors rather than to the company (and, therefore, to shareholders).

BEFORE IT GETS BETTER

The fact that the interests of the directors are often divorced from the interests of the company can lead to many dangers for shareholders. When there is a takeover who do you think the directors are thinking of most – themselves or the shareholders?

The tragedy is that company directors often change companies in order to make them bigger – not because this makes sense for the company but because it means that the director can demand a bigger salary and bigger bonuses. Company directors frequently award themselves huge bonuses when a takeover goes through – even though there may be no evidence to show that the takeover is of any benefit to the shareholders. It is common for company directors to expand and move into other areas of business (often into areas where the company has no experience) in order to increase the turnover (and the directors' fees). These expansions often lose the money which is being made by the profitable basic business.

Today's bosses maximise profits by moving the company's headquarters to Bermuda or Liechtenstein and the workforce to China but they use the company's money as their own; spending huge amounts of other people's money on giving themselves and their pals a good time. (These days most so-called multinationals aren't multinational at all. They are set up with their financial headquarters in a tax haven so that the parent company won't pay any taxes or have any legal liabilities or responsibilities.)

The good news is that there are early signs of revolt against all this greed. In May 2002 over half of GlaxoSmithKline's investors voted against the chief executive's contract. His pay package was £8.46 million but his contract would have also given him compensation of £22 million if he was fired. Since it seemed unlikely that he would be fired without having done something seriously wrong, even to some in the City of London this seemed a rather large reward for not doing your job properly.

These sums have lost all connection to the pay of workers or even ordinary executives.

For it is difficult to sustain an argument that anyone employed in a company should receive more than 20 times the wage of the lowest paid employee.

In the end the people who lose out (and who must pay these massive salaries) are the other employees (who must share a smaller pot of gold), the customers (who must pay higher prices to fund these absurd salaries and bonus schemes) and, most of all, the investors: the people who own the company.

* * *

There is a mistaken belief (common even among employees and investors) that the directors are entitled to do as they like because they are the company's owners. This is not true, of course. Many company directors don't even hold shares in the companies they run. The whole thing is a confidence trick – with rewards far removed from quality or value. A director can earn over $100,000 for a very part time job. One highly paid American director sits on 195 boards. Nor are the highly paid institutional money managers the real owners. They are merely 'managing' investments for the real owners – the small savers whose unit trust, investment trust, insurance company or pension fund really owns the shares. The investors are the people who own a company. They are the people who put up the risk money and they are the ones who deserve the greater part of any profits. But in today's world the investors seem to come last; they are derided by customers and employees and dismissed as irrelevant by the highly paid directors.

* * *

Directors and other senior members of staff aren't the only ones taking advantage of company shareholders. The Government has for some time used a quota system to force companies to employ people who would not otherwise be employable. This typically patronising piece of interference is done not through generosity or compassion but to help reduce the amount of money the Government must hand out in benefits. The Government also forces companies to collect taxes, to distribute (and bankroll) benefits and to organise pensions. None of these things are the real responsibility of an employer.

* * *

'The government that governs best taxes least.'
THOMAS JEFFERSON, FORMER PRESIDENT OF THE USA

* * *

One in four employees in the UK now works directly for the Government (if you include people working for local governments the figure is even more frightening) and since two out of every three new jobs being created are for the Government that figure will rapidly get worse.

Since New Labour came into power in 1997 they have added several hundred thousand employees to the State payroll. Britain's productivity has been destroyed because the New Labour Government has hired far too many new State employees. How long before Britain is as bad as France where one in three employees work for the State?

Britain's apparently impressive growth rate, and low unemployment figures under Labour have been almost entirely due to the growth in the number of people employed by the Government and to the fact that the Government has given its own employees massive pay rises while those working in the private sector have been limited to much smaller pay rises. State employees are treated like a superior class. (Just as they were in Russia a few decades ago). They get five or six week vacations (plus a host of bank holidays), index-linked pensions, free car parking, medical care and as much sick time as they want. (In contrast, the self-employed must struggle and fight. There are thousands who have not had a holiday for years. On a skiing trip I met a man who ran a small television shop. Every day he had to be back in his hotel room at 4 pm to talk through the problems encountered by the man he had left in charge.)

There are many problems with the dramatic rise in the number and importance of state employees.

The first, and most obvious, is the fact that government employees are not productive. Teachers, civil servants, diplomats, spin-doctors, policemen, outreach workers, equality advisers, regional bureaucrats, firemen, soldiers and NHS employees *may* do vital jobs but they don't make money for the country. They cost money. It's like running a huge country house with masses of servants. None of the servants bring money into the house. They exist (in theory at least) to make the house run more smoothly for the inhabitants.

The second problem is the fact that for years the Government has been offering its employees exceedingly generous index-linked pensions and has, consequently, created an elite class of pensioners who are immune to the nation's economic problems. The present and future working population must pay the bill for these pensions (a bill now amounting to hundreds of billions of pounds) and it is perfectly clear that they cannot and will not continue to do this for long. (All Government pensions are paid not out of taxes paid by the pensioners themselves but out of taxes to be paid by today's and tomorrow's workers.)

Today, the real workers (the people who contribute to a nation's wealth) are shrinking in number, while the eunuchs (whirling around the political leaders as advisors, administrators, quango sitters and bureaucrats) are multiplying. The cost of keeping the eunuchs (and all the drones who live on benefits) will, as I forecast back in 1988 in a book called *The Health Scandal*, soon become intolerable. The Government should understand that bureaucrats produce nothing of economic value – they are economic eunuchs living off the imagination, enterprise and work of the producers – and it is crucial to keep their numbers down to a minimum.

* * *

'This spending of the best part of one's life earning money in order to enjoy a questionable liberty during the least valuable part of it, reminds of the Englishman who went to India to make a fortune first, in order that he might return to England and live the life of a poet.'
HENRY DAVID THOREAU

* * *

During the last few years New Labour has encouraged a credit binge in a desperate attempt to keep the economy alive and kicking and to keep a recession at bay.

The apparently strong British economy is fuelled by credit – and has been ever since Labour came into power. Government borrowing has been rocketing as the Labour Government has rapidly increased its own spending while taxable profits have steadily fallen. Between 1997 and 2003, the first six years after Tony Blair marched into Downing Street, the country sank steadily into a financial crisis. The aggregate debt of Britons went up from £497 billion to £897 billion – a rise of around 80% – during the first six years of Blair's Government. Profits made by British companies have been going down steadily in the same period.

The credit financed binge has been dependent on low interest rates and the availability of low cost imports (mainly from China). What the Labour Government probably wasn't aware of was that the low cost imports were destroying Britain's own manufacturing industry. 'When China awakes, she will astonish the world,' said Napoleon. Modern politicians, neither so astute nor so far-sighted, have failed to see what the French Emperor had seen.

Following the Government's example many families now have a year's worth of salary on their credit cards and are using credit cards for a host of daily expenses. It is now by no means uncommon for people to use credit cards to pay for legal expenses, health care (such as cosmetic surgery) or for buying shares (many people are still paying off credit card debts for dot com losses). The banks send out millions of pre-approved credit card offers in every post. All the recipient has to do is sign a form and they will receive another new credit card. The line between solvency and bankruptcy has never been thinner. Very few people have any spare cash at all. They have no pension savings and have borrowed so much on their homes that the slightest fall in house prices would be disastrous. One quarter of current pensioners are so short of money (thanks to New Labour) that they have had to go back to work. Many of the rest are living in misery and would go back to work if they could. One in fifty say things are so bad that they have contemplated turning to crime.

* * *

We may seem to be getting richer. But we aren't. Today's two income family has less discretionary income than yesterday's one income family. Today's average family has far more financial instability than yesterday's average family. Britons are getting poorer and less financially secure.

* * *

The Labour Government claims to want people to save for their retirement (and it desperately needs them to) but, as usual, Labour Party policy isn't honest or logical. The Labour Party has consistently and deliberately (and deviously) attacked those who have put money aside for their pensions and has created a pensions crisis. Possibly through sheer incompetence. Possibly simply because they spotted a huge potential source of income and decided to help themselves.

Before they were elected in 1997 New Labour promised that they wouldn't raise taxes. It was, of course, just one of their many lies. Ever since coming into power they have done very little but raise taxes –

though rather than do it honestly they have done it the New Labour way, through scores of sneaky stealth taxes. It was one of their sneaky taxes which has helped destroy the value of millions of pensions (though it has not, of course, adversely affected the pensions of Government ministers).

When New Labour came into power in 1997 one of the first things they did was put an extra tax on pensions. At the time I warned that this would lead to a collapse in the value of pensions and a long-term shortfall for future pensioners. That, of course, is exactly what happened. Labour Party greed, stupidity and ignorance created a huge problem for the future. The New Labour pension tax ruined pension funds and was poorly thought out. Companies ended up having to pay more into their pension funds to make up the shortfall which resulted from the Government's tax changes. The New Labour change ended up by wrecking pension funds and encouraging pension scheme closures.

Individuals with their own pensions have seen their savings halved in value during the lifetime of the Labour Government. Many have simply stopped putting money into their savings plans, discouraged by the incompetence and dishonesty of the investment industry, the dishonesty and greed of the Government and the fact that means testing provides a real incentive for workers to spend everything they earn and to put nothing aside into their pension fund. Those who have never bothered to save for their old age now see no incentive to do so. If you save money (having paid tax on it) you then have to pay tax on the interest or dividends you receive. If the investment 'experts' don't lose your money for you then the Government will tax it. And then, when you're old, the Government will cut your pension and your benefits if you have saved. The message the Government has given out is that it is much better to spend your money than to save it. Let the State take the strain.

Companies which have provided their workers with pensions for decades are, as a result of the Labour Party's actions, beginning to ask themselves why they are doing this. Many large companies now have such huge pension debts that most of their profits now go not to shareholders but to retired pensioners. The direct consequence of the New Labour changes are that many large companies with thousands of employees have discovered that they are effectively in the pension fund business – managing investments for their pensioners – rather than the business they thought they were in. Many companies have been dragged close to bankruptcy by their pension fund shortfalls and in most cases these problems were caused by the Labour Party intervention in 1997.

Many Labour Party supporters sneer when there is talk about the rights of shareholders. They regard shareholders as parasites, leeching off the backs of the workers. The truth, however, is that anyone who has a private or corporate pension, an endowment policy or savings invested in a unit or investment trust is almost certainly a shareholder. The only people who aren't directly affected when share prices fall are the people who have a Government pension and no investments. When share prices fall pensions and companies all become weaker.

The result of this remarkably short-sighted piece of political mismanagement is that the provision of pensions for British workers will fall increasingly upon the shoulders of the already overburdened taxpayer.

Incidentally, the annuity which pensioners must purchase by law is the final insult for those who have put money aside for their old age. Pensioners receive a poor return for their money, which they must hand over to the insurance company providing the annuity. Worse still, the money paid out to pensioners seems certain to drop still further as insurance companies give the best deals to those with 'impaired life prospects' (those who smoke or who are grossly overweight). Taking high risk individuals out of the equation will mean that pensioners who have looked after their health will receive even smaller annuity payments. Since annuity payments are for life pensioners must take an enormous gamble with their life's savings when they choose to turn their pension fund into an annuity.

The people who will really suffer for all this will be workers currently in their fifties or younger who are not members of Government-backed inflation-proof pension schemes. Within a decade or two British pensioners will fall into two distinctive groups: those former Government employees who have inflation-proofed Government pensions (who will be the new rich) and those who are dependent upon corporate or private pensions (who will be the new poor).

In 2003 New Labour announced new legislation specifically designed to punish those who had saved enough money to give them a pension which might rival a Government minister's pension. (Naturally, Government ministers would be exempt from the new legislation).

Why Everything is going to get worse

Finally, since millions of elderly people are now mortgaging their homes in order to live (since their pensions are inadequate) the next generation (their children) will not be able to rely on receiving any inheritance. This is a serious problem since many of those children have made no plans of their own for their retirement.

* * *

Theoretically, taxes are the price we pay to live in a peaceful, civilised, democratic society. The idea is that we hand over a percentage of our earnings to the government so that it can look after us and provide us with an effective and reliable infrastructure. It is the Government's job to take care of the things that it can take care of better than we can, for example: building and maintaining roads and providing policemen to protect our security.

Modern taxes were invented at the end of the 18th century to pay for the Napoleonic Wars and the rates at which income tax is levied have been rising remorselessly ever since. Today, income tax is more of a fine for doing well than a genuine taxation to pay for the essentials of the State. Most taxpayers know they aren't getting value for money but are being ripped off by the State. We are overtaxed and underserviced.

Tax is, and always has been, a disincentive to work (though politicians who have no work experience don't understand that) and has traditionally survived only because those who pay taxes realise the importance of having a strong and effective national infrastructure and are generous enough to want to help those who cannot work and look after themselves.

Citizens were encouraged to believe that if they paid taxes then their government would look after them even if they fell sick or unemployed. Workers were encouraged to pay their taxes as a sort of insurance policy; they were buying a safety net. The idea was that we would all, together, share the risk of bad times.

That was the theory.

In practice taxes are no longer quite so rational. The costs of providing sick pay and benefits have spiralled out of control. This has happened partly because the number of people genuinely needing support has increased (instead of becoming healthier our society has become sicker) and partly because the lazier citizens have simply taken advantage of the system to avoid work, while pressure groups representing their interests have insisted that payments to the unemployed and to those

200

receiving sick pay should be increased way beyond the basic cost of living. Today, those who are on benefit expect not just to be fed and housed but also to be provided with television sets and free cars.

∗ ∗ ∗

Taxes in Britain are higher than ever. Under Denis Healey, Chancellor of the Exchequer in the Labour Government of the mid 1970s the Government took 34% of the national income. When New Labour took office the Government was taking, and spending, 38% of the nation's available wealth. Today, Blair and Brown are grabbing 42% of the national cake, and the percentage they are taking is rising fast.

What are they spending it all on?

Well, in 1996-7 social security cost the country £76 billion but by 2002 it was costing £111 billion. The cost of running the NHS went up in the same period from £34 billion to £50 billion (sadly, most of that extra expenditure went on higher wages for administrators so there was little or none left for improving services to patients).

In its first two terms Labour introduced 60 tax rises and increased the tax burden by £54 billion. During that time it was generally agreed (in just about every survey done) that every aspect of our national infrastructure had deteriorated. Some of the extra tax was used to give public sector workers huge pay rises (as much as 40%) but much of the extra tax revenue has been used to pay for more red tape. (Indeed, red tape is the one item for which productivity has gone up under Labour.) The problem, of course, is that red tape interferes with commercial and industrial productivity and, in the end, weakens a nation's economic strength.

The Government collects huge amounts of taxes and spends most of it (unproductively) on welfare, entitlements, corruption, huge salaries and vast perks for politicians and their hangers-on, membership fees of the EU, and subsidies for industries which, if they really cannot survive without subsidies should be allowed to die quietly.

The Government's ability to waste money never fails to astonish. For example, taxpayers have for years been paying for the building of a new parliament in which Scottish politicians could strut and run a new EU region (they think they're running a quasi independent nation, but in practice of course they are simply running a region of the EU). The costs of this building went up from an estimated £40 million to over £400 million. If a private company had been building something and the costs had gone up from £40 million to over £400 million heads would have rolled and questions would have been asked. But public money is not regarded as real money by the people who are in charge of spending it. People who themselves have never handled more than a modest salary or a small mortgage suddenly find themselves handling millions (or even billions) of public money and because they don't have any experience of such sums they treat it all as if they were playing a huge game of Monopoly, spending a million here and a million there without a thought for the hard-working citizens who have had to scrimp in order to pay their tax bills. There have been similar obscene overruns on the building of a new European Parliament building.

Almost 10% of British taxes, including the money raised by VAT, go directly to the military to pay for wars against Iraq and Afghanistan. Britain's Trident nuclear weapons system alone costs us £1.5 billion a year and the total cost could be £45 billion. What is it all for? Tony Blair's enthusiasm for war (and for supporting his new friends in America) has cost British taxpayers billions of pounds and, worse still, committed taxpayers to spend billions more on reconstruction and policing in Iraq. This burden will weigh heavily on a country which will almost certainly continue to hover in or close to recession in the next few years.

Worse still Britain, unlike America, is not going to benefit financially from the war. (America will end up controlling Iraq's oil and since the USA has quite illegally decided to keep most of the rebuilding work for itself, American corporations – largely controlled by George W. Bush's chums – will make billions out of selling their contracting services to Iraq. Iraq is one of the richest countries in the world and yet the people of Iraq will remain in poverty, denied clean water, decent food and proper medical services while Americans benefit for years to come.)

The cost of running Whitehall (the centre of Britain's uncivil nonservice) has soared way over budget and now costs £18.6 billion a year. In other words around 6p in the £ on the basic rate of tax simply covers the Government's own basic running costs. Any business which tried to operate with such huge overheads would have failed years ago. There are currently 516,000 clerks of various ranks working in Whitehall. At the height of Victorian power, when Britain had an Empire to run, there were just 1,628 civil servants. In 1900 when the Empire covered a quarter of the globe the foreign office had 142 staff. Today the Foreign

Office employs 5,620 people. It is, therefore, clearly overstaffed by 5,478.

Too many of the so-called 'specialists' and 'consultants' now providing advice have no experience of running a business (or, indeed, much experience of life itself).

* * *

Wastage and incompetence is also a problem at local government level. Local council wastage has gone through incredulous, past funny and bizarre and into totally unbelievable. For example, changing a light bulb in a council building can cost £50, involve five people working in three different buildings and take up to five weeks.

Local councils are just as guilty of wastage and incompetence as central Government; they spend money on the wrong things too. Many, for example, provide fitness and leisure centres, competing directly with private operators of health clubs. This is nonsensical. The only services local councils should provide are the ones (such as public libraries) which commercial operators are unlikely to provide.

Council taxes have risen to absurd levels (with residents paying more and more money for less and less) and will continue to rise because staff salaries and benefits have risen so much that massive rises will be needed merely to pay for salaries, perks, sick pay and pensions of administrators, bureaucrats and their assistant photocopier operators. Councils are having to increase charges but reduce services because of the vast numbers of people who are employed. Just walk into any council building and you'll see hordes of well-paid bureaucrats sitting on their backsides staring into space. The ones who move about do so as though walking with lead boots on their feet. One Welsh council advertised for a 'senior photocopying assistant' offering a pay scale 20% higher than that which a qualified nurse would receive and 15% more than a qualified teacher. In 2003 it was reported that one British council had 450 employees being paid more than £40,000 a year.

Local councils are now paying their administrative staff hugely inflated salaries (many have doubled in the last two or three years) and naturally, highly paid executives need more assistants. So the amount of money needed to pay the base costs has rocketed. As any businessman knows it is crucial to keep base costs as low as possible. Council staff, most of whom have no experience whatsoever of running a business, and no interest or incentive in saving other people's money, simply put up the rates.

In the bad old days councillors did their work out of a sense of public service; today's councillors are forever voting to give themselves massive pay increases.

Naturally, local residents start to complain about this; wondering why they are paying such huge bills and what they are getting for their money. The council's executive administrators cannot cut costs without sacking themselves or taking huge pay cuts (which they are obviously not about to do) and so the only alternative is to cut the number of services provided. It is difficult to do this without upsetting the ratepayers (who will, not unnaturally, become irritated by the knowledge that they are paying more for less). And so the council spins.

* * *

Today's politicians are in politics for the money. They have no passionate yearning to improve the world. Since they have no other source of income, backbenchers are compliant and scared of upsetting the power holders. Those in power feed greedily at the trough, helping themselves to the goodies and dishing out perks to their friends. Under New Labour the expenditure on entertaining and on servants has risen massively. Tony Blair's two parliamentary pensions will be worth £100,000 a year. (Former Tory Prime Minister Lady Thatcher receives an official pension of £17,535 a year.)

In order to save the Labour Party from its own financial incompetence it seems certain that British taxpayers will soon be forced to bankroll political parties to the tune of £30 million a year. The Labour Party is, at the time of writing, £8 million in the red (this, remember, is the party running the country). New Labour pledged, before they were elected, that they would only ask taxpayers to pay for their party if there was cross party support for the idea. However, this pre-election promise seems likely to go the way of all the others.

The white collar government employee, the pointless representative of Orwell's Big Brother, is the man who has most benefited from six years of New Labour. Public sector salaries are rising at double the rate of private sector pay (for whom inflation and increased taxes mean that their spendable income has fallen). Public sector wages are rising at 5% a year, compared with 2.7% a year for private sector workers.

In some areas – for example local government and NHS management – senior public sector wages are rocketing. There are, of course, also the final salary pensions (which taxpayers will have to fund). And council workers may be given grants to help them buy homes.

If you want to become rich and secure become a local government officer or a social worker rather than an entrepreneur. In the old days public sector workers traded wealth for security. Now they get both.

In some British towns spaces in open air car parks are kept for the free and unrestricted use of councillors and people working for the council. Business people looking to park must go elsewhere. Uniformed security officers look after the vehicles. At weekends, when the car parks are open to the public, the security officers are removed. The EU and New Labour have created a two-tier world. The people who work for European, national, regional, or local government on the upper tier and the rest of us on the lower tier.

* * *

Just collecting council taxes in England and Wales now costs £600 million a year. That, believe it or not, is the administrative cost of sending out the council tax bills and banking the cheques. (And remember that most councils now send out just one bill a year and expect council tax payers to send in their cheques on time.)

* * *

Thanks to taxation and the benefits system modern Britain has been divided into two groups: those who pay and those who receive. And today there seems to be little or no correlation between the two groups. The takers (those who receive) know what they are entitled to. They have become adept at working the system to their advantage. They know how to get extra for this and extra for that. They know their way around the rules. They know where to find legal help to aid them with appeals at tribunals. And, because they do not have to work for a living, it does not matter to them so much if they have to sit for five hours in a hospital out-patients' department. The workers are less happy about things. Indeed, those citizens who have realised that if they want their children to have a decent education, or if they themselves want decent health care, they will have to pay extra, are angry. They are paying their taxes but they are getting nothing in return.

WHY EVERYTHING IS GOING TO GET WORSE

✳ ✳ ✳

Tax authorities are becoming ever more aggressive and are constantly changing the rules (which are increasingly incomprehensible). The inevitable result is that more and more innocent people are being hurt. Businessmen who have been working on projects for years suddenly discover that the Government has changed the rules. Within hours a carefully developed project can crumble into dust. Entrepreneurs live in fear that a new law may turn them into outlaws overnight. An increasing number of companies go bankrupt because suddenly introduced legislation makes them unviable. If companies had warning of new changes they would be able to adapt. When there is no warning there is no time.

Governments around the world (but particularly in the UK) have been flexing their muscles for some years now – changing rules, punishments and penalties so rapidly that no one (not even the specialists) can keep up, introducing retrospective legislation (which means that nothing in your past is safe) and turning civil liabilities into criminal ones. Retrospective tax legislation brought in by New Labour means that even the past is now filled with uncertainties. (Governments only ever bring in retrospective legislation which helps protect the system. They never bring in retrospective legislation which will be of any help to individuals.) The British Government should take note of a recent ruling from the Canadian Supreme Court which decided that the Canadian Government's tax department is bound by that nation's six year statute of limitations for collecting tax bills. In other words tax collectors must obey the same laws as everyone else.

The tax authorities in every country seem to delight in proving themselves irrational, cruel and heartless. Consider, for example, the case of 'The Singing Nun', who had a huge hit record in 1963. In the USA alone this genuine singing nun sold over two million copies of a record called *Dominique*. Her record royalties of around £100,000 were all handed over to her convent. However, the tax authorities in Belgium subsequently insisted that The Singing Nun (whose real name was Jeanine Deckers) was herself responsible for the tax on the money that had been earned. They demanded £70,000. Ms Deckers, who didn't have any money, appealed to the convent for help (the convent being a convent was not liable for tax) but the convent told her that her earnings had all gone to a mission in the Congo. Poor Jeanine was threatened with imprisonment and the tax authorities continued to hound her until the 1980s. She left the convent but every time she tried to get a job the tax authorities leapt on her and demanded money. When she eventually gave up and killed herself in 1985 she left a suicide note saying: 'We go now to God. He alone can save us from this financial disaster'. How can one explain the minds of the tax officials who would persecute such a decent, honest woman in such an indecent and dishonourable way? Always expect the worst and you will never be disappointed.

'When I said I was being investigated by the tax authorities my family wanted to know what I'd been doing wrong,' wrote one reader. 'The trouble is that no one else in my family has got a job. They don't understand that these days you don't have to do anything wrong to get investigated by tax people. I know three honest, hard-working people whose lives were devastated and virtually destroyed by tax investigators. One was told to empty his pockets out on the taxman's desk. Another had to give a list of everything he'd bought his wife and children for Christmas.'

(I should, perhaps, point out that the one time I was investigated by the Inland Revenue they ended up giving me back a fairly large cheque. It turned out that I had paid far too much tax. My former accountants later explained this by saying that it wasn't their fault because they had been using 'out-of-date textbooks'. You will not be surprised to hear that I fired the accountants.)

The ruthlessness of the tax authorities could, perhaps, be better accepted if the tax people themselves were without fault.

However, they are not:

♦   The tax authorities admit that one in four tax returns was processed wrongly in 2002. The Inland Revenue aims to get things right just 75% of the time.

♦   In 2002 the Inland Revenue sold its own buildings to a company based in a tax haven.

♦   In 2002 the Inland Revenue had a huge problem with national insurance contributions threatening millions of workers' entitlement to a full state pension.

♦   In 2003 the Inland Revenue caused a political crisis when they failed to make prompt payments of tax credits.

- ◆ In 2004 the Inland Revenue admitted that they had made mistakes affecting the national insurance contribution payments made by 10 million taxpayers. (The Revenue only took over responsibility for national insurance contributions in 1999.)

- ◆ In 2004 the Inland Revenue admitted that more than one million company car owners had been given the wrong tax codes. The errors were blamed on a 'programming error'.

- ◆ The Inland Revenue charges one rate of interest on money it is owed and another, lower rate on money it owes. Why? Has the Inland Revenue become a bank?

It seems unreasonable, therefore, for the Inland Revenue to pounce on taxpayers who have unwittingly made a small mistake on their annual return. (It is particularly unreasonable of them when one realises that the tax forms and accompanying literature have been widely described by accountants as 'incomprehensible'. The incomprehensibility of tax rules can be judged by the fact that those who make calls to the Revenue's own advice line will know that the responses and opinions offered by Revenue employees will often vary even though the question remains the same.)

Governments (and their tax collecting employees) sometimes seem to forget that it is, by definition, taxpayers who pay all the bills. They forget that taxpayers deserve to be treated with just a little respect and decency and not to be treated as criminals. It's time for taxpayers to stand up for themselves.

Tax collectors should not be above the law. They should be forced to be more competent and more kindly and to treat taxpayers as honest and decent citizens until proved otherwise (rather than treating them as crooks whatever the circumstances). A little courtesy wouldn't go amiss either. Every year, as far back as my teen years, when I had part-time jobs, I have received an income tax demand on or around Christmas Eve. Apart from being a nasty unseasonal shock the income tax demand usually arrives just after the tax office bureaucrats have gone on holiday so that if there are queries (if, for example, the bill is for £1,000,000 instead of £17.67) no one can be reached until the New Year.

And why don't Governments ever say 'thank you' to taxpayers? Without taxpayers Governments would have no money and no power.

Before It Gets Better

***

The truth is that our current system of income tax is outdated and unfair. Stamp duty taxes on share purchases are a tax on hope, ambition and faith in British industry. The capital gains tax and the congestion charge imposed on Londoners both cost more to collect than they yield in revenue. When a tax costs more to collect than it produces for the exchequer it stops being taxation and becomes revenge.

To argue that people who are rich should be taxed at a higher rate because they are rich is as fair and as logical as arguing that athletes who can run fast should have their legs chopped off so that it will be fairer to others, or that good golfers should have an arm removed. It is the philosophy of jealousy rather than equality. But that is the taxation philosophy now operated in the UK. It is a dangerous game to play. As taxes go up and services go down so a growing number of people are voting with their feet. And it's the biggest and best taxpayers who are leaving. The wealthy are leaving the UK (and the USA) in record numbers and the implications should worry both Governments. In the USA the top earning 1% of USA taxpayers pay 37.4% of all individual federal income taxes collected, but they earn only 20.8% of all taxable individual income. It is clear, therefore, that the wealthy pay a high percentage of the total. The country will miss them a lot if they leave. Add to this the fact that top earners are constantly facing frivolous lawsuits simply because they are wealthy, and are also constantly at risk of having their assets seized by the Government for one absurd reason or another, and it isn't difficult to see why so many people are leaving these countries and setting up overseas. If the top 10% of taxpayers leave the country, taxes for the rest of the nation will triple. (If the number of non-working, non-earning, non-taxpaying asylum seekers continues to grow the taxes for the rest of the nation will increase even faster.)

Governments claim they aren't worried by the exodus of top earners. They should be. As the top earners go so the taxes paid by the rest must rise dramatically. It will not, I suspect, be long before governments stop their residents moving their own money out of their home country. Currency restrictions have in the past been used for this purpose in Germany, South Africa and in the UK.

Paying tax is, these days, a meaningless, bitter chore which most people resent because they know that the hard earned-money they contribute will not be spent wisely but will be wasted, stolen, frittered away and given to the greedy rather than the needy. More and more workmen have discovered that they are better off if they pack up working after two or three days each week. The tax credits and benefits they receive from the Government more than make up for the loss in earnings.

Like many I now regard tax as a sort of protection money. I don't expect to get anything back for it. (I know that if I need half way decent medical care or competent dental care I cannot rely on the NHS but will have to pay extra.) But I pay up because I know that if I refuse to pay men in uniforms will come round to my house at 4 am They will, I expect, break down my door and cart me off to a small room. Paying tax is no longer a privilege or a duty. It has become a chore and we pay not because we believe in it but we are too frightened not to pay.

It is hardly surprising that more and more people now believe that by paying taxes they are contributing to the strength and stability of an irreversibly, irretrievably corrupt system. We have taxation without representation and the politicians who remember their history will know what that leads to.

We have now reached a position where the Government can remain in power without any votes from taxpayers. It is possible for a political party to obtain, and retain, power simply by relying on the millions who receive their weekly pay cheque from the Government. (I'm talking about the millions who receive their money without having to work for it.) So many people are now on benefit that their votes can easily keep a party like New Labour in power indefinitely. (New Labour recently announced plans to lower the voting age to 16. This, of course, would give voting rights to schoolchildren and students – most of whom would vote for the political party likely to hand out the most money in benefits and grants. Allowing 16-year-olds to vote would further weaken the power of the tax paying working minority.)

This clearly isn't just. The people who pay the money have no say in what happens to it; they are, very effectively, disenfranchised. It's as if the recipients of charity funds decided where the money went, while those donating money had no say at all. The Government's expenditure is effectively decided by the people who receive it.

A fairer alternative would be to give the vote only to people who pay income taxes. This would mean that any would-be Government would *have* to listen to the wishes of the taxpayers. Taxpayers could probably force this change on the Government by refusing to pay any taxes until the appropriate changes were made.

Alternatively, a tax on consumption would be a much fairer way to raise money for Government spending. Income taxes only produce half the Government's income so the loss would not be difficult to make up with raised consumption taxes. With a zero rate of income tax the world would be a far better place. There would be far less fraud, virtually no need for accountants, less time wasted on preparing accounts, more productivity and more jobs available.

A tax on expenditure would be simpler, far cheaper to operate, more efficient and fairer (those spending more would pay more). It would encourage savings, reduce time wasting, make business easier, and would produce a system which would be far less stressful, worrying and confrontational for honest citizens. There would be far less opportunity for fraud and so the Government would benefit enormously.

The present system means that we get taxed on our earnings; if we save we get taxed on any interest or dividends we receive; if our savings make enough profit we have to pay capital gains tax (and, remember, the collecting of this costs more than it raises); and when we die our beneficiaries may pay tax on what we leave. This is a nonsense. Lottery winners, who acquire their money solely by chance, get their money tax free. But if you save money from your after tax earnings and leave it to your relatives they will have to pay yet more tax on it. Where is the sense in that? Where is the incentive to work, to save, to invest or even to plan for the future? Our Government is encouraging laziness and gambling. We should get rid of taxes on investments (that would encourage people to save) and put a flat tax on spending.

Taxpayers could force the Government to make these changes either by refusing to pay their taxes (if just 10,000 people refused to pay their tax bills no government would dare risk putting them all in gaol) or by refusing to cooperate with government departments.

* * *

Revolutions often start for relatively simple reasons. The American revolution didn't begin because the Americans wanted democracy. The Americans revolted because they were fed up of high unemployment figures and they wanted more money. Simple.

Big Brother thinks he is safe today. But he isn't. Remember the Roman Empire, the French Revolution and Berlin in the 1930s? In all these cases the middle-classes rose up because their values had been destroyed. Moral and financial collapse often leads to big changes.

As I mentioned at the beginning of this book, the end of the Roman Empire began when the workers (the middle-classes) were ignored and the authorities put all their effort into pleasing the drones. Something similar happened in France when the middle-classes were impoverished by the actions of Louis XV. Ignoring the middle-classes led directly to the French Revolution and the arrival of a man on a white horse called Napoleon.

The middle-classes tend to be quiet and easily put upon. They are easily ignored and often forgotten by politicians. They can be resilient and long suffering. But, like all living creatures, they have a breaking point.

There will come a time (and it is not far away now) when ordinary, hard-working citizens of Britain will wake up one morning, look around them and suddenly see the squalor, the unfairness of life, the huge taxation burden they are being forced to bear, the impoverished quality of the services they and their families receive from the State and the contempt with which they are treated by the endless rows of State bureaucrats who have leeched and bled the nation dry. They will look around, they will see all this, and they will say: 'Enough!'

* * *

The introduction of, and the opposition to, the poll tax changed the balance of power in Britain.

Few people dare say it but the poll tax was actually a wise and fair tax. The idea was that the occupants of a house would pay for council services according to the number of people using those services. The poll tax would have meant that if there were eight working people living in a council house (and taking full advantage of a range of local services) they would between them have paid more tax than an 80-year-old widow living alone. The poll tax, possibly the fairest tax ever created in Britain, was successfully opposed by people who had become accustomed to getting something for nothing and wanted to carry on in the same way. In the end the poll tax disappeared (and perhaps helped to destroy Margaret Thatcher) because a relatively small number of noisy protestors (all receiving benefits and hardly any of them working) realised that they would have to start paying for the benefits they were receiving. They had the time to protest, the money to get them to where they wanted to go and excellent motivation.

Cowardly ministers backed down, abandoned a sensible innovation and reverted to a punitive and unfair system which rewarded those who take and penalised the elderly and the hard-working.

In some ways the demise of the poll tax heralded the beginning of the end for Britain. For it was then that those who opposed the poll tax realised the power they had at their disposal, and it was then that new politicians realised that they could rule Britain without taking any notice at all of taxpayers.

* * *

And then there is the problem of the asylum seekers.

Actually I don't think the term asylum seekers is particularly appropriate. Most of the people pouring into the UK in search of asylum aren't really looking for asylum. Thousands of people who label themselves 'asylum seekers' are coming from countries which we have just bombed in order to get rid of mad, bad tyrants. The Government can't have it both ways. It can't claim to have liberated Iraq and Afghanistan and yet continue to accept asylum seekers from both these countries. (Unless, of course, the people seeking asylum are claiming that they are running away from the Americans.) Even after the so-called end of the Second Iraq War, people from Iraq were coming to Britain as asylum seekers.

Britain now has over 500,000 permanent legal migrants a year (this figure does not include illegal asylum seekers). Many of the 500,000 people pouring into Britain every year are not running away from the firing squad. They are coming here because they rather fancy our welfare system. Many are, to put it bluntly, beggars rather than asylum seekers.

How many *illegal* immigrants are there? No one knows. But there have been estimates that another 500,000 people in the UK now live with friends and sleep on sofas.

In 2003 it was reported that the average asylum seeker received £16,000 a year tax free. This isn't only unfair, it is also unsustainable. Moreover, it is not merely the cash payments to newcomers which are helping to destroy our economy. One family of asylum seekers has cost the country £350,000 in failed legal bids, lawsuits, social security benefits and police protection. All of this is, of course, paid for out of public funds. Legal aid for asylum seekers was, in late 2003, costing taxpayers half a million pounds a day.

Although many asylum seekers prefer to return home for medical treatment (only in very few countries is health care worse that it is in the UK) asylum seekers are destroying what is left of the NHS. Many family doctors are so under pressure because of the floods of foreigners pouring into the UK, that they are giving up. There are more than 3,000 vacancies for GPs, Half of all GPs want to retire early because of the stress. Even illegal immigrants can be an enormous source of financial cost to the NHS. For example, one illegal Iraqi immigrant was crippled by a crash in a stolen car after his application for asylum was rejected. The total cost of looking after him is now expected to run into millions. The hospital Trust responsible for the cost of his care has a £150 million annual budget to care for 170,000 people. How many taxpaying Britons will die on waiting lists because of the amount of money being spent on this man's care? The Government doesn't seem to understand how all this is affecting the public view of asylum seekers and other immigrants (and how it will, eventually, lead to an enormous and frightening surge in the amount of racism in Britain).

The Government doesn't even seem to understand the motives of some of the asylum seekers themselves. For example, it announced that if asylum seekers whose claims for asylum had been rejected didn't leave the country, their children would be taken into care and looked after by local authorities. Was this really intended to be a disincentive? 'We will take your children into a hotel, feed them, clothe them, educate them and provide them with a full range of health care at our expense.'

* * *

I do not for a moment deny that we should help people less fortunate than ourselves. Despite the exhortations of our Prime Minister (who has, I seem to remember, told us not to) I still give money to beggars. But I don't want the Government to tax me in order to give money to beggars. That's compulsory charity. And if we've got to have compulsory charity then I would, if you don't mind, like to have a say in the way my money is going to be given away.

Since we are constantly being told that there isn't enough money to go round I rather think that when the Government is handing out our money they should make British citizens who are old, infirm or sick a priority. I would go further. I think the Government should give priority to the people who have, for decades, paid into the system and who did so in the rather naive belief that they would get something back.

International polls show that Britain is regarded with contempt by foreigners. Britain attracts far more refugees than any other country, not because they admire us in any way but because our financial benefits are better. Twice as many asylum seekers want to come to the UK as want to go to the USA. The Government says it is actively encouraging foreign workers to come to Britain because migrants bring money into the country and therefore contribute positively to the economy. This is not true. Civil servants told the House of Commons international development select committee that migrant workers send around £3.5 billion a year home to their families, rather than spending it in the UK. The migrants who do bring money into the country (rather than taking money out) are less than 1% of the total and largely consist of Americans, Arabs and Japanese who are rich and who come to Britain for the tax benefits. (Bizarrely, if you live in Britain but aren't British, the UK is a tax haven.)

The authorities support and protect immigrants but do little or nothing to integrate them into our country. The obvious way to integrate immigrants is to offer them citizenship of our nation but, bizarrely, that is deemed unacceptably racist. Incredibly, newcomers to the UK are encouraged to ignore our history, language and culture. In deference to the feelings of foreigners, Britons are told that they must not show their flag. Schools are told that they must teach immigrants in their own language and that English history should be suppressed. Some English children are now being taught in Urdu in English schools. Those who delicately suggest that true citizenship must surely include obligations as well as rights are reviled as racists.

The Government makes things far worse by fostering the view that anyone who worries about any of this is racist and by encouraging incomers not to bother sharing our way of life or our values – they encourage multiculturalism which is, in the end, the father and mother of racism. No one dare ask why immigrants want to come to the UK if they don't want to live like us. Could it be that they just want the money? That, at least, is the implication.

Why has New Labour allowed so many migrants to pour into Britain? Why is it allowing 72 million citizens of East European countries free entry to Britain (and our generous benefits system)?

It is worth remembering that very few immigrants will ever vote Tory. And politicians (of both parties) have, in the past, regularly altered constituencies and boundaries to their benefit.

* * *

Despite the claims of the Government, prudence is neither valued nor appreciated these days. New Labour has introduced means testing for everything. Under New Labour a massive 38% of British families now receive a means tested benefit.

Means testing is a very 'statist' way to distribute money. It is, of course, grossly unfair because it means that people who have saved or contributed most in taxes and national insurance payments tend to get least in return. There is an inverse relation between what you pay in and what you get out. If the Government was an insurance company it would only pay out to people who didn't have anything and hadn't bought any policies.

Means testing (now a basic principle of New Labour Government) is invidious and destructive and, in the long-term, counterproductive. It removes all incentive to work or save. In fact it means that there is a huge disincentive to do either.

Those who use the system know that if they do have money left over they should keep it safely out of sight.

New Labour is so wedded to this awful principle that they have even introduced it from birth. The Government has announced that it is giving between £250 and £500 to every baby born in the UK. The sum depends inversely on the earnings of the parents. This is, of course, grotesquely unfair since it means that the children of working parents are discriminated against from birth. The appalling unjust principle of means testing has even been introduced into our legal system. Our courts hand out vastly different fines according to the income of the accused and the Government is planning to introduce means testing into speeding fines too. Instead of a flat rate fine motorists will be fined according to their incomes. No account will be taken of circumstances, responsibilities or commitments.

The bizarre structure of tax credits and Child Support Agency payments means that a growing number of workers have discovered that they are better off if they work less. For example, a bus driver in South Wales who was working five days a week for a total take home pay of £120 discovered that he if dropped his working week to 3 days he would end up with a take home pay of £186. Can anyone blame him for taking the second option?

The unfairness of means testing becomes particularly obvious in old age. Pension benefits are means tested to death and the result is that there are now huge incentives to give up work and to stop saving.

If you work hard all your life, pay tax on your earnings, and manage to save a little of your after-tax earnings, the Government will refuse you help when you grow old and frail. The Government will tax you to death on your savings (and, indeed, beyond) but will deny you help when you need it. Having taxed you for decades it will then insist that you sell your home and use your savings before it will provide you with help or support.

On the other hand, if you work hard but spend all your money then the State will look after you. It will make sure that you don't starve and if you fall ill it will look after you. If you grow too frail to look after yourself the State will provide you with a bed in a nursing home.

And if you decide not to bother working for a living at all, but to spend your life living on Government handouts, then the Government will continue to look after you in your old age. When you grow infirm and need care the Government will give you free nursing care.

This is bizarre, irrational and unfair and it leads to resentment and injustice; worse, it leads a large proportion of the population to regard improvidence as the only rational course of action.

* * *

One of Britain's biggest growth areas is the number of people receiving Government benefits.

Handouts to support young single mothers now cost the state £22 billion a year. The system encourages single parent families. Hard-working taxpayers can't afford to have children (because they either have to give up work or hire expensive nannies) but the irresponsible and feckless have as many children as they like and get Government support for them all. Having children has, in 'benefit mad Britain', become a profitable business. The costs are met by responsible taxpayers.

In 1975 just 8% of families were single parents. Now 26% of all families with children are single parents – mostly without jobs. Just why taxpayers should pay anything – let alone so much – towards the costs of bringing up other people's children has never been satisfactorily explained.

The New Labour Government does nothing to change any of this because it suits them. No New Labour functionary ever asks whether it is fair or reasonable to dole out huge chunks of taxpayers' money to women whose only achievement is having children. No one ever asks why the Government should endorse, encourage and subsidise unprotected promiscuity.

New Labour has now decreed that children are living in poverty if they don't have friends round for tea at least once a fortnight, own a bicycle and go on a school trip at least once a term. So payments for single mothers must rise. Surely the elderly, especially those who have already paid into the system, deserve to be given priority? (Incidentally, the astonishing increase in the rate of children diagnosed as suffering from asthma may be partly blamed on the fact that parents – or mothers – with asthmatic children may claim enhanced benefits.)

New Labour provides these benefits, not through compassion, but because those on benefits are New Labour's core voters (they don't take much interest in politics but they know that if a Tory Government gets in they might get less in benefits). New Labour (the most irresponsible and wasteful Government Britain has ever had) doesn't expect to get votes from taxpayers. And they don't care. They can get by without those votes.

New Labour know that this system keeps people weak. Single mothers aren't going to march and campaign against wars. And people bent double under taxes won't have the time or the energy either.

* * *

Advice To Help You Make The Most Of Your Money

1. Be careful not to buy too much insurance. The extended warranties so beloved by electrical stores are a perfect example of fear being used to sell us an expensive product we probably don't really need. The small print is usually complicated and far too daunting to read in the time available. And so we hand over another substantial sum for an over-expensive extended warranty. (The fact that many stores now make a considerable portion of their profit from selling these

warranties should tell you something about their value to the customer.)

We have been brought up willing to pay to avoid risk. And some risks (the big ones) are always worth insuring against. Most of us need to take out public liability insurance because if a slate falls off our roof and lands on a passer-by the resulting claim for damages could bankrupt us. Most of us need to insure our homes against fire because if our house burns down we won't be able to afford another one. This sort of insurance doesn't usually cost a great deal (because the risks are quite small) but it is worth buying.

But much of the insurance we are sold doesn't fit into that sort of category. Most of the time we insure ourselves against losses which will not seriously embarrass us. And our excessive zeal for insurance cover means that we end up buying multiple cover for the same risks. The expense of these accumulated policies can be horrendous.

The variety of risks against which one can now take out insurance is apparently unending. Every time you buy one insurance policy the company from which you bought it will try to sell you another policy, covering areas that weren't included in the first policy.

Most of us – particularly those who are careful and honest – will be better off if we put the premiums into a special savings account and use that to pay for plumbing costs, heating repairs and so on.

And since it is probably not worthwhile making a claim against an insurance policy unless the claim is considerable it makes sense to agree not to make a claim for small sums, in return for a discount on the premium. (Remember, too, that insurance companies now tend to put up premiums when they pay out. A small claim can lead to an annual rise in premiums which matches the one-off payment.)

Finally, remember that insurance companies are routinely dishonest. They lie. A lot. When they tell you the cheque is in the post they are probably lying. When they tell you that the claims forms are in the post they are probably lying. When they tell you that your claim is being processed they are probably lying. Insurance companies lie (and make life exceedingly difficult for anyone trying to make a claim) for one very good reason: they hope that if they make things difficult for you then you will get bored and go away without them ever having to pay up.

2. If you are looking for a job remember that a post with a central or local government is the only sort of job that offers real security and a reliable pension.

   If you don't fancy working for the Government, self-employment may sound dangerous but in the future it will offer more security than employment with a company – particularly a large international one. The self-employed don't have to retire and can't be made redundant. New, strict employment rules and regulations mean that companies prefer to keep their number of full-time employees to a minimum.

   Remember that if you are self-employed you don't have to concentrate on one type of work. Most skills are saleable and the fees you can charge will depend on the need for your skills, the number of other people doing the same thing, how good you are and how much you want to do it. Build up your own portfolio of work. More and more people are discovering that having a portfolio of several jobs gives them more wealth, more pleasure, more independence and more security than struggling to make a living out of a single activity. But remember to take time off occasionally. Employed people get holidays, weekends off and bank holidays but many who are self-employed find it difficult to relax. Your health and productivity will improve if you put aside a day, or even half a day, a week for yourself.

3. Be loyal to individuals rather than to organisations or countries. If you have a good relationship with someone at your bank and they move to another bank then consider making the move with them.

4. Don't ever retire. If you already have retired then you should consider unretiring. If you are planning retirement from a full-time job look for small part-time jobs to take up.

   And why should you ever retire? Retirement didn't exist before the 1930s. The concept of retirement was invented in the USA during the great depression of the 1930s. The idea was to convince older workers to stop working in order to open jobs for young people.

   The retirement age was fixed at 65 by Chancellor Otto von Bismarck of Germany because the average age of death at the time was 63. He rather meanly decided that 65 was the age when German civil servants could collect a government pension. In Japan the official retirement age was set at 55. (At the time life expectancy there was 43.)

Today retirement causes misery because millions simply don't know what to do with themselves. Poor pensions mean that many are now living in penury. When the idea of retirement was introduced most people had physical jobs. Today, most people have jobs which require thought rather than action. Retirement is an unnecessary anachronism. Much wisdom and experience are wasted.

5. Most people end up working not for what they need but for what they think they have to buy in order to keep up with friends and neighbours who are, in turn, working harder than they need (frequently at jobs they hate) to keep up with *their* friends and neighbours.

6. Ask yourself this simple question: 'What is money for?' Think carefully about the answer. You can only do two things with money: spend it or save it. If you are doing the latter you need to know why.

7. Money can buy you freedom, independence and time. Money can give you the opportunity to say 'No' when you want to say 'No'. Money can give you a voice. The more money you have, the more your voice will be heard.

8. What do you need? What are you prepared to do to achieve those needs?

9. Amazingly few people understand money management which, although it isn't taught in our schools, is one of the most important skills anyone can have. Most people think they can trust the experts; they think that money management is boring, too complex, or beneath them. Most people think that you need years of training to understand shares, bonds and money markets. None of this is true. Most spectacularly successful investors have never had any proper or orthodox training. And if you do decide to manage your own money you will have one huge advantage over everyone else: you will always care more about your money than anyone else will.

10. When you buy something make sure it justifies the cost. Work out how many hours you have had to work to pay for it. For example, if you buy a car which costs £10,000, divide your hourly income

into £10,000: that gives you the number of hours you have had to work to earn that car.

11. Don't worry about what anyone else gets paid.

12. Before you invest in a company check out the directors' holdings. Do they have a large investment in the company – or are they just paying themselves huge salaries and giving themselves options which they sell whenever they can? As a general rule directors who believe in a company will have the equivalent of more than one year's salary invested in the company. If the people who are running the company don't have enough faith in it to own shares, why should you? The fact that a director invests £10,000 in shares in his company means nothing if he is being paid £500,000 a year by the company. (If I was running the country I would insist that directors had at least 10% of their personal wealth tied up in each company with which they were involved as a director.)

13. Traditional investment rules all rely on hindsight. In practice, it is forecasting and predicting skills which really count.

14. Investment is more about timing, asset class allocation and diversification than reading company accounts. Diversification is the major key since it is this which provides some protection against the dishonesty which is now so endemic within all aspects of the investment industry.

15. Don't allow money experts to decide which investments you should hold. There is a risk that they will 'churn' your money (buying and selling to make extra commissions).

16. Never take investment advice from anyone who isn't a self-made millionaire and/or considerably richer than you are. What does the guy in your local bank know about investments? If he is so good why isn't he rich, rather than sitting behind a desk telling you what to do with your money?

17. Don't trust analysts, brokers or bankers. They are all getting rich out of finding new ways to take your money from you. Many professional money managers are in their 20s. The words 'twenty-five' and 'billion pounds' do not go well together.

18. Remember that whenever you buy a share it is because someone

else is selling it. And when you sell a share someone else wants to buy it.

19. If your goal is to become financially secure then you can do it.

20. You can either eat seeds or you can plant them. Money is like seeds.

21. Let your profits run and cut your losses. (If an investment is making you money then keep it. If it is losing money then sell it.) Most investors lose money because they buy at the top, (they feel comfortable knowing that everyone else is buying then). They then hang on as the share drops because they don't want to accept that they have made a mistake. The value of an investment (whether a bond, a share or a house) has nothing to do with what it is worth but with what people think it is worth. The two things are not necessarily connected.

22. Just because a share price has fallen a long way doesn't mean that it is cheap.

23. If a share price halves in value it will have to double in value to get back to where it was.

24. Learn to differentiate between investments and speculations.

25. It is usually more important to get the general area of investment right than to pick the right investment.

26. Schemes specifically designed to help you avoid tax are usually poor investments.

27. Timing is almost everything in investing. Buy today what you think others will want to buy tomorrow.

28. Make sure that you manage your money – don't let it manage you.

29. If you own a house don't ever confuse it with your investments.

30. Most investment professionals (actually 75% of them) somehow manage to do worse than average; worse than they would have done if they had simply invested your money in every share available. When you remember that the professionals have a number of advantages over you and I (they pay lower commission rates, they have direct access to company boards and they get company information before it is released to ordinary investors) this failure suggests a considerable level of incompetence.

31. If you have a pension or an insurance policy you probably own shares.

32. £100 put under the mattress in crisp new notes in 1928 would now be worth £72,500 to a collector of old bank notes. Following the rules isn't always the best way to make money.

33. All investment is gambling, the only thing that changes is the extent of the risk. If you leave your savings in a sock under the bed you are gambling that inflation won't eat it all up.

34. If you are a cautious investor consider putting 80% of your money into very solid, safe, boring investments and investing just 20% of your money in risky things like shares.

35. Don't put more than 5% of your wealth in a single investment. If you don't have enough money to put it in 20 different investments then just keep it in the bank.

36. Don't invest in anything you don't understand. And don't be too greedy.

37. As far as money is concerned, don't trust anyone but yourself and be wary of yourself.

38. If you aren't prepared to take small losses you will probably have to accept big losses.

39. Widely-known information is useless because it is widely known. The secret of good investing is good forecasting. Most professional investors and analysts have proved themselves to be very poor at this.

40. Keep your eyes open and use your daily experiences to help you make investment judgements. For example, on a flight to Paris a few years ago two strangers came up to me and asked me where I had bought the electronic organiser I was using. (The devices were new at the time.) When I got to Paris a Frenchman asked me the same question. I immediately telephoned a broker and bought shares in the then relatively young company making the device. Two or three years later, after the shares had risen dramatically, I needed to call the company with a minor technical query. Getting through to speak to someone was a nightmare. In the end I gave up. And two minutes after I'd decided to give up I sold the shares. Both were good decisions.

41. Investment is a long-term business. 'We've had some good centuries and we've had some bad centuries,' said one family investor. Trading (buying and selling frequently) uses up capital because of the dealing costs. It is generally agreed that Jesse Livermore was probably the greatest trader of all time. And it is generally agreed that Warren Buffet is the greatest investor. Livermore killed himself because he had lost his money. Buffet is one of the richest men in the world.

42. If you buy when others want to sell and you sell when others want to buy you will get rich.

43. There is as much risk in doing nothing as there is in doing something. Whatever investment you choose there is risk. Even with money under the bed (or in the bank) there is the risk that inflation, taxes and charges will destroy the value of your savings. There is no escape from risk. All you can do is try to maximise your opportunities while keeping your risks to a minimum.

44. The biggest purchase you will ever make will probably not be your house or your car but your pension. And yet most people spend weeks worrying about a house purchase and buy a pension in minutes.

45. More people who have money lose it through investing badly than lose it through frittering it away on luxuries.

46. Don't expect a bank to protect your interests. Banks cannot look after the interests of staff, shareholders and customers at the same time since the interests of these three groups are often opposed (even though some people may be staff, shareholders and customers). The shareholder wants the bank to make huge profits. The staff want a big cut of the profits. The customer wants the bank to do everything for free.

47. The investments you own don't know that you own them. They won't care (or be hurt) if you sell them.

48. When selecting an investment try to go against the crowd. If you buy an investment which everyone else agrees is worth buying then you are probably paying too much. This is true for every investment you can think of – including bonds, shares and property.

Chapter 9
Our Disappearing Privacy

Governments all around the world are now busy collecting as much information as they can on their citizens. The fake war on terrorism has given Governments an excuse to collect (and exchange) information on us all.

Make no mistake about it, these are dark and difficult times. Anyone whose beliefs are considered politically inconvenient or who protests about any government action is likely to be listed as a dangerous dissident. For example, the British Government has for a long time classified animal lovers as 'terrorists' while the American Government now classifies peace marches and protests as 'terrorist' events.

'They have taken us much farther down the road toward an intrusive, Big Brother-style government – toward the dangers prophesied by George Orwell in his book *1984* than anyone ever thought would be possible in the United States of America,' said USA Vice President Al Gore in early 2004.

Our privacy has gone. Nothing you tell your doctor is private. Nothing you tell the Government is private. Government departments even boast about how much they know. In recent television advertisements the British Government warned us that they now know where we all are and what we are doing. If you're living with someone and haven't told the authorities they will know. If you haven't bought a tax disc for your car, they will know. Big Brother has become so arrogant that he wants us to know that he knows.

Credit card transactions, mobile phones, loyalty cards, and CCTV cameras mean we can all be tracked virtually every inch of the way and every second of the day.

It is now clear that CCTV cameras neither prevent crime nor lead to arrests. So why do we have so many? How much do they all cost? Who watches the monitors? And, most crucially, if they don't prevent crime or keep citizens safe what are they for? The only logical conclusion is that they are to spy on us; to take away yet another aspect of our privacy.

* * *

The Government collects information about us in a thousand different ways.

For example, everyone in the UK needs to have a television licence if they own a television. The British Government licenses televisions in much the same way that in Communist Czechoslovakia the Government used to licence typewriters. The money is used to support the BBC (though, as an aside, many are beginning to question why an organisation which broadcasts commercial-style eye candy, publishes popular books and magazines and whose independence is frequently questioned, should be financed in this way).

The licensing authorities who collect the money for the BBC seem to assume that everyone in Britain must have a television set and so even people who don't have sets still receive pretty nasty letters demanding money and threatening prosecution. However, this scatter gun approach hides the fact that they do actually have a pretty good idea of who does own a TV set. (The scatter gun approach is designed to scare anyone they've missed into paying up.)

For many years the authorities pretended that they knew who had a TV set because they had fleets of special detector vans driving around the country. This was one of the great cons of the 20th century. Did you ever see a detector van? Do you know anyone who ever saw one? Exactly.

In practice, the authorities find out who's got a television set in a much simpler way. They have a database of people who've bought TV sets. Where do they get that information from? The people who sell them, of course. Just try buying a television set without giving your name and address and you'll see what I mean.

* * *

The Government and your local council are constantly collecting information about you. They don't just use it to make sure that you've bought a television licence, of course. They use it to make sure that you pay your taxes and your council taxes and they use it to check up on you in a hundred different ways.

All that is bad enough. But it gets far worse.

The Government and your local council also *sell* the private information they've demanded from you.

Nothing you tell the Government is private. Nothing you tell your local council is private. As far as the authorities are concerned the word 'confidential' doesn't exist. The Government actually allows local councils to sell information from the electoral register to credit reference agencies and to commercial groups. Isn't that outrageous? Your local council can demand that you give it private information about you and your family. If you don't give them the information they demand they can take you to court and fine you. But when you have handed over your private, confidential information they will then sell it (with or without your approval) to anyone prepared to pay for it. You cannot stop them selling the information they have forced you to give them.

The result is that if you have a home address anywhere in the UK your friends and your enemies can find out where you live within seconds, either by using the Internet or by using a relatively cheap disk which contains the names, addresses and telephone numbers of everyone on the electoral roll. And don't assume that having an unlisted telephone number stops people getting hold of it. There are many commercial telephone numbers which will, when you dial them, 'capture' your telephone number and tie it in with your name and address. The number that you thought was private will then no longer be private.

* * *

When confronted with all this, the reaction of many is to say 'Well, I've got nothing to hide. Why should I worry?'

The truth, of course, is that the innocent have just as much to fear as the guilty. Indeed, they probably have more to fear since the guilty are usually prepared for the problems they may face.

British and American gaols are full of citizens who are innocent but who have, often through no fault of their own, fallen foul of the system.

Can you really guarantee that you will never cross paths with someone (possibly a lunatic) who will bear a grudge against you?

If you don't protect your privacy when you don't need it, you certainly won't be able to get it when you do need it.

* * *

'If a nation values anything more than freedom, it will lose its freedom; and the irony of it is that if it is comfort that it values more, it will lose that too.'
W. SOMERSET MAUGHAM

* * *

Your home address and financial history, the names and details of the people you live with, your birth date, your former addresses and the details of the people you've shared a home with are all kept on file and are updated every time you buy a new fridge, CD or a gallon of petrol.

Credit firms often assume that people who share a flat are financially linked. If you are a millionaire and you live with a penniless drug addict you'll both get rotten credit histories. One spendthrift teenager still living at home can ruin his parents' credit rating.

Naturally, the computers also keep a full record of everything you buy (unless you pay cash). If you ever have problems paying a bill the computers will know. If you move house they will know before your relatives have received your change of address cards. When you sign an application form for a credit card or a mortgage or a bank loan the fine print no one ever reads gives the bank the right to make a credit check. Your records will list all your applications for credit.

And don't think that you have nothing to worry about because you've always paid your bills. One study showed that around one in ten files contain an error.

* * *

Look at what happens when you visit a hotel these days.

In the old days they used to give you a huge metal key. To try and stop you taking the key away with you by mistake the hotel would attach a piece of metal or wood to the key.

As far as the big hotel chains are concerned that's all history now. Though there are still some independent and smaller hotels which allow guests to use bits of metal to open doors most big hotels now hand their guests little bits of plastic that look like credit cards.

Credit card type hotel room keys differ from hotel to hotel but some of these cards are packed with more information about you than you might want them to have. They contain (in addition to the number of the room you have been allocated) your name, check-in and check-out dates, home address and credit card number and expiry date. There is enough information on one of these cards to enable someone to steal a great deal from you. None of this information will be eradicated unless you hand in the card and a new customer is assigned the same room.

Personally, I think that putting even part of a customer's address on one of these 'keys' is reckless on the part of the hotel. If a crook gets hold of your 'key' (even for a few moments) he can obtain vital, personal information about you. All he has to do to obtain your full address is to put your name and partial address into a computer. There are plenty of readily available software packages which will then provide him with your full address. Once he has done this the crook knows where you live. From the 'key' he knows how long you will be away.

My advice is simple: once you receive once of these cards don't ever let it out of your sight. And when you leave the hotel take the card with you and destroy it as quickly as you can. If the 'key' is left lying around you could be in trouble.

* * *

A few years ago it was possible to travel without giving your name. You could simply buy a blank ticket, board a plane and go where you wanted to go without the Government, the airline and the rest of the world knowing where you had gone. These days, of course, you cannot possibly buy an airline ticket without giving your name. You will also be expected to provide various forms of proof showing that you are who you say you are.

This change was made, it is claimed, to stop terrorists travelling. This is a nonsense. The change was made long before the Americans decided that terrorists were a threat to their safety. When the changes were originally made they were blamed on drug-smuggling-money-laundering criminals.

As usual, to find out why the change was made all you have to do is look to see who benefited from the change. And that's not difficult to work out.

First, the airlines benefit because unused non-refundable tickets cannot be sold or transferred to someone else. In the old days you could simply give or sell an unwanted ticket to someone else. These days, if you can't fly the airline keeps your money and sells your seat to someone else.

Second, the Government likes to know where its prisoners (sorry, citizens) are at all times.

It has been claimed that American citizens now have less privacy than German citizens had in the 1930s. This is true of British citizens too.

* * *

A snooper's charter has been introduced to give spying powers to local councils, quangos and the Royal Mail. Local councils can, for example, now legally employ undercover agents to spy on you. They can spy on your telephone calls and your e-mails and they can find out where you used your mobile phone and whom you rang (and why). Of course, the technology isn't perfect yet. They can't yet tell which room you were in when you used your mobile phone. But they're getting there.

It isn't just official bodies who can collect information about you. Private companies can now buy images and information collected from space satellites.

And why do you think all those stores have loyalty cards? Did you really think they wanted to reward your loyalty? The loyalty card you so dutifully produce when you do your shopping enables the supermarket to know exactly what you buy, how much you pay for it and how often you buy it. They have your home address, of course. You can't get a loyalty card without giving them that. And they have access to your age, your hobbies and your bank details. They can tell your interests and peccadillos from what you buy. If you buy your clothes from them then they know what size socks he wears and what size bra she wears. And their computers can make judgements about you based on the information they receive.

WHY EVERYTHING IS GOING TO GET WORSE

So, for example, if a woman of childbearing age suddenly stops buying tampons the computer can decide that she may be pregnant. And so the store will send her a special offer on nappies.

You may find all this quite amusing and enormously useful. You may not mind the store selling your details to another non-competing establishment. You may like the idea of receiving letters offering you breast-enlarging surgery at a special price (that purchase of a 36A bra was a giveaway that you might be in the market for a boost). You may be mildly amused to know that the computer has worked out that you have dinner parties once a month. You may be delighted to receive letters or telephone calls offering you a special price membership of a local slimming club (they know your dress size). And you may not mind the computer, the store, and everyone working there, knowing that you've stopped buying condoms and are presumably getting ready to start a family.

But remember this: once you've lost your privacy you can never get it back. And there may, one day, be something you don't want the world to know about it.

By then it will be far too late.

* * *

Computers are now very much part of our lives and we have, by and large, grown accustomed to their growing importance in our world. Although we are conscious of the explosion in computer crime, most people still think it is something that happens to other people. Many believe that using e-mail is more secure and more private than sending a letter through the post. They're wrong on both counts.

When a leading Internet security firm surveyed 167 home PC users in the UK they found that 95% of the computers had been 'visited' by hackers within the previous month. On average there were 56 hacking attempts on each of the 167 PCs. In only eight cases – out of the 167 computers surveyed – was there no attempt to hack in.

Corporate computers are, if anything, even more susceptible to hacking and the most widely used hacking tool can even take remote control of a PC and steal data from it.

It is safe to assume that if you use a computer and are linked to the Internet then whatever is on your computer will be available to, and read by, a wide variety of strangers.

Before It Gets Better

The World Wide Web is the least private, least confidential method of communication ever invented. Graffiti is more private than e-mail. Do not put anything into an e-mail that you would not like to see in your daily newspaper. The e-mails of around 100,000 people a year are currently being spied on in Britain. No one whose private Internet accounts and telephone records are being accessed by police, security services, Inland Revenue and Customs and Excise knows that they are being investigated (though it was revealed that Transport Department officials had sought damaging personal information on members of the Paddington Survivors Group – a small collection of citizens who had survived a serious rail crash and had set up a campaigning group).

The New Labour Government has given huge numbers of civil servants and local council and quango officials the right to check Internet use and telephone records. The Government refuses to divulge anything about the use of e-mail interception.

It isn't only the Government you need to worry about. Commercial and private organisations may dump 'spy' programmes onto your computer so that they can keep an eye on every site you visit and every e-mail you send.

Many computer users think they can avoid viruses and other complications by not downloading unknown attachments that accompany e-mails. Sadly, that's not enough. Today, viruses can travel inside the subject line of an e-mail. As soon as you try to read the message your computer is toast.

Millions rely on having installed firewalls and anti-virus software (some of which can cause a computer to slow down or crash) but even these are little protection against anyone determined to get into your computer. And they are no protection at all against government agencies. The bottom line is that the Internet is now fundamentally insecure.

Personally, I much prefer the fax machine to e-mail. Messages arrive in an easily readable form. I can see them when they arrive but I can deal with them when I am ready and I can read them easily and without being interrupted by advertisements. Most important of all, fax messages are far more private and confidential than e-mails. Fax machines are faster and more secure than the Internet (though they should still be regarded as non-private).

Old-fashioned mail (a letter in an envelope with a stamp on the outside) is the most private way to communicate.

If you are worried about outsiders hacking into your computer to spy on your private work you should keep one computer for Internet access and one computer for private work – never, ever connecting *that* computer to the Internet. Even then you aren't completely safe because technology is available which enables hackers to get into your computer from outside your home. (This sort of technology is, however, fairly expensive and the risk of this happening is much lower than the risk of your computer being accessed through the Internet.)

Anyone sending an e-mail should remember that any such message can (and probably will) be read by all sorts of people – including governments. Moreover, e-mail messages cannot be burnt or shredded. Once an e-mail message had been sent it exists for ever; eternally captured, carved in cyberspace. How many careers and lives have been ruined already by hastily written and long-forgotten e-mails? E-mails are about as private as stuff written on a wall with a spray can – but much longer lasting. They can never be erased.

The American Government and the British Government have both given themselves the right to look at every e-mail you send or receive. They can also check out your banking records, the sites you visit on the Internet and what you buy. The authorities in both countries are compiling comprehensive computerised dossiers on every man, woman and child in the USA and the UK.

* * *

Many of the paedophiles now being arrested worldwide were caught because they used credit cards to access Web sites catering to their needs. Accessing those Web sites might not have been illegal when they did it but that won't protect them from prosecution and possible imprisonment.

The authorities have targeted paedophiles because they are a 'safe' target. No one is going to protest on behalf of paedophiles. Everyone is revolted by the idea of children being abused.

But the way the law has been used to target paedophiles can now be adapted to arrest other Web users.

So, for example, the authorities might decide that anyone who has, in the past, bought a book about terrorism should be arrested. Or they might decide that anyone who collects guns (even fake ones) is a threat to society and should be arrested. Or they might start arresting people who have visited sites offering information on martial arts. The possibilities are now limitless.

Just because something isn't illegal today doesn't mean that you can't be arrested for it in ten years' time.

* * *

You have no privacy when you go into hospital or visit a doctor (unless you give a false name or refuse to answer any personal questions). Your medical records are now pretty much on open view to policemen, social workers, hospital porters, administrators, bureaucrats and anyone who wanders around carrying a clipboard and wearing a white coat.

Putting medical records onto computer has, in my view, really opened them up to a wide audience. Those little cardboard envelopes doctors used to favour for the storing of medical notes and letters may have been clumsy and crude but they worked and they were much easier to protect.

* * *

Have you noticed that although big companies will frequently refuse to do business with you until they have gouged every shred of private information they can think of from you, they will clam up when you ask *them* for any details. They regard their privacy as far more important than yours.

'It is not our policy to give out names or numbers,' is the standard reply when you ask the person to whom you have just bared your soul for their details. When you ask them why they will use the magic word 'security'. (As in: 'We can't give out that information for security reasons.')

An employee of one large financial institution which will probably prefer to remain anonymous once refused to accept a Post Office box number as my personal address. I tried everything I could think of (including explaining that both the Inland Revenue and Customs and Excise people are happy to write to me at a Post Office box number) but the voice in a suit was adamant, insisting that only people who had something to hide would use a box number and that the bank regarded anyone using such an address as intensely suspicious and possibly criminal. 'OK,' I sighed at last, 'I'll write and put my case to the chairman. What's your address?' There was a long pause before the voice in a suit answered.

The institution's address was, as you have no doubt guessed, a Post Office box number.

It was the only time in my life that I have heard anyone blush.

* * *

An increasing number of businesses now use the 'security reasons' argument as an excuse to invade our privacy.

For example, I recently telephoned three separate estate agents to ask them to send me property details. Each of the three insisted on having a telephone number before they would post the details. When I asked them why they needed a telephone number they all said it was for 'security reasons'. When I asked what 'security reasons' were involved with sending me a piece of paper advertising a property, they insisted they couldn't send the particulars without a telephone number. Resignedly I gave them a number and equally resignedly I took repeated harassing telephone calls from all three agents during the following week.

* * *

Remember that many companies which make a great fuss about demanding your private details in the name of 'security' will, when they no longer need your private information, just toss their paperwork, unshredded, into a dustbin. Professional thieves will then steal the paperwork and use it to create a fake identity in your name.

* * *

People in authority tend to have double standards when it comes to privacy. They don't rate your entitlement to privacy as very high but they regard their own privacy as essential. This general and widespread phenomenon is well illustrated by what happened in America.

Police who were investigating a fellow officer who was suspected of using drugs searched through the woman's rubbish bin to see what they could find. When they found a used tampon they sent it to the police laboratory to be analysed.

There was a public outcry when this became known but the police chief defended his force's actions by claiming that once rubbish has been put on the kerb it is 'abandoned in terms of privacy'.

However, guess what happened when a local newspaper dug through the rubbish left outside the homes of the police chief, the mayor and the district attorney and recovered a mass of financial statements and personal material?

You probably guessed right. The mayor called the newspaper's actions: 'potentially illegal and absolutely unscrupulous and reprehensible'.

It's that old 'them' and 'us' thing again.

* * *

One significant consequence of the Government's apparent obsession with terrorism is that the banking zealots are becoming increasingly hysterical. More and more decent, tax paying citizens are receiving threatening letters from banks and investment companies who claim to be hunting for the money laundering terrorists among their customers.

The standard letter received usually reads something like this: 'If you don't provide documentary evidence of your identity and address within 30 days your a/c will be closed (you will be charged costs and any losses which result will be yours).'

Customers are told that they must take their passport to their bank so that it can be photocopied (thereby increasing rather than reducing the security risk). It's hard luck for those who don't have passports.

Some customers have been told that they must in future show proof of their identity if they want to pay in a cheque (don't even think of paying in cash because that will immediately brand you as a terrorist) or move their own money to another account in their own name. One investor received a scary letter from the wretched institution holding her account telling her, quite arbitrarily and without any excuse, that: 'your funds will be returned to you at the current market value or the original investment amount, whichever is lower'.

This sounds to me like an institution trying to make a profit out of an alleged security clamp down.

New money laundering rules prevent many pensioners from opening new accounts at all. Many have been left angry, humiliated and embarrassed after being told that they cannot open accounts because they cannot provide the long list of documents the bank demands. Many pensioners can't produce passports because they don't travel abroad. They can't produce a driving licence because they no longer have a car or drive. And they cannot produce a utility bill or rates demand if they live with relatives, in a nursing home, rest home or sheltered accommodation.

Even younger customers face huge problems if they move house and go to live in a new area. Without those damned utility bills, opening a bank account becomes impossible. And, in some areas, it is impossible to get the utility companies to connect you up to their mains service unless you show evidence of a bank account.

One couple who wanted to put £3,000 into a small account offered the bank their passports, utility bills and bank statements. These were all verified, copied and sent off but the application was rejected because the bank demanded that the application be accompanied by a 'cheque with a zero balance made out to yourself'. No one at the bank could explain what that meant.

* * *

Government rules mean that banks can be fined if they are too lenient with people opening new accounts, and bank staff are liable to criminal proceedings, but the absence of any firm guidance means that each member of staff tends to interpret the non-existent rules in their own way. It is all rather as though motorists were told that they would be fined for speeding but not told what the speed limits were.

The FSA (the Financial Services Authority, which makes up the rules) has suggested that a driving licence and passport are enough but it does not give firm guidance about this. The rules about precisely which identity papers to accept has been left to the Joint Money Laundering Steering Group. They have left banks free to interpret the rules in their own way. So, the end result is chaos.

* * *

The absurd new money laundering rules have added huge costs and inconveniences to our daily lives. But so far the authorities haven't caught any money launderers or stopped any terrorists with their new rules.

'I don't see a lot of terrorists and money launderers going to gaol,' said one leading financial expert who specialises in bank regulation. In fact money laundering continues to take place faster than ever. Most money laundering takes place not in funny little countries no one has ever heard of but in the USA (which is known around the world as the world's largest tax haven because there is no tax at all on the investment income of non-USA residents) and the UK.

So what is the point of these expensive infringements of our freedom? I can't believe that anyone with an IQ higher than their shoe size genuinely believes that any of this has anything to do with criminals or terrorists.

These absurd new rules have been introduced to frighten us and to control us. And because the Government wants to gather every scrap of information it can about its citizens.

Don't let them kid you that they are doing this in the name of security. If they were worried about security they wouldn't be so quick to flog your confidential information to anyone prepared to pay for it. Selling off private information is hardly the way to stop terrorists making up fake identities.

* * *

Even when you've got a bank account the absurd new security rules turn the simplest request into a Kafkaesque nightmare. These days when I ring up the bank to ask them something about my account I end up speaking to a stranger. Since he is probably sitting in a call centre somewhere in Madras it's not entirely surprising that he's a stranger.

Before he will tell me anything about my money he will insist on interrogating me; asking me questions which some idiot at the bank has devised to enable me to prove that I am me. The last time I took this impromptu examination I failed miserably.

The first question he asked was: 'What was the last cheque that went through your account?'

How can anyone possibly know the answer to that? Even if I can remember the details of the last cheque I wrote (unlikely) how am I supposed to know which cheque was presented last? How am I supposed to guess which cheque the bank processed first?

I took a wild guess and got it wrong.

On to question two.

'How many standing orders do you have on your account?' he asked.

I took a guess and was wrong and that was that. The guy wouldn't speak to me any more and for the rest of the day I kept looking out of the window expecting to see a police van disgorging policemen carrying assault rifles.

I would have rung up my own branch to complain but they either don't have a telephone or else the number is too secret to share with customers.

Naturally, the banks pretend that all this secrecy is to stop terrorism. Equally naturally I don't buy that. I don't know the number of the last cheque to have gone through my account but something tells me that if Mr bin Laden had an account with the Fondling -under-Water branch of my bank he would know the answers to everything they'd ever be likely to ask him.

***

A few weeks ago I wanted to open a second account at a bank I use. They sent me a fistful of forms to complete. I rang them up and this time somehow managed to pass the examination. 'You've sent me some forms to fill in,' I said. 'But I've already got an account with you. I just wanted to open a second account.'

'If you want to open a new account then you must complete all our security questions and prove you are who you say you are,' replied the robot at the other end of the phone. 'We need your driving licence or passport, two utility bills and your last bank statement. Copies will not do.'

'But I've already got an account with you,' I repeated. 'I'm the same person as that person. Same name, same address, same date of birth, same everything. I just want another account number and another cheque book.'

'You must complete our forms and send us proof of identity,' insisted the woman.

'But I've already got one account with you,' I pointed out again. 'If you need me to prove who I am to open a second account why do you accept my identity for the first account?'

'It's the rules,' said the woman. 'If you want to open an account you must complete our forms and send us proof of identity.'

'Including the last bank statement you sent me?'

'That's right.'

'You want me to post back to you the very same bank statement that you posted to me last week?'

'Yes.'

'And then you'll post me details of my new account?'

'Yes.'

'That will satisfy your security checks?'

'You must also send two utility bills and either your passport or your driving licence.'

'I pay the utility bills by direct debit, through your bank,' I told her.

'We still need copies of the bills,' she said, rather snottily. 'And your driving licence or passport.'

'They might get lost in the post,' I told her. 'And besides, what if I need them while you're looking at them?'

'Our security regulations are set by the Government.'

'They're not,' I told her.

'Do you want the country over-run with terrorists?' she demanded, ignoring my entirely accurate interjection.

I paused and counted to ten. 'Instead of opening another account,' I said quietly. 'Can I please close the account I've got with you?'

'You'll have to write to us,' she said.

'Then you'll send me a cheque?'

'Yes.'

'Where will you send the cheque?'

'To the address on the bank statement.'

'But you don't have any proof that I'm that person,' I pointed out. 'If you had proof that I was that person then you wouldn't need more proof that that person was me in order to open a new account.'

'It's for your own security,' said the woman. 'Do you want the country over-run by terrorists?'

* * *

'Liberty means responsibility. That is why most men dread it.'
George Bernard Shaw

* * *

I had a nightmare.

'I'd like to open an account for a friend of mine,' I said.

'He'll have to come into the bank to be fingerprinted,' said the teller.

'He doesn't have any arms,' I said.

'That's all right. He can have an iris scan,' said the woman.

'He can't,' I said. 'He lost both eyes in the same accident that took his arms.'

'I'll talk to the manager,' said the teller, still cold but now rather suspicious too. 'Maybe we could accept three utility bills instead of two.'

'He doesn't have any utility bills,' I told her. 'He lives in a hospital unit. The hospital pays the gas and the electricity bills.'

'If he doesn't have any utility bills then he can't open an account,' said the woman.

'He's got a compensation cheque he needs to cash,' I told her.

'It's for his own protection,' she said. 'Does he want the country over-run by terrorists.'

* * *

New laws have turned accountants and financial advisors into snoops for the Government and have made it hazardous for anyone to consult an 'advisor'.

Consider, for example, the Proceeds of Crime Act 2002 which applies to independent financial advisors and to accountants as well as to bank managers and solicitors.

Theoretically, this new piece of legislation is supposed to have been passed in order to counteract money laundering, drug smuggling and terrorism. If you believe that then you probably believe that there are fairies at the bottom of the garden too.

In the bad old days you could trust your accountant. You could tell him things and rely upon something rather old-fashioned called 'client confidentiality'. He wouldn't talk about your financial affairs at the golf club and he wouldn't go running off to the police or the Inland Revenue every time you asked him for advice.

However, under the new law any accountant or advisor who suspects (suspicion is all it needs) that his client is guilty, or could be guilty, of tax evasion is obliged to report it immediately to the National Criminal Intelligence Service. If an accountant fails to report his suspicions to the State authorities he becomes a criminal himself and liable to a lengthy prison sentence.

This whole Big Brother scenario is made particularly absurd because every suspicion, however tiny, must be reported to the authorities.

So, for example, if your accountant suspects that you might have put *one* private letter through the office franking machine then he knows that you are evading tax on the cost of the stamp and he is legally obliged to report this to the authorities.

All other employees – even junior employees – of the accountant's firm are also obliged to make a report if they have any suspicions that you might, just might, have ever done anything even ever so slightly against the law.

And this new law also applies to banks, solicitors and financial advisors.

If the employees of a bank, a solicitor, a financial advisor or an accountant have the faintest suspicion and they *don't* tip off the authorities, then they are liable to a gaol sentence of up to 14 years. That's 14 years as in 168 months.

And the report must be made secretly.

If your accountant, bank manager or solicitor tips you off – and tells you that he has had to report you to the authorities, or even that he might have to report you because he suspects that you might possibly have done something wrong – then he becomes liable to an extra five years in prison. (To save you hiring an accountant that means that he then becomes liable to 19 years in prison. That's 19 years as in 228 months.)

The junior tea-maker at your accountant's office is also liable to the same prison sentence. As is the junior coffee-maker at your bank and the junior photocopier assistant at your investment adviser's office.

Obviously, this new legislation will very effectively destroy any trust that might have existed between client and accountant or financial advisor. It means that millions of honest but slightly forgetful citizens will be reported to the authorities. And, inevitably, it means that the authorities will be so overwhelmed with petty incidents that they will be less likely than ever to catch any real criminals. And that is, of course, precisely the opposite of the alleged intention of the legislation.

* * *

As if all that wasn't bad enough the Government has now set up something called the Assets Recovery Agency. New Labour Party Ministers don't talk about this one very much but this agency, yet another little piece of Government with jack boots on, has the power to seize private property from individuals who cannot explain how they have accumulated every penny of their wealth.

Think about that.

The Agency does not have to prove or even suspect that a crime might have been committed. And its employees have the right to turn up and take what they want from your home or business, and to empty all your bank accounts. (You may or may not have the right to stand and watch.)

Of course, if you can prove where you purchased every piece of furniture in your house, and exactly how you earned the money with which you paid for it, then you have nothing to worry about. If you can show where the money came from to buy that £250 worth of premium bonds you've had for years then there is absolutely no reason for you to be concerned. If you know (and can prove) exactly how and when you paid for the clock in the hall, the fridge in the kitchen and that old pair of trousers at the bottom of your wardrobe you can sleep easily at night. If you have boxfuls of receipts and cheque stubs going back to the days when you had a paper round then you can forget all about this legislation.

On the other hand, if you might have difficulty remembering, explaining or finding any of the paperwork then you could be in big trouble.

All this is, of course, being done to stop Muslim fundamentalists attacking prominent American landmarks.

* * *

One of the most significant consequences of the incident of 11/9 has been that the New Labour Government has taken advantage of the so-called 'terrorist threat' to introduce identity cards.

(I call the threat 'so-called' because there have been fewer terrorist attacks in Britain since 11/9 than there were in the few years preceding it. This fall in the number of terrorist incidents in Britain could well be due to the fact that the Americans are now very slightly less enthusiastic about supporting the IRA.)

The irony here is that even the Americans themselves have rejected the idea of introducing identity cards. They are presumably aware that countries which have introduced ID cards have seen no increase in security or reduction in terrorist attacks.

The USA Congress inserted the following line in the bill which created the now much despised Department of Homeland Security: 'Nothing in this act should be construed to authorise the development of a national identification system or card.'

Before It Gets Better

The New Labour Government frequently claims that we should accept identity cards because the French have them. Apart from the fact that they do not bother to explain why this has anything to do with their suitability for Britain there are many flaws in this particular argument.

The identity cards the French use are quite simple, more like the flimsy bits of cardboard that the Nazis were so fond of, than the high-tech credit card style devices that New Labour plans to introduce. It is quite wrong to suggest that the cards the French use compare in any way with the cards Britons will have to use.

The identity cards being introduced by New Labour will use iris recognition technology to identify the holder. Plus fingerprints. The French ID cards do not contain fingerprints or eye scans.

The New Labour ID cards will contain a microchip with every bit of information about you that the authorities can find. Your medical history, dental records, police record, banking records, address, telephone number, tax records, age, credit card details and, of course, a personal number similar in style to the one the Nazis used to tattoo on people. (New Labour has already proposed giving every newborn British child an identity number.)

The French ID cards do not include any electronic records, they are valid for ten years and only 51% of the population even have them. French identity cards can be used to support claims for state benefits, banking transactions and (in place of a passport) for travel around Europe. They are, indeed, a sort of poor man's passport – perfectly acceptable for people who just want to travel on the European mainland.

New Labour's identity cards (also known as smart cards) will ultimately replace credit, debit and cash cards, keys, passports, driving licences, national insurance cards, medical records, tax records and even cash.

In the Brave New World envisaged by New Labour, we will carry nothing with us but our New Labour smart cards. Mr Blunkett and his lieutenants will know where you are, what you earn, what you spend, what you wear and where you sleep.

Another flaw in the New Labour argument is that identity cards are voluntary in France (as they are in most of the European countries which have them).

British ID cards, the ones New Labour are introducing, will probably be compulsory.

Why Everything is going to get worse

It seems only a matter of time before some bright young Minister at the Home Office points out that tattoos on our forearms would be cheaper, easier and more reliable than ID cards.

Better still, he will doubtless suggest, we could all have little chips inserted under our skin. They will 'sell' this to us on the basis that it will mean that if we ever get lost the authorities will be able to find us very quickly. They will also point out that since we won't be able to lose our tattoos or our 'chips' we won't have to face the cost and inconvenience of obtaining replacements. I have no doubt that millions of citizens will accept these arguments and eagerly queue up to be tattooed or to accept their implants.

There is a another difference between the French ID card and the identity card which New Labour plans to introduce.

French ID cards are issued free but Britons will have to pay a minimum of £25 to prove that they are living in a police state.

The overall cost to taxpayers for setting up the system is forecast to be between £3 billion and £30 billion. On past record, this probably means that the final bill will be at least ten times as much as the highest of these two figures with 50% added on for additional unforeseen costs.

* * *

The real problem with the New Labour ID cards is that no one has yet explained why we need them and how we will all benefit.

The Government claims that their new ID cards (complete with fingerprints and iris recognition capability) will stop terrorism, money laundering, asylum seekers and identity fraud. If they really believe this then they are even more stupid than most people already suppose them to be. I suspect that the Government is, as usual, simply lying through its collective teeth.

The truth is that ID cards will make life easier – not harder – for terrorists, money launderers, asylum seekers and identity fraud cheats.

The big flaw in the whole argument is, of course, the fact that in order to obtain an ID card you must first prove your identity.

How do you do that? Well, naturally, you must use your passport or your birth certificate – the very items which are so easy to forge or to obtain illegally.

The Government's ID cards will merely legitimise fraudulent papers.

Those wanting to pretend to be someone other than they are must be cheering enthusiastically at the prospect of Britain forcing its citizens to carry and use ID cards.

***

I have a host of fears about ID cards. Obviously, the threat to civil liberties and human rights is paramount.

But does anyone out there know if iris scans are safe? Has anyone checked? Will repeated iris scans be safe – particularly when performed by the sort of incompetent, poorly-trained half-witted thugs now employed to police borders and search for nail files? Not as far as I know they haven't.

What possible long-term damage could eye scanners do? How many people will be blinded before scientists discover the dangers? Even if the equipment is safe, what risks will be there when it is faulty (which it often will be) or ill-maintained (which it often will be)?

Frequent travellers will have their irises scanned a lot. What risks will they run? Remember doctors once thought X-rays and cigarettes were perfectly safe. I can remember when they said mad cow disease wouldn't affect humans and when they insisted that benzodiazepine tranquillisers couldn't possibly be addictive.

My advice, if you are told you have to have an eye scan, is to insist that the person doing the scan sign a form accepting full legal responsibility for any damage which might be done to your eyes. If they refuse to do this make a written note yourself of the date when the scan was performed, the place and the name of the operator.

Put the risks aside for a moment and we are still left with the fact that iris scans are really of very questionable value. Iris scans can be duplicated and forged. How will the police stop crooks switching the iris scan on your ID card and enabling a terrorist or identity thief to take over your life completely?

Finally will the Government sell advertising on ID cards? Will they sell all the information on ID cards to commercial companies? What happens if someone steals your ID card? What happens if you just lose your ID card?

***

Much of this is being done to please the Americans. Legislation passed in the USA after 11th September 2001 (the excuse for every piece of freedom threatening, oppressive legislation passed anywhere in the world since then) says that from October 2004 other countries will either have to include fingerprints and retinal information on their passports or lose their right to participate in the USA's visa waiver scheme. (The fascists really should get their act together. Do they want iris scans or retinal scans? They probably don't realise this, but there is a difference between the iris and the retina.)

Regardless of the fact that no right minded individual wants to visit the USA these days, New Labour and the EU are bending over forwards to keep the Americans happy and are obeying the instructions from Washington to the letter, while pretending that the decisions they're making are their own. It seems likely that before very long the EU will introduce the same rules for the other 350 million citizens of the new European superstate.

Personally, I think we should all resist the idea of being fingerprinted and eyescanned. ID cards won't stop terrorism, asylum seekers or money laundering any more than they will stop foot and mouth disease or mad cow disease. As any expert will tell them (if only they would listen) ID cards will make life easier for terrorists, asylum seekers and money launderers. ID cards will merely give the State more control over us and reduce us still further to numbered pawns; pitiful drones with no rights, no individuality, no freedom and no privacy.

We have to stop the march of the fascists somewhere and for me ID cards mark the line.

✳ ✳ ✳

Identity theft is now the fastest growing white collar crime in the UK and the USA.

The principle is simple: a crook gets hold of your personal details (name, address, date of birth will do for starters) and then pretends to be you. The more information he has about you the easier he will find it to steal your identity, and then your money and your reputation.

Identity thieves operate in a number of ways. They may use stolen documents to open an account in your name. More simply they may steal credit cards which have been posted to you. Some acquire information by 'shoulder surfing'. They stand behind you when you use a hole-in-the-wall cash machine and make a note of the number you tap in. They will then distract you and steal your card. Sometimes they will trick a hole-in-the-wall cash machine into holding your card and then disgorging it when you have gone. (If anyone ever distracts you or interrupts you while you are getting money out of one of these machines, press cancel and go away.)

Crooks sometimes have confederates working in restaurants or hotels. When the establishment takes a legal impression of your card the crook's accomplice will take a copy. The details can then be used to purchase goods by mail order or to obtain a replacement card and start an alternative identity for the real card holder. The crook may notify the issuer that their card has been stolen and ask for a new one. Naturally, they take the opportunity to report a change of address.

Stealing documents is a favourite way to steal someone's identity but most crooks don't bother taking the risk of stealing documents these days. Instead, they go through dustbins and bin-bags looking for discarded documents which can be used to re-create an identity. Fraudsters now routinely raid dustbins for information – targeting private and business bins. In one major survey it was found that 53 out of 71 local authorities had reported 'bin-raiding' in their area. A check on 400 dustbins in Nottingham found that a fifth of the bins held enough details of credit cards for transactions to be made by a crook.

One major hazard is that banks and other financial institutions which have finished with paperwork dealing with your life may just dump the unwanted paperwork outside their offices. (There is some irony in the fact that institutions which put such great emphasis on security should, in practice, be a source of a good deal of crime.)

Already completed application forms sent out by banks, loan companies and credit card companies are another major source of crime. All the thief has to do is sign the application form and then ring up and report a change of address.

If he has a copy of one of your bank statements or utility bills the fraudster can easily open an account in your name. (Banks have made life relatively easy for thieves by introducing absurdly insecure identity checks which rely on utility bills.)

Another favourite trick of fraudsters is to contact your bank, pretend to be you, and have all your mail (including new bank and credit cards) sent to their own new address.

Banks have made this fraud easy by using call centres and absurd questioning techniques to identify customers. In the simple old days, when customers had to telephone their own local bank, the bank staff would know their customers and would know that Fred wasn't really moving to Delhi.

A survey conducted by the USA Federal Trade Commission, estimated that more than 27 million Americans have had their identity stolen in the last five years. In 2002 alone 10 million Americans were victims of identity theft. The chaos caused by all this can be judged from the fact that it took 300 million hours to sort out the problems. Consumers are estimated to have spent $5 billion in out-of-pocket expenses trying to re-claim their identities and the cost to banks and businesses was ten times that much. Two thirds of those involved said that their credit card accounts had been misused and one in five said that thieves had tapped into their current or savings accounts and taken money out. Around a third of those whose identity had been stolen reported that new accounts had been opened in their names and that other frauds such as renting an apartment or house, obtaining medical care or getting a job had all been committed in their name.

It gets worse.

Thousands of thoroughly respectable citizens have been arrested and handcuffed in public for crimes committed in their names. Some victims have taken years to get their lives back on track and to erase misdeeds from official records.

* * *

These new laws, which remove our privacy, our confidentiality and our freedom, have nothing whatsoever to do with terrorism. Those who claim they do are either extremely stupid or else they believe that we're all extremely stupid.

Terrorists pay cash. They don't use credit cards in their own names. If they need a false identity they will provide the necessary paperwork (complete with as many utility bills as are requested) without a blink and they will obtain a new identity easily and quickly.

The truth is that all these new regulations are designed solely to keep an eye on you and me and on what we are doing; to control every movement we make; to know where we are and why; to know how much money we have and where it is and what we are doing with it; to cut down on tax evasion and on perfectly legal tax avoidance schemes and, in short, to spy on us and to control us.

Identity cards and computerised records will enable the authorities to swoop on people who don't pay parking fines or who attend unauthorised street parties or buy or sell food at a fête without having obtained a special licence from the appropriate council inspectors, or who sing 'happy birthday' in a pub without first obtaining the appropriate (and very expensive) licence from the authorities.

These new laws, which so effectively remove every last vestige of our civil liberties and our human rights, will never stop terrorists and, more importantly, were never intended to stop terrorists (any more than the previous tranche of similarly oppressive laws were really intended to stop money launderers or drug smugglers).

These new laws are being created to keep you and I busy, worried and quiet. They exist to create fear and panic. They help fascist governments and they help the multinationals; they enable politicians to stay in power and they enable businessmen to make bigger profits. But they do not – repeat not – make us safe.

If you want to see a politician or a policeman blush ask them how many terrorists or money launderers or drug smugglers all these dictatorial, freedom crunching new laws have enabled the authorities to arrest. How many terrorists have been taken out of circulation in exchange for so much of our freedom?

Since they will doubtless be too embarrassed to reply I will tell you the answer. It isn't 1,000. It isn't 100. It isn't 10. It's none. None. As in not one.

$$* * *$$

A favourite trick of the politicians introducing all these oppressive new laws is to claim that anyone who questions their legislation is either a terrorist or is helping terrorists or is sympathetic to terrorists.

That nasty, evil trick, which is in truth a contemptible piece of spin which should always be treated with disdain, is too often taken seriously by people who really should know better. The truth is that if the terrorists want to destroy our society and to smash our civilisation then their work has been done for them by the politicians and bureaucrats who have introduced so many unnecessary and intrusive new laws.

Privacy is not a perk. According to Canada's Privacy Commissioner, the right to be anonymous is at the very core of human dignity, autonomy and freedom. Privacy (like freedom) is a basic human right. And yet it is a basic human right which your Government has taken from you without your approval or your permission.

Being private takes a lot of energy. If you don't organise your privacy when you don't need it, the chances are that when you do need it you won't have any left and you won't be able to get it.

We all take great care to protect ourselves against disaster. We take care about what we eat. We buy insurance to cover the no-claims bonus on our car insurance. But we have allowed governments (and others) to take away our privacy. We have allowed ourselves to be exposed to thieves and crooks who will, with great pleasure, part us from our money and, if it suits them, our lives.

The Government keeps a lot of secrets from us. They say they do this for 'security'.

So, why aren't we allowed to keep secrets from the Government?

Our security depends upon our privacy.

* * *

Advice To Help You Protect Your Privacy

1. The claim that 'you've got no need to hide anything if you are honest' is one of the commonest and most stupid things ever said. Your personal security is crucial. If you are reckless with private information you might get away with it. But you probably won't.

2. If you don't already own one you should go out now and buy yourself a shredder – and you should use it. I was delighted when I read that the shredder was the most popular Christmas gift in 2003. You should shred all financial details which you don't need to keep – that includes monthly accounts and statements from your bank or your credit card company, credit card receipts, invoices from utility companies and other sources, receipts from cash machines, blank stationery carrying your name and/or your address and all letters which have anything on them which you would not be happy to see published in a national newspaper. If it can be read (and anyone is ever likely to read it) then you must shred it unless you need to keep it. If it's embarrassing then shred it. Even junk mail can be hazardous – you should shred unwanted and unsolicited applications for bank products, loans and credit cards. (Many of these arrive with your details already filled in.) If you

don't have a shredder tear the paper into as many pieces as you can (making sure that you tear across essential pieces of information). Mix the pieces up, divide them into three or four piles and then put each pile into a separate public rubbish bin.

3. Do not use visiting cards. If one of your cards falls into the wrong hands the recipient will find it easy to impersonate you.

4. To protect computer work from hackers you might like to consider using two computers. Use one for the Internet and e-mail and a second computer for your own original work. This is the best way I know of to protect your computer (and therefore your work) from hackers and viruses.

5. Remember that fax machines are quicker and more private than e-mail. A fax will be seen the moment you send it and the recipient doesn't have to turn on his computer and check on his e-mails to find your message. Messages aren't lost as a result of viruses and you don't have to print anything out because it is already available as hard copy.

6. When preparing passwords avoid obvious dates and names. If you use a password to protect an account make sure that it is something unusual (don't just pick your telephone number, birthday or pet's name). Never, ever disclose your private password to anyone – including a bank official or a policeman. Keep your passwords secure.

7. Be very cautious when using a cash machine. If someone is standing close by, or tries to engage you in conversation, stop your transaction, remove your card and leave. If you have any difficulty in inserting your card do not proceed with the transaction. One new trick employed by fraudsters is to place a device over the card slot on the ATM. The device will clone your card and catch your personal identity number. If you think this has happened contact your bank immediately.

8. Protect your identity and your personal security. Be suspicious of anyone who asks you for private information (such as your address, telephone number, date of birth etc.). Some of the people who ask for this sort of information are crooks. Regard the rest as stupid and incompetent.

   Financial institutions (and even stores offering cards) want customers to fill in a mass of personal details. One I saw recently asked for (among other things) name, address, bank account details, security password, date of birth and passport number. The institution claimed that it wanted this information to protect its customers from fraud. This is nonsense. (As is the claim that all this information is required by law). If you give this much information to any institution you will expose yourself to fraud and, in particular, to identity theft. If an institution demands this much information from you tell them that their demands are a threat to your personal security and that you are taking your custom elsewhere for 'security reasons'. What institution will dare question your determination to protect your own security? Security is the excuse for every new law which takes away our liberty and our privacy. We can use the same excuse to protect our privacy and our liberty. If enough people refuse to comply with these absurdly intrusive demands then the institutions concerned will stop making them. Get into the habit of refusing to give out personal information. Banks, shops and government officials will often demand more information than they are legally entitled to. Only ever give out information that you have to give out.

Remember that when they have finished with your private information banks, store and others are quite likely to toss it out in the rubbish – allowing identity thieves to help themselves to your identity and your money. Remember, too, that private detectives, lawyers and journalists can pretty easily get hold of the details of any bank account you have.

Banking privacy works one way. They won't tell you anything. But they'll share your secrets with anyone who wants them.

9. If you are posting something valuable avoid the temptation to put on extra postage. (That's an immediate 'give-away' to crooks that the item contains something valuable.) Don't put sticky tape on the backs of ordinary envelopes because that too tells thieves that the envelope contains something 'special'.

10. If your home is ever searched, or you are ever investigated by the police, your computer will be taken away. (You may not get it back for weeks, months or years – or ever. Even if you do get your computer back your work may have been erased, distorted or ruined.

If you run a business and have essential work, files or records on your computer you could be ruined by this. The lesson is clear: keep copies of your work elsewhere.)

11. Keep a 'crisis' list of telephone numbers and addresses that you might need in an emergency. We all buy fire insurance but are pleased if we never have to use it. Know how to deal with crises – and hope you never have to use the knowledge you have acquired. A good precaution is never wasted. Preparations you don't use are nevertheless good value.

12. When filling in a form which asks for your age or date of birth, write either 'legal age' or 'over 21'. (A few years ago forms actually had a box which offered this alternative.)

13. If you have to give information about yourself which is going to be fed into a computer there are a few simple ways to confuse the system. Follow the example set by senior actresses and alter your birth date by a year or two. Try using your middle name. Or just give an initial rather than a name. Remember, however, that changing your name in order to deceive someone or to defraud them is strictly illegal.

14. Paying cash is fine for privacy but it draws attention to you. This is particularly likely to be a problem at airports. Many airlines will refuse to take cash at all. If you want to travel but don't want the entire world to know where and when you are travelling buy your ticket with cash from a real life travel agency with a real shop and real people working in it.

15. If you want to make sure that strangers can't check your telephone to see whom you last called try this: hang up when you have finished your call, then pick up the receiver and wait for the dial tone. Punch in a single digit and then put the phone down. If anyone uses the 'last number called' service they will find your single digit number.

16. If you want to keep your address private use a PO Box. You may have some minor problems when using a PO Box but persevere. These days quite a number of private organisations also offer a mailing address service.

17. If a bank (or any other institution) demands unreasonable amounts

of information before accepting you as a customer, walk away and go elsewhere. Every time you do this you increase the chances that the bank will reduce its unreasonable demands on future customers.

18. Do not consult an accountant, a financial advisor, a lawyer or a doctor and expect anything you tell them to be treated as confidential.

19. Keep your personal computer files on a removable hard drive or disk. If you do this you will never have to leave valuable files on your computer ever again.

20. Remember that more and more places (including many hotels) are now bugged. Lobbies, lounges and elevators are often fitted with cameras and audio bugs.

21. Remember that if you work for an institution or company and your computer belongs to the company you work for then so does the information on your computer. Your boss is entitled to read everything on your computer and to check out a list of all the Web sites you have visited.

22. There is no such thing as 'deleted' as far as a computer is concerned. Many networks routinely store back-ups of all the mail that passes through them. Everything you say in an e-mail or a visit to an on-line discussion group can, and will, be read by hundreds or thousands of other people. A full record of every Website you visit will be kept. This information may come back to haunt you in ten, twenty or thirty years' time.

23. When you buy a new computer do not fill in your own personal details. If you do, and then subsequently dispose of the computer, you may be held responsible for the activities of others.

24. When you delete a file from your computer you delete only the address. The file remains on your hard drive. You can buy as many programs as you like to erase the file but it will still be there. You can format your hard drive as often as you like and the information will still be there. I have nothing whatsoever to hide or to protect (except my personal privacy) but when I want to get rid of a floppy disk I remove the plastic disk from inside the casing and cut it up into tiny pieces. I then put the various pieces into different dustbins.

When I buy a new computer I remove the hard drive from the old one and smash it to pieces with a hammer. (Even this may not be enough since a fragment of discarded plastic or silicon from a CD ROM might yield a considerable quantity of text. Experts claim that even burning a CD might leave ash particles large enough to contain readable data. However, I reckon that if someone is so eager to read my old mail that they want to try to resurrect a hard drive I have hammered into a misshape then they are welcome to try.)

5. E-mail is never private. Nothing you can do to your e-mail will stop other people looking at it. You can use a fictitious name, you can buy the best encryption software available, you can put your e-mail on disks or you can send your message as a photograph but if people want to read your e-mail they will.

The very idea of privacy on the Internet now seems quaintly old-fashioned. Those who expressed surprise and reservations when it was revealed that Google, the world's most-used Internet search engine, was introducing a new e-mail service which would allow Google's computers to 'read' user's e-mails in order to send out targeted advertising, were described as 'privacy activists'.

E-mail is permanent, public and can always be traced back to you. It even seems certain that at least some of the anonymous re-mailers may be sting operations run by government agencies and designed to trap people who want to keep their e-mail private. Naturally, no one knows which ones are the stings. Hackers can break into the systems used by re-mailers. It is now widely believed by privacy experts that the USA Government collects, scans and stores all messages (including codes) that travel between computers. E-mails can linger for decades. They are widely used in civil and criminal cases. If an e-mail which you have encrypted is used against you the prosecutor will want to know why you felt the need to encrypt the message. The court will assume that you had something to hide. The safest way to end a confidential message is to write it on paper, fold it several times, wrap it in a page torn out of a magazine, put it in an envelope, stamp it and mail it.

6. Viruses can now be transmitted in the subject line of an e- mail. You don't have to open an attachment for your computer to 'catch' a virus.

27. Many rogue transactions involving credit cards are a result of cloning done when a consumer uses the Internet. Other forms of cloning are done in pubs, restaurants or service stations. A crooked employee puts the card into a machine called a skimmer which reads and then stores the information on the card. The skimmer is sold to another crook who downloads the information onto a computer and then transfers the details to replica bank cards. The counterfeit cards are frequently used by illegal immigrants. Much of the fraud which involves credit cards and the Internet originates in the USA and you should not expect the authorities there to take much interest in your problems. Report any incidents or suspicions to your bank or credit card company immediately in order to protect your reputation and credit rating and to recover any money taken from you fraudulently. A new type of card is now being introduced in the UK which will make card cloning more difficult. Actually the card isn't all that new. It was introduced in France a decade ago, since when card fraud has fallen by 80%. No one seems to know just why it took ten years to bring the technology to the UK.

Chapter 10

When Progress Isn't Progress At All

ociety needs to convince us of the importance of progress because without progress industry would slow down, consumption would fall, axes would collapse and governments everywhere would have less money o spend. (We, of course, would get the chance to learn to enjoy our orld and our lives.)

We have created a world and a society which now controls us. Our resent and our future are controlled by the social structures we have evised. Our institutions and our establishments need progress in order o gain more power.

We like to blame the invisible 'them' for our graceless state but there re no invisible 'them'. The men and women who have positions of uthority in our society are as tortured by what is going on as everyone lse. They suffer as you and I suffer. The power is now vested in the nstitutions themselves.

And in order to grow in size and power the institutions we have reated needs progress. Without progress we would not need to keep uying new gadgets. We would not throw away perfectly serviceable lothes or replace perfectly reliable motor cars.

Politicians tell us that progress makes our lives better but, as usual, hey are lying. Progress is only good because it's good for them.

Technological changes have utterly altered our way of life. But have they always improved it? Steam engines and spinning jenny revolutionised the world. They led directly to factories, assembly line back-to-back housing, overcrowding and the spread of deadly infectious diseases such as consumption, fixed working hours, formalised schooling and the welfare state. Would anyone really argue that all of those were 'good' things?

Inevitably, anyone who works for any company or institution will insist that progress is synonymous with 'better'. Even if you put aside the fact that judging something 'better' than something else must always be subjective, this is clearly nonsense.

Is a supermarket, where the customers have to select their own food, queue to pay for it and then carry it home, better than an old fashioned grocery shop where the customers handed their list to the grocer and then went go home and made a cup of tea while they waited for the delivery boy to cycle round with the required groceries?

Is serving yourself to petrol better than having a pump attendant fill your tank?

Is life really better now that we have 100 satellite television channels?

New opera houses and concert halls may look very 'modern' but why are the acoustics in new buildings so often far inferior to the acoustics in buildings which were erected hundreds of years ago? What sort of progress is that? Why do architects insist on tearing down everything that is traditionally British and putting up soulless, concrete replacements in their stead? Our towns and cities used to have a quaintness about them which locals and visitors alike found charming. It was, very often, the quaint areas which provided the town or city with a heart. Today, all in the name of progress, the hearts have been torn out of our cities to make way for new administration blocks. (Why are the council offices and the Post Office invariably the ugliest buildings in any town or city? Why did the architects of France's National Library (completed in 1995) not realise that a glass exterior would prove disastrous for the fragile books the building was intended to house? (The direct sunlight through the glass walls damaged the books so much that yellow shutters had to be hung inside the walls.)

Progress, officially, is having a car radio which automatically changes itself to the station which gives the best reception – regardless of what you want to listen to.

Progress has enabled us to replace spoons with little plastic sticks

hich don't stir properly but which do melt when placed in hot fluid. Is
at progress which we should welcome?

Is sport more entertaining now that players and pitches are festooned
ith sponsors' logos and advertising hoardings? (Where does all the
xtra money go? Why do footballers need to be paid £100,000 a week
) do something most of them would happily do for nothing? Do modestly
lented cricketers deserve to be paid a fortune to spend their lives playing
game most people happily pay to play?)

Do pesticide enriched apples taste better than ones which were grown
1 a local orchard and picked from the tree by hand? Does sliced bread
ste better than home baked bread? Do pies bought in a packet taste
etter than home-made pies like mother used to make?

Is your life more enjoyable now that business contacts can telephone
ou when you are lying in the bath, sitting on the beach, watching a
lm or having dinner in a restaurant?

What the supporters of progress really mean is that progress is
ood for business or offers some advantage in terms of money or power
) the part of the social structure to which they are tied. Progress is,
ronically, essential to the status quo.

Progress means that life in general and 'things' in particular become
nore complicated and more likely to go wrong. Progress means that
he 'things' you bought yesterday (and were happy with) are outdated
nd useless within months – and cannot be repaired because the parts
ren't available.

Progress means that more and more people have to exchange a
ich, varied, wholesome healthy lifestyle for one which is hollow and
lled with despair and loneliness. Progress means deprivation for people
ut strength for our social structures. Progress means that the jobs
eople do become more boring and less satisfying. Progress means more
ower to machines. Progress means that things are more likely to go
rong. Progress means more destruction, more misery and more tedium.
'rogress means more damage to our planet. Progress means more
oxic stress.

Those who worship at the altar of progress make two simple but
ital errors. They assume that man must take full advantage of every
ew development and invention and they assume that he must always
earch for a better way of tackling everything he does. Neither of these
wo assumptions is soundly based.

Why Everything is going to get worse

Just because man has invented computers, supersonic jets and atomi
bombs he doesn't have to use all these things. There is an assumptio
that science and technology are wonderful things which invariabl
improve our lives enormously. It is a false assumption.

* * *

There is, among most observers and pundits, an almost universa
belief that computers have been unreservedly beneficial to mankinc
and that they have led (and will continue to lead) to wonderfu
improvements in the way we live.

Many experts claim that computers are the third big revolution.

First, there was the agricultural revolution.

Then, more recently, came the industrial revolution, which began i
England and which led to the invention of factory machinery (an
factories).

The information revolution (based on computers) really started i
the 1950s and the 'experts' say it has improved our lives just a
dramatically as the other two revolutions.

But are we really all better off because of computers?

I don't think the judgement is quite as easy to make as some expert
would have us believe.

Government officials and politicians are all keen on computers. Th
'system' loves computers because computers enable the system to kee
track of where we all are and what we are doing. Computers enabl
the bureaucrats to see what we're earning and what we're spendin
our money on. Governments use computers to increase their knowledg
about us; that knowledge gives them an enormous amount of powe
Computers have removed almost every last vestige of personal privac
and personal security.

Big companies like computers for the same reason. Computers enabl
corporations to increase their knowledge of their customers and t
maximise the profit potential of every transaction.

It is perfectly true that computers now dominate our lives. But ha
the effect been entirely positive?

Some experts have made startling predictions about the futur
dangers of technology. Some have claimed (quite wrongly in my view
that by the year 2020 even cheap computers will match huma
intelligence. Bill Joy, co-founder of Sun Microsystems and co-creato

BEFORE IT GETS BETTER

of the JAVA programming language has argued that there is a high risk that new technologies will result in the extinction of the human species. (I don't agree with that either.) But what about the recent past, the present and the immediate future?

How many times over the years have you heard promises of the paperless office?

A decade or so ago pundits were claiming that by the end of the millennium we would all be working at home. The office, they argued, would be little more than a memory.

In reality, nothing much has changed. Most people still commute and go to an office which is equipped with desks, telephones and filing cabinets. Electronics have changed the appearance of the office, and they have changed the way we do our work, but they haven't really changed our lives very much at all. And have they changed our lives for the better?

Computer experts tell us with great enthusiasm that computers double in power every eighteen months. But computers still crash so often that most users regard such incidents as 'normal'. We have learned to accept that computers are unreliable and temperamental. Cock-ups are so commonplace that no one notices. The Government is forever forking out millions for computer systems that don't work properly. The latest screw-up was £450 million for a faulty computer system at the Child Support Agency. In 21st century Britain failure is one of the few things which isn't an option; it comes bundled in with the software. Even when human error is ignored, computers are still woefully impractical and unreliable. Would we accept television sets, washing machines or cars which were as unreliable as computers are?

Not long ago I decided to try out a new personal digital assistant (PDA) which had e-mail capability. The manager of the shop which sold me the device assured me that it would take very little time to set up. I responded by offering to pay him to set it up for me. It took him and a colleague (a professional PDA expert) four full days to make the PDA operational. Even then it did not do the things it was supposed to do. I took it back to the shop and demanded (and received) a full refund.

* * *

I believe that those who are unblinkingly enthusiastic about computers are wrong.

WHY EVERYTHING IS GOING TO GET WORSE

Computers (and other pieces of modern technology) have not improved the quality of our lives. On the contrary, they have reduced the quality of life for most people. Millions who used to be able to get home and relax now feel they must spend their weekends, evenings and early mornings collecting e-mails and working on their laptops. Mobile telephones have made it possible for us to call for emergency help wherever we are (though whether or not we can get help is another matter) but mobile telephones have also done irreparable harm to our social lives, our privacy and our ability to relax and 'get away from it all'.

Mobile telephones have made everyone's life nastier, noisier, more annoying, more brutal and unarguably shorter and have in many ways done far more harm than good. Even the people who don't own or use them are harmed by them.

Why have so many people suddenly found so much that is so urgent in their lives? Just walk through any average city and you'll see every other person talking on the phone. In a restaurant I once watched two diners sitting together and talking throughout three courses on their mobile phones. Were they talking to one another? Did they find face-to-face communication impossible? Or did they find one another's company so unbearable that they could only stomach their food while talking to third and fourth parties? And loudly, of course. Do people who speak on mobile telephones only ever converse with deaf people?

(Computer people really don't strike me as being the brightest in the world. When in 2003 a virus damaged the computers of many customers of Microsoft, and made it impossible for them to access the Internet, the company advised these unfortunates to download a remedy from the Microsoft Web site. Did the Microsoft employees not understand that without access to the Internet their customers wouldn't be able to access the Microsoft site and download the patch they needed to get access to the Web?)

Some companies undoubtedly do benefit from computer technology. Companies which deal directly with the public may benefit if their software enables them to keep records of their customers' likes and preferences.

But most companies have actually lost money since computers were first introduced. The increase in computer power has led to a marked slowdown in productivity growth in all western economies during the last thirty years. One reason for this is that most companies have spent money on equipment which does far more than they could ever need. Another reason for the fall in productivity is that many employees now spend a large proportion of their working day surfing the Internet, playing computer games or dealing with (and simply deleting) unwanted e-mails.

Around a trillion e-mails are now sent every year. Three quarters of these e-mails are spam – anonymous, unsolicited e-mails which are sent out in bulk. Around 350 billion pieces of spam are mailed out from America every year and most of the spam which clogs British computers and adversely affects British productivity comes from Tony Blair's best friends, the Americans. Naturally, the American authorities do little to interfere with American businessmen sending spam to the UK (and, indeed, to the rest of the world). The EU recently made it illegal to send spam but this new law will have no effect whatsoever on e-mail sent from the USA.

Spamming continues because it is hugely profitable. One American spammer sends out around 10 million e-mails a day. From those 10 million e-mails he receives around 50 orders a day for cyber eavesdropping software. As a result he earns around £500,000 a year. His business costs are virtually nil since he is effectively subsidised by companies and individuals who have to pay while they delete his unwanted e-mails.

(Although the American authorities don't seem to care much about Americans inundating foreigners with e-mails they have made a fairly pathetic attempt to stop junk e-mails within the USA. Americans who don't want to receive junk e-mails will be able to send their e-mail address to a Web site and say that they don't wish to receive any spam. They can give a list of specialist areas in which they are, or are not, interested. Unbelievably, American bureaucrats seem to believe that this system will deter unwanted e-mails. It does not seem to have occurred to them that spammers will merely use offshore servers, harvest all the e-mail addresses of people who say they don't want e-mail and e-mail them anyway.)

It is largely because of unwanted e-mails that many busy people (including a surprising number working in both the computer and the telecommunications industries) have admitted that they do not use e-mail at all.

WHY EVERYTHING IS GOING TO GET WORSE

It was, for example, announced in September 2003 that the head of one major British telecommunications company had instructed his 2,500 employees to speak face-to-face or use the telephone rather than using e-mail. Indeed, staff were actually banned from sending each other e-mails. The company boss said that this would save each employee three hours a day and would save his company millions.

Other firms, realising that it is possible for employees to send copies of e-mails to a thousand colleagues simply by pressing a single key, are now following suit. The worst spammers are in fact those working for a company (rather than those sending e-mails in from outside). Employees who send jokes and photographs to colleagues are helping to destroy corporate productivity.

Although I have had a Web site for many years (and have had an Internet presence since the early 1990s) I have never been an enthusiastic user of e-mail. Just opening and reading the day's e-mails can take several hours. And there is an urgency about e-mail which I find alarming. Several years ago I remember opening a series of e-mail requests from one reader. The first e-mail demanded advice on some subject which I have long since forgotten. The second e-mail, timed about ten minutes later, demanded to know why I hadn't replied to the first e-mail. The third e-mail, timed another ten minutes later, was ruder and wanted to know again why I hadn't replied. The final e-mail, sent less than half an hour after the first request, was angry, indignant and threatening.

***

The World Wide Web was created by an Englishman (and given free to the world) but a company currently backed by the American Government now controls it. (The Internet itself was created by the American military and there are those who believe that the original idea was to create a computerised system which would eventually enable the American Government to build up computer files on everyone, and find a way to read everyone's correspondence. If that was the aim it has been remarkably successful.)

The company currently running the World Wide Web will, in a few years, become independent but meanwhile other countries worry that the World Wide Web is dominated by American 'culture' and 'values'. The rules for the way the Internet and the World Wide Web are used are made behind closed doors, based on USA policy and ruled by American laws. The number of Internet Service Providers is falling rapidly and the monopolistic companies taking control of the World Wide Web are now selling different levels of Internet access. It is likely that Web sites containing 'marginal' content (content which isn't associated with the Government or big business) might soon be marginalised. There seems no doubt that governments everywhere (but particularly those in the USA and the UK) regarded the potential for information exchange and mass market communication offered by the World Wide Web as a serious threat – and something to be controlled and contained.

Although I recognise that the Internet does have numerous good features I would still argue that it has been wildly oversold. Instead of becoming a tool for freedom it has become little more than a marketing medium for pornographers. Well over three quarters of the traffic on the World Wide Web is related to porn sites.

There are several reasons why the Web doesn't have much of a future.

The first is that the initial Web businesses, run by entrepreneurs who thought they could get rich out of mining this particular communications seam, wrongly believed that all they had to do to get rich was to accumulate market share. They thought that if they dominated the market they would win all the subsequent battles. They were, of course, quite wrong and if they had known anything about business history they would have known that the first entrepreneurs in a new business area usually go bust – leaving the second and third tranche of operators to make the profit.

Believing that they had to win market share at all cost these young businesses gave away their product. They gave away information, software and whatever else it was that they were supposed to be selling. Since most of them were young, naive and totally inexperienced they thought that they would be able to work out a way to make money later on. (The young Web entrepreneurs can be excused their naivety on the basis that they were inexperienced and ignorant. The bankers and venture capitalists who supported their businesses cannot be excused on these grounds and must simply plead guilty to being amazingly stupid.)

One of the best examples of Internet hubris was exhibited by boo.com – an $800 million Internet company which had 400 employees.

Boo was widely respected as one of the most exciting Internet companies (the boss advised Tony Blair on e-commerce) and yet on their very best ever day (with a 40% off sale operating) they managed just 1,078 orders. (A figure that Publishing House has exceeded with around 1% of the number of employees).

The boo.com Web site was rated Number 1 in the world for ease of access but it is alleged that it took a staggering four minutes to download.

When the company received a thank you letter from a customer they were so excited and delighted that when a book was written about the boo.com site the letter was published in the book.

∗ ∗ ∗

Many of the delightfully naive young entrepreneurs who planned to become millionaires through Web sites thought that they would be able to make a fortune out of selling advertising to other Web based businesses. They didn't stop to wonder where the money would come from to pay for the advertising if everyone was giving away their product for free.

Some of these young entrepreneurs had never even run a lemonade stall in summer and had no idea at all of how the world operates. They genuinely thought that the rules would be different for the Internet. They thought that they were changing the way the world operates.

The big problem was that by giving away their product they devalued the value of Internet information. As a result most users of the Internet still expect to get material free of charge from Web sites. Some become indignant and outraged if they are asked to pay.

The result is that much of the material available on the Web has been put there by lobbyists and public relations groups trying to sell a specific product or a particular line of thought. It is now extremely difficult to find honest, trustworthy material on the Internet.

Some search engines are alleged to have compounded the problem by allowing people to buy positions on their search lists. This, inevitably, has devalued the reputation of search engines and will, eventually, mean that search engines themselves will be doomed. It is as though the public library accepted bribes from corporate sponsors to respond to specific requests for information by providing specific material. Once people realise that a request to a search engine may simply produce a list of advertisers, or a list of sites which have paid to be selected, or a list of sites run by people whose primary skill exists in ensuring that their site comes top of a search list, rather than an objective list of relevant sites, users will stop using search engines. Without search engines the Internet becomes unwieldly and incomprehensible. Eventually, most people will pretty well stop using the Internet.

(The availability of free information on the Internet has had an effect on other areas of life too. Internet users have become so accustomed to the idea of obtaining 'free' information that they resent having to pay for it, wherever it comes from, and are seemingly unaware that the value of information for which you pay nothing invariably matches what you paid for it.)

* * *

The early Web-based corporations thought that they were entering an entirely new area of marketing. They were not, of course. Web businesses are simply mail order operations which, instead of advertising in magazines and newspapers, advertise on the Internet. Web companies still need all the usual back-up associated with a mail order operation.

The stupidity of those operating early Web-based companies is, to my mind, best exemplified by the fact that numerous entrepreneurs thought they could get rich by selling pet food and cat litter over the Web. If they had stopped to think about what they were doing, and had realised that they were running mail order businesses, they would have surely realised that selling extremely cheap but extremely heavy to post items could never work in a mail order operation.

* * *

Although the Web started off being promoted as a tool for freedom and free speech things haven't turned out that way at all.

Back when the Internet was still young many pundits believed that it would give power to the people. In the beginning it seemed that the Web would enable people to find out whatever they wanted to know about specific, professional areas. It would mean that experts would have to justify themselves and it would empower patients and consumers. It would, said the experts, boost democracy.

In 1990, writing in his book *Powershift*, Alvin Toffler forecast that communication systems, global, ubiquitous, mobile and interconnected, would make it impossible for governments to manage ideas, images, data, information or knowledge. I'm afraid that Toffler underestimated the ability, the power and the determination of governments to stay in control. The Internet did promise much in this area but all that has changed. Governments now control the World Wide Web and have given themselves the legal right to study all Web communications. Nothing is safe from their prying eyes and the legal responsibilities of Web site owners are now awesome. The Americans (as usual) insist that their authority is now global and they have arrested people who aren't American, living in countries outside America, because they have broken American laws. Those who operate Web sites are legally responsible for everything that appears on their sites and anyone who still allows chat rooms to appear on their Web site must be immensely brave.

Today, it is clear that the medium which was supposed to empower us has done exactly the opposite. The Internet enables bureaucrats, politicians and lobbyists and lawyers to find out everything they want to know about us while, at the same time, making it pretty well impossible for us to find out what we want to know about them.

* * *

Computers attract the sort of nerdy figures who used to spend their weekends dressed in anoraks writing down engine numbers. But instead of just cluttering up railway station platforms the nerds have turned nasty. Today's nerds don't have the imagination or the skill to create good sites so they use their basic skills to destroy other people's work. Hackers, usually unemployed and living on state handouts, spend their days either trying to damage Web sites or creating and then sending out viruses designed to damage the integrity and reputation of the Internet. Nerdy hackers are curious people. Why would anyone obviously keen on computers be so desperate to destroy the viability and popularity of the thing they are keen on?

The Internet will survive of course. It is a medium and it isn't going to disappear. But in practice it will survive as a tool for advertisers, propagandists, amateurs and pornographers.

Futurologists are still making great claims for the Web. They still believe that it will change our lives. They are utterly wrong. Unless you are a pornographer (or a porn user) the Web will have made little impact on your life. And the Web will make relatively few, small changes to our day-to-day lives in the future.

BEFORE IT GETS BETTER

It is possible to argue that computers have done far more harm than good in every possible way – and that we would all be better off if computers had never been invented at all.

Before you dismiss this thought ask yourself this simple question: In how many ways have computers really improved (not changed, mark you, but improved) your life? And in how many ways have they made it worse?

* * *

What the computer enthusiasts perhaps don't realise is that the technology that people think is going to change the world rarely does change the world – at least, not in the way that was envisaged. The great influences on us come not from military or political leaders but from the thinkers who change the way we look at life, and from the inventors of simple, humdrum things which change the way we live in real, practical ways.

When they were first introduced, cars, steamships, trains, aeroplanes and the telephone were all said to bring hope for making the world a fairer and more decent place. It would be easy to argue that all of these have done exactly the opposite and there is no reason to believe that the Internet and the computer will be different. The Web has no past, an overstated present and a future which is nowhere near as rosy as its advocates claim.

It has never been the 'obvious' advances which have changed our lives. It has always been the little things which have produced the greatest social changes; and they have often done this quite unexpectedly.

For example, which do you think changed our lives more: the candle or the computer?

I'd give my vote to the candle. The candle gave us light and the ability to continue our lives after dark. The candle gave us the use of the night.

Which do you think changed our lives more: the computer or the chimney?

I'd say the chimney.

The chimney changed our social lives by making it possible for us all to have individual fires – and, therefore, individual homes. It made it possible to have a fire indoors without setting fire to the furniture. Before the chimney was invented people used to live in large halls where the

271

smoke from the fire would billow around before eventually leaking out through doors or windows. People would huddle together for warmth. The chimney changed all that.

I'd also say that central heating has changed our lives far more than the computer. Central heating has completely altered the way we use our homes. When we just had a fire we all had to huddle around it. Now we can do our own things in our own rooms.

Even when bits and pieces of technology do change our lives they often do so in ways that the original designers didn't envisage.

For example, the mobile phone enabled young people to leave home but retain some security and stability. The mobile phone also made it possible for people to move around and yet stay in touch with their relatives and friends. And the mobile telephone made it possible for us to speak to people without having the foggiest idea where they are.

In so many cases it is not the technology itself – nor the immediate effect it has on us – which is important, but the unexpected social effects.

For example, the microwave oven enables families to cook their meals separately. As a result, families no longer have to eat together. This may be progress, but is it a good thing?

Sometimes the things which change our lives are remarkably simple.

If I had to be dragged back to the 19th century one of the few modern luxuries I would want to take with me would be the paper handkerchief.

And I would argue that the invention of the ordinary lead pencil has had a greater impact on our world and our lives than has the invention of the computer.

* * *

We are taught to have respect for science and technology. We are taught that science and technology have all the answers to the problems of today and tomorrow. We are told that science can help mankind conquer the future and that technology can help man deal with the problems that have been created by the present and the past.

But the people who tell us all this are wrong; sadly, woefully, ingloriously wrong. Science and technology are, in practice, the cause of a great deal of stress.

Ironically, science and technology are now largely dedicated to solving problems created by science and technology.

Science is no more than a tool and like any tool it can be a force for evil as readily as it can be a force for good.

It is science which has enabled us to destroy much of our world. It was science which gave us the ability to conquer, control and exploit nature. It was science which gave us pollution. Science gave us penicillin but it has also given us benzodiazepine tranquillisers. It was science which gave us concrete and high rise tower blocks and endless ribbons of motorway. It was science which gave us road traffic accidents and air crashes and a thousand different varieties of death and destruction. It was science which gave us nuclear power and the ability to destroy ourselves. It was science which turned the poppy into heroin and the coca leaf into cocaine. It was science which gave us landmines and cluster bombs. It was science which gave us chemicals which blind and drugs which numb and destroy the brain.

And it was science which gave us genetic engineering.

Genetic engineering threatens our existence and our future.

Genetic engineering has been sold to us as offering us the opportunity to have cheaper food and a greater choice.

Really?

Before the genetic engineers appeared on the scene there were more than 500 types of apple grown in England. Now there are less than 30, though it is true that that number will soon be supplemented by genetically modified apples which will never rot. We are not told what those apples will taste like. Or what their vitamin content will be. Genetic engineers don't concern themselves much with taste or goodness. They are more concerned with profit. (That, you see, is what genetic engineering is really all about.)

Genetic engineering means that a woman can now choose the sex of her baby. (This facility is illegal in Britain but British women who want to take advantage of it simply go abroad.) Those who promote this as a choice ignore the fact that the consequences for the planet could be catastrophic.

In health care, technology has taken the place of caring and the 'p' word that matters is 'profit' not 'patient'.

* * *

We have (quite rightly in my view) a deep-rooted suspicion of technology.

WHY EVERYTHING IS GOING TO GET WORSE

After he had finished creating his monster, Mary Shelley's Dr Frankenstein said: 'Now that I had finished, the beauty of my dream vanished, and breathless horror and disgust filled my heart.'

Would that today's scientists shared the sensitivity of Dr Frankenstein.

By the year 2006 meat and milk from cloned animals will probably be on sale. An American Government report, from the Food and Drug Administration, has concluded that: 'Cloned animal products appear to be safe for consumption'. Consumers should be terrified by the carefree way with which the American Government includes, but ignores, the word 'appear' in this sentence. The long-term effects of eating cloned meat and milk are, of course, unknown.

In the UK the Government planned a public debate on genetically modified crops in order to dispel what they called the 'myths' surrounding GM foods and to please (largely American) companies desperate to sell their GM food to British customers. The aim was to prove that the public were happy to eat GM food, but, as always, the Government got things badly wrong. Of 37,000 responses received from British citizens less than 2% said they would be happy to eat GM food. There was very little support for the commercialisation of GM crops and the survey revealed widespread distrust both of the Government and of the multinational companies involved. Most people responding to the Government's request for comments said they wanted more research and incontrovertible proof that no harm would come from the technology. It was clear that most electors believe that the only people who will benefit from GM technology will be multinationals and politicians. Voters expressed concern that ordinary people and farmers would all lose out while there would also be irreversible damage to the gene pool.

Naturally, since the results weren't what they wanted, the Government decided to ignore the evidence of its own survey and announced the approval of genetically engineered crops despite the widespread public opposition.

There is no evidence to show that GM food is safe, and much to suggest that it could be dangerous. Worse, if GM crops and food do turn out to be dangerous then the dangers may well be irreversible. We may change our planet permanently – and for the worse. There is very little upside and an enormous downside.

Before It Gets Better

✳ ✳ ✳

It was science which gave us unemployment and which took away from millions the natural pride, pleasure and quiet satisfaction that can be obtained from a day's work well done. It was science which turned skilled craftsmen into miserable machine minders; removing pride, self-expression and satisfaction from their lives.

Science created all these problems. And now science pushes us to search for new answers and solutions. And as it pushes so it creates new problems and new fears.

When we use science to help us live better, happier, cleaner, safer and more contented lives then science can be a powerful force for good. But too often science is an end in itself rather than a force for good. Too often science aids only scientists; too often science adds nothing to the quality of life.

Those who believe implicitly in progress believe that we must always endeavour to use every new nugget of information we obtain. They believe that if man invents a faster way to travel then the faster way to travel must be better than the old way. They believe that if man invents a quicker and more effective way to kill people then we must use this quicker and more effective weapon of destruction. They believe that if man invents a faster way to do mathematical equations then all our industries must be adapted to take advantage of this new technology.

These assumptions are not based on logic or fact.

Progress for the sake of progress often simply means change for the sake of change. Change is not always for the better.

Nor is there much sense in the belief that man must always busy himself looking for better ways to do things.

To some extent, the problem lies with the definition of the word 'better'. What, exactly, does it mean?

Is a television set better than a radio?

Is a motor car better than a bicycle?

Is an aeroplane better than a yacht?

Are modern motor cars, equipped with electric windows and air-conditioning, better than ancient Rolls Royce motor cars equipped with neither of these facilities?

Is artificial turf better than real grass?

Are artificial flowers better than the real thing?

Are people wiser, happier and more contented now that electric toothbrushes are available?

Are people more at peace than their ancestors now that the compact disc player has been invented and marketed?

The truth, of course, is something of a compromise. Some advances are good. Some new technology is helpful. Some new developments really do improve our lives. Some progress reduces pain and suffering.

Progress can be a boon as well as a burden. It would be stupid to claim that all progress is bad. Progress is good when we use it rather than when we allow it to rule our lives. The Luddites aren't always right. But they aren't always wrong, either.

Progress is neither good nor bad unless we make it so.

But society isn't interested in the truth. And it certainly isn't interested in any compromise. Society needs uncontrolled progress in order to grow. Our society's institutions have an insatiable appetite for progress. And the people who acquire their power and their status and their wealth from those institutions do what they are expected to do. Our world is no longer controlled by people. It is controlled by the structures we have created.

The real problem is that we are no longer allowed to choose between those aspects of progress which we think can be to our benefit and those which we suspect may be harmful. Our society wants progress and that is what it gets.

Chapter 11
The Power Of Fear

Our ancestors lived in a world about which they understood very little and where they were constantly in danger. They had many things to be afraid of: being eaten alive by wild animals to mention but one.

We, in contrast, should lead relatively fear free lives.

But all the evidence firmly shows that fear plays a much bigger part in our lives than it ever played in the lives of our ancestors.

Fear is the most fundamental cause of pain and distress; it is the father of a whole range of destructive and damaging emotions including: jealousy, guilt, sadness, greed, bitterness, anxiety and prejudice.

Why are we so much more afraid than our ancestors?

The main reason is that we are constantly being *made* to feel afraid.

Fear rules our emotions and our lives. It is always there. Fear of redundancy. Fear of losing the house. Fear of arrest. Fear of facing some bizarre, untrue allegation. Fear of a tax investigation.

So, where does all this fear come from and why?

To find the answer remember Lenin, for he it was who first pointed out that if we don't understand why something is happening, and we want to know why, then we should simply look to see who is benefiting.

There are plenty of suspects, for fear is very useful to all sorts of people. Fear encourages us to spend money and to accept progress and

277

change. Fear helps to keep us weak but it helps to keep society's institutions strong. Fear divides us and cripples us, but gives our social structures strength. Today we are never allowed to forget our fears for an instant. Every representative of every social structure uses fear to manipulate us. 'The mass of men lead lives of quiet desperation', wrote Henry David Thoreau and the desperation comes out of fear. Fear helps our society to sustain itself and to increase its power.

It is no accident that industries, advertising agencies, politicians, experts and television commentators all contribute to our daily ration of fear. They know that one of the best ways to get people to do something which they might not choose to do is to frighten them. Fear is one of the most potent forces used to control us and to manipulate our emotions.

But the commercial exploiters of fear are just the beginning. They're just after money. It is politicians who exploit fear most ruthlessly. The politicians want our hearts, our spirits and our freedom. They want to control us so that we become obedient and unquestioning; allowing them to retain their power (and all the perks that go with it) without ever having to explain, apologise or, in the end, take any notice of what we want.

They know that when we are overwhelmed with trouble we fear everything and turn in on ourselves, desperately hoping that someone will take over and sort out our troubles for us. This is why patients and relatives hand over their trust so completely to doctors and nurses. The wild animal goes into a corner and faces the wall; we just shut the door and watch television.

When did you last hear a politician, pundit or expert offering undiluted comfort and reassurance? They never do, do they? The fact is that politicians spend much of their time *deliberately* making us afraid. They use fear, the most potent of all forces, to manipulate our emotions and to control us. They use fear to justify what they call 'progress'.

The two weapons by which leaders traditionally took and held onto power were wealth and violence (or the threat of violence). The king who has gold and an army is in a strong position to retain his position. As long as he keeps control of the gold and the army he is unlikely to have to face much in the way of an uprising.

But the underlying weapons which leaders use to hold onto power have always been fear and ignorance. If you keep people frightened, and you don't tell them what is going on, you will, inevitably, have power over them. The biggest fear our politicians have is losing the power they have; they know that the wealth and status they enjoy is not personal, it comes with the office rather than because of any personal qualities they might possess; they have to keep us frightened in order to keep their own fears at bay.

Our political leaders use four weapons to keep control of us.

First, they use money to control us. Since they don't have any money of their own they use the money they have taken from us. Indeed, not only do they use our own money to control us but they use the threat of taking away what money we have left to keep us quieter still.

Second, they use force to control us. We know that if we disobey them we will be punished. Even when their orders are unfair, unjust and not at all what we (the public) want the consequences are the same. We have to obey or we will be thrown into prison. Those who dare to demonstrate on the streets know that they will be confronted by thousands of policemen. And demonstrators know (or should know) that they will be photographed, identified and possibly visited at home. Sometimes the force involves batons and rubber bullets. Sometimes the force involves intimidation.

Third, they use ignorance. They refuse to release essential information on spurious 'security' grounds. And, of course, they lie. They lie endlessly. They tell us that we are being threatened and must go to war to protect ourselves. They tell us that without our nation's membership of the European Union we would all be destitute. They lie shamelessly and without end.

But, finally, and most of all, they use fear.

For personal and professional reasons politicians have good reason to know all about fear.

'It is not power that corrupts but fear,' wrote Aung San Suu Kyi, human rights activist and democratic leader of Burma, writing in *Freedom from Fear*. 'Fear of losing power corrupts those who wield it...'.

Frightened politicians deliberately want to keep the rest of us afraid because then they can convince us that all the new laws they are passing (laws which are taking away our freedom but which are giving them and the institutions they represent more power) are essential. The politicians need the new laws to satisfy the lobbyists, who are wandering around the corridors of power with their pockets stuffed with currency.

It is the lobbyists who, in the end, control much of the legislation which is passed. Of course, the lobbyists themselves don't benefit much at all (though they get their salaries and their bonuses). It is the corporations they represent which benefit. In other words laws are passed not because they are what the people want but because they are what the corporations want.

* * *

'On rencontre sa destinée souvent par des chemins qu'on prend pour l'eviter. (We often meet our fate on the road we take to avoid it.)'
JEAN DE LA FONTAINE

* * *

Politicians keep us frightened, cowering in our homes and malleable, in a number of different ways.

1. They deliberately allow the level of street crime to rise.

Do you find that difficult to believe? Think about it. Ask the village idiot how he would cut crime on our streets. He'll tell you that he'd put more policemen back on the beat. It's the obvious answer. And it would obviously work. So you have two choices. Either politicians are even more stupid than the average village idiot (possible but improbable) or they deliberately don't put policemen back on the streets because they don't want crime levels to fall. And look at Labour Party policy towards punishment. The Labour Government's latest scheme is to allow burglars to go unpunished if they apologise to the householders they have burgled. OK, answer this: are politicians really so stupid that they don't see that when crime goes unpunished criminals will flourish? Of course they aren't. The only alternative conclusion is that they know exactly what they are doing. The Labour Party want more crime because they want you and I to be too frightened to think of anything but staying alive and hanging onto whatever possessions we still have. Politicians make us frightened in order to encourage us to allow them (and the social structures which they operate) to have more power. Every new law they pass gives them more power and means that we have less freedom. Police chiefs like us to be frightened of criminals because that gives them an excuse to demand more money, more assistants, bigger offices and more power. The police force (as an institution) thrives on high crime figures. Think about it: if there was no crime there would be no need for any policemen.

2. They deliberately exaggerate the risk of terrorism.

Politicians and police chiefs frighten us about street violence in order to encourage us to give them more power. They know that in order to keep us frightened they need to keep crime figures high. So that's what they do. Politicians want us to be frightened of terrorists for the same reason. For a few years politicians used the 'drugs war' as an excuse for scaring the daylights out of us – and taking away our freedom. Now they've got a much better way to create fear: terrorism. Politicians make us frightened of our unseen enemies abroad (even if the enemies are imaginary or of no real threat to us) because by making us frightened they can grab more power – and stay in charge for longer. Fear is a potent weapon and the availability of television and radio means that we can be frightened more speedily and more effectively than ever before. Fear helps our society to sustain itself and to increase its power. Fear wins elections. Oh, how the politicians love terrorists.

Ignoring the reality (that there is far less terrorist activity in the UK than there was a few years ago when the largely American funded IRA was in full swing) British politicians have used the threat of terrorism as an excuse for a whole library of new anti-freedom laws. New Labour want to terrify us all so much that they can push through any legislation they like on the grounds that it is 'for our own protection and security'. If we protest about losing our freedom we can be dismissed as unpatriotic. If we make too much noise we can be thrown into prison on the grounds that we are a threat to the safety of the nation. Much of the most oppressive legislation in the world has been passed on the grounds that it is for the security of the State (with a capital S). But only fascists care about the State. The State doesn't bleed; it doesn't have friends and family; it doesn't care and it damned sure doesn't matter. Those of us who really care about human rights don't want to see the State take precedence over people. (The State is not the same thing as your country.)

The Government spends a fortune deliberately frightening us about the threat from terrorism. In fact terrorism kills fewer Britons than horse riding. There are hundreds of things which kill more Britons than terrorism. Bicycle riding. Fishing. Swimming. Tony Blair starting unnecessary wars kills more Britons than terrorists do. And if you really want to look at the big killers you can forget terrorism completely. Nothing, is done about the perils of eating meat which, the Government knows darned well, causes cancer and kills as many people as tobacco. Warning us about the hazards of eating meat would upset the mighty meat industry.

It seems appropriate here to remind readers that the same Tony Blair who seems so worried about the threat of terrorism, is the same Tony Blair who allowed advertising for tobacco to continue on Grand Prix cars after his party coincidentally received a huge donation from the bloke who runs Grand Prix racing and who stood to lose lorry loads of loot if the tobacco advertising was banned. And it's that very same Tony Blair who is so keen on the European Union – an organisation which has used billions of pounds of taxpayers' money to subsidise the growing of tobacco.

In February 2003 (just before Blair started his war on Iraq) the Government suddenly and, rather conveniently, decided that there was going to be a terrorist attack at Heathrow airport. The Labour Government claimed that terrorists were planning to plant a bomb on a plane. The logical thing to do would have been to increase the number of foot patrols, to search the toilets regularly, to have metal detectors at the entrances to all public buildings and to make sure that no one went aboard an aeroplane carrying a bomb. However, the Government responded to this alleged potential attack by sending a stream of tanks to the airport. It would be difficult to imagine a move more likely to create fear and panic.

Within hours our television screens were showing an endless circle of tanks driving round and round Heathrow airport. Now, think about it carefully. What could a row of tanks do against terrorists planning to plant a bomb on a plane? What were they planning to do? Drive the damned tanks up the steps and onto the plane? What possible military reason could there possibly have been for sending tanks to stop terrorists planting bombs in lavatories or restaurants at an airport? You're right. Absolutely none. Sending tanks to Heathrow had nothing to do with terrorism. But it had a great deal with fear, politics and Blair's planned invasion of Iraq. Photographs and film shots of tanks were far more dramatic – and far more frightening – than photographs of bored looking security officers inspecting briefcases. And that's why the tanks were there. To frighten us and to panic us into accepting the need for a war against Iraq. In the end there was, of course, no attack on Heathrow airport and the tanks were driven back to their base having crunched up the roads and terrified the lives out of millions of ordinary voters. But the tanks had served their purpose. They had managed to convince us that we were about to be invaded and that we needed to defend ourselves. Millions of people were terrified unnecessarily to help justify Blair's unjustifiable war on Iraq. (Scare tactics of this type are not always necessarily designed simply to frighten the electorate into accepting whatever the authorities might want to do. In February 2004, after a series of British flights to America had been cancelled for 'security' reasons there were some suggestions that these alerts – all of which had involved British airlines – had been of considerable commercial advantage to American airlines.)

Today, we all accept as 'normal' many things done in the name of 'security' and 'the war on terrorism'. At airports squadrons of hired thugs confiscate nail clippers, though no one has yet bothered to explain just how or why a terrorist would choose to try and hijack an aeroplane with nail clippers when there are surely many far more satisfactory ways to exert illegal influence over the crew. (On the plane the cabin staff will happily sell you the ingredients to make a Molotov cocktail within minutes of the ground staff confiscating your nail clippers. And I lost all faith in airport security when, five minutes after my small bladed penknife had been confiscated by a trio of scowling, intimidating security guards, a smiling stewardess handed me a stainless steel knife with a blade three times as long and twice as sharp as the one in my confiscated penknife).

'Terror alerts' are sounded at regular intervals. They have them in red and in orange. There are Grade I alerts, Grade II alerts and heaven knows what else. Announcements of the most exciting alerts are accompanied with pictures of soldiers jumping out of helicopters or shooting at empty buildings on a firing range. By the law of averages some sort of incident (or possibly just an arrest) will occasionally coincide with the latest alert, thereby giving the other alerts a sort of spurious and entirely unjustified credibility.

Small countries trying to pay off the interest on their international debts by building up a tourist industry are likely to wake up one morning and find that planes don't stop at their airport any more because New

WHY EVERYTHING IS GOING TO GET WORSE

Labour has decided that there is going to be a terrorist attack in their country.

In practice, judging by the Government's track record, the safest place in the world to visit is usually the place that Blair et al have just announced will be the site of the next terrorist outrage. But these warnings, handed out apparently arbitrarily to keep up the fear level at home, ruin business for months or years to come in the poor country whose name has been pulled out of the hat. (It isn't just tourist businesses which are being wrecked by anti-terrorism laws. America now refuses to accept shipments of goods as varied as jeans, sports shoes, perfume and prescription drugs lest they be counterfeit. The argument is that terrorists might make money out of selling counterfeit products.)

When the Government announced that there was going to be an attack on London the next attack actually took place in Bali. (The Government was out by 8,208 miles with that warning.) Then, when there was a warning about an attack in Malaysia, a bomb went off in Kenya. (That time they were out by just 4,104 miles.) When the Government warned that New York and Washington were next the attack actually took place in Saudi Arabia. (That attack was 5,130 miles off target according to her Majesty's Government.)

Our Government doesn't have the foggiest idea what is going on. During the last decade, more Britons have been killed travelling in Spain and America than have been killed by all the terrorist attacks put together. Drunken teenagers and trigger happy American policemen are a far greater hazard to British tourists than terrorists are or ever have been but the Government isn't likely to tell you that.

The main reason they don't tell you the truth is that you'd yawn. And that wouldn't do at all; the Government wants you frightened out of your skin. Keeping us all frightened has enabled the Government to give itself the right to search motor cars without reason other than high handed nosiness. (And don't try to console yourself with the thought that you are innocent. These days no one is innocent – not even you. If they can't find any heat-seeking missiles tucked away in your boot they'll take the opportunity to arrest you for having an empty windscreen squirter bottle.)

Peace activists are arrested if they dare set foot in an airport and under yet another raft of exciting new laws are soon to be arrested if they congregate in groups of two or more in a local cafe. (I am not joking.) The Government has started compiling a blacklist of trouble-makers. It's easy to get on the list (just annoy a neighbour so much that they warn the police that you might be a troublemaker). But it's impossible to find out if your name is on the list, and impossible to get your name off the list once it's on. Write a letter of protest to the BBC or your local council or your local newspaper and you will probably find yourself on at least one blacklist.

Terrorism (or rather the threat of terrorism) has enabled politicians to create their ideal situation: a war without end. As George Orwell foresaw in *1984*, a permanent war is a dream come true for oppressive politicians. When a country is at war politicians have a great excuse to introduce new legislation. They can (and do) get away with taking away our freedom in order to defend it. (They make it sound as though they are putting our freedom in a very safe place so that they can bring it out again when the fighting is over. They never do anything of the sort, of course. Once politicians have taken some of our freedom away they never, ever return it. We will never be as free as we were, unless or until there is some sort of peaceful revolution.)

They build up our fears, exploit them and use them to introduce endless new laws to keep control of us. The modern politician isn't interested in making life better for the electors. The modern professional politician is carving himself a career. He needs to keep us frightened so that he can stay in power. Power gives him a kick but it also feeds his vanity and fills his bank account.

In order to conquer our fears we need to know what we are afraid of; we need to be able to focus on them. If we don't even know what we are supposed to be afraid of then we will soon be afraid of everything. And that's exactly what the politicians want. They want us afraid because they can use our fear.

You can help yourself to a world free of fear. The basic way of tackling and conquering fear is to build up your inner strength so that you are better able to cope – and so that you know that you will be better able to cope. But you must also be able to identify, isolate and study your fears. Our greatest fears involve the unknown. Know your fears and you will move a long way towards conquering them. I hope this chapter has helped you to understand how 'they' use fear to manipulate you.

Chapter 12
The Myth Of 'Them'

In the year after I left school, and before I went to medical school, I worked in Kirkby, Liverpool as a Community Service Volunteer. It was quite a culture shock for me. A week or two after leaving my smart, provincial grammar school I found myself living in a stark dormitory town where the shop windows were all protected with wood and wire, where the police station was barricaded behind barbed wire and where the bus drivers would not enter the area after dark unless they were accompanied by at least one police patrol car. The first thing I learnt was that most of the young people who lived in that town felt totally alienated from authority. They lived in a different world to the world I'd left. They lived in a world where justice was meted out with a half brick and where anyone in a uniform was the enemy.

At medical school I set up and ran a nightclub and the lessons I had learnt in Liverpool were reinforced.

It was supposed to be a youth club but the sort of teenagers I was trying to attract didn't go to youth clubs. So I called it a nightclub. I hired a disc jockey who played loud music and because we couldn't afford to buy chairs put old beds around the edge of the dance floor. One night there was a fight. A group of boxers who were training nearby came into the club determined to cause trouble. The youths who were members of the nightclub, and who now regarded it as theirs, resented this intrusion and fought back. I tried to stop them, fearing most of all that they would get hurt, but they wouldn't stop. They fought so hard and with such determination that the boxers retreated. Most of the teenagers were badly injured. Some were badly cut, others had broken bones. But they had fought on unflinchingly.

'You could have ended up in prison,' I pointed out later to the ones who weren't by now in hospital. 'You could have ended up dead.'

'So, what?' said one, who had blood pouring down the side of his face. 'What does it matter? We haven't got anything to lose.'

And at that moment I understood.

Their anger was so total, and their sense of not belonging so complete, that they had no fear. They had nothing left to lose and so they fought to protect the one thing they had: the club. They felt that the rest of the world was 'Them'. They had lost all respect for authority and they had lost all faith in the structures of our society: justice and liberty were not things society provided but things society tried to take away.

* * *

When I look around and listen to middle-class Britons I can hear the same anger rising; the same sense of injustice; the same frustration. Everything is getting worse. Things don't just *seem* to be getting worse. They *are* getting worse. Much, much worse. The quality of health care and transport are deteriorating rapidly. The crime rate is soaring. Politicians lie more than ever before. Institutions which are trusted to look after our money fritter away our savings through incompetence. What is left they steal. They create rules which are incomprehensible and then punish us severely for the slightest infraction. There is no doubt that a state of 'Them and Us' has been created. The workers contribute. The bureaucrats and the scroungers take.

And what has happened to our country? It should provide a safe infrastructure – transport, health care, security and so on. It should look after us if we get into trouble abroad. But it doesn't do any of those things. The New Labour State has no conscience and has divorced responsibility from authority. To our leaders today 'honesty' and 'integrity' are now just words in the dictionary. Your Government doesn't love you any more. In the immortal words of George W. Bush, if they are not for you then they must be against you.

You can be loyal to your country but your country will no longer be loyal to you.

What happened?

Who are these people who have stolen our country? Whose country do they think it is anyway? Who gave them the right to do this? The New Labour Government seems to exist to put up speed cameras to raise money to put up more speed cameras. Everything it does has to make a profit. Trains, hospitals, libraries, museums all have to make a profit. The concept of providing a service has gone. So, why do we need a central government at all? If the infrastructure is expected to make a profit, and to be run privately, what is the point of government at all?

In the world of New Labour you should no longer expect your country to look after you, or to provide you with education, justice or healthcare. You and I are on our own. You are a citizen of the world but you have to be your own country; you must defend and protect yourself and your family and your friends.

What's going on? Are we victims of a major international conspiracy organised by a consortium of bankers, industrialists and politicians?

* * *

It isn't difficult to support the conspiracy theory. Most people have, I suspect, now heard of The Bilderbergers: a secretive group of leading politicians, major bankers and multinational bosses who meet in secret at regular intervals.

Wherever they meet the private meetings of the Bilderbergers are protected by state security, even though no details of the meetings are ever published. The discussions are held in total secrecy. The media ignore these meetings. Maybe this is because it is impossible to find out what is going on. Maybe it's because there is pressure from on high. Maybe it's because some of the people who attend these meetings own large chunks of the media.

It is hardly surprising that conspiracy theorists believe that the Bilderbergers control the world. The obvious question is: 'If there is so little to hide, why spend so much time and effort hiding it?'

There are many conspiracies active at the moment but I don't believe there is *one* conspiracy. I believe that the second war against Iraq was the result of a conspiracy organised by religious extremists and greed industrialists but I don't honestly believe the Bilderbergers are running the world. My scepticism is inspired largely by the fact that the people who attend simply aren't bright enough to run the world. Is there anyone in the New Labour Government bright enough to boil an egg? Could George Bush find his way home alone in the dark?

By and large the sort of people we tend to regard as conspirators are lying, manipulative and deceitful (all the necessary qualities for a successful conspiracy) but they are also greedy, self-serving and hypocritical (qualities which do not make for good conspirators). The people who are usually found on the conspiracy theorists' lists are driven not by great passion but a small passion – themselves. At a Bilderberger meeting, there are, I suspect, a lot of small greeds and ambitions rather than one big one. I just don't believe that the sort of people who turn up at Bilderberger meetings are clever enough, committed enough or competent enough to run an effective conspiracy.

* * *

The popular alternative theory is that we're in a mess because our leaders' are grossly incompetent and really have no idea what is going on around them. The cock-up theory (as it is usually described) has its attractions.

But this alone doesn't explain why things have got so badly so quickly. Why should public servants, industry bosses and politicians all become incompetent at once?

I think there is a third main explanation.

* * *

I think the institutions have taken over; and instead of us running them for our benefit, they are now running us.

This has happened for a variety of reasons.

First, political correctness means that common sense policies are not pursued. The people who are supposed to be running things find themselves following policies (which are usually supported by legislation and therefore given some spurious legitimacy) which add nothing to the quality of our lives but which, on the contrary, make life grey, unsatisfying, frustrating and (ironically) deeply unfair.

Second, over-bureaucratisation means that we have weak leadership. The people who seem to be in charge of our institutions aren't in charge

at all. There is no one actually running the EU – just as I don't belie
there is really anyone running the NHS. Both organisations are no
out of our control. The EU, in particular, satisfies all the requireme
for a truly fascist society. When the needs and rights of the individ
take second place to the needs and demands of the state (or, in the ca
of the EU, the superstate) the state has become unarguably fascist. T
bureaucrats working for the EU exist only to create rules. It is wh
they do. They have no experience of the real world and no understandi
of how their new rules affect people's lives. And they don't care. In fa
they love chaos and confusion – because chaos and confusion give the
an excuse to create new laws. They love making new laws becau
when they make more laws they give themselves more power. And t
more complicated the rules become the easier it is for them to arg
that they need more staff and bigger offices. And if they have mo
staff (and more authority) they deserve to receive more pay. The I
bureaucrats are the perfect example of modern administrators gatheri
authority without responsibility. Those working for the EU ha
enormous amounts of authority but no responsibility at all. Every mir
bureaucrat is a state sponsored despot; this is fascism (or communis
at its very worst.

Third, the need to produce short-term profits means that commerc
organisations must follow policies which lead to short-term advanta
– even if those policies are disadvantageous for customers, employe
and shareholders. The long-term interests of these three groups a
pushed aside in favour of the needs of the corporation. Naturally, t
rewards paid to the select few individuals who serve the corporatio
needs most assiduously become obscenely over generous. It is, after
in the institution's interests to ensure that the directors who defend t
institution should be well rewarded. Short-termism has always bee
problem in central and local government where the overriding aim
politicians is usually to get re-elected (it is alleged that this was Blai
first aim when moving into Number 10, Downing Street) but it h
increasingly become a serious problem in industry where compan
now desperately need to produce a constant stream of quarterly profi
Large corporations are like huge rudderless tankers; they plough
regardless, unstoppable and unsteerable; the captain and crew reduc
in practice, to the status of mere passengers.

Fourth, pressure groups operating on behalf of very specific intere

ave become extremely powerful and effective. Lobbyists are no longer
asy to identify. A few years ago lobbyists all wore smart suits, carried
riefcases and hung around the corridors of power, waiting to invite
oliticians to lunch (and more). These days lobbyists are more subtle.
hey found pressure groups and give them innocent sounding names.
hey create 'campaign' groups which often sound as though they are
un by concerned citizens and they recruit concerned citizens to run
1em. And, of course, lobbyists working for large corporations help put
elected politicians into power. This has been happening for years in the
JSA. (There are, astonishingly, between 15,000 and 20,000 full-time
rofessional lobbyists working in Washington, USA.)

Naturally, the lobbyists put malleable, corruptible people into power,
o that they can get them to do exactly what they want. (Hands up
1nyone in the world who genuinely believes George W. Bush plans his
wn policies and organised his own election campaign. Then, hands up
1ose who believe that George W. Bush is just a rather dim-witted front
1an for a bunch of Zionists, neo-conservatives and oil-men.). An honest,
assionate, caring politician (were there such a beast) would be of no
se at all to the manipulators.

The eternal danger has always been that politicians will do things
olely in order to win votes (rather than because it is the right thing to
o for the future of their community). Plato and de Tocqueville both
varned about this. But that danger has been replaced. Today there are
wo dangers. First, that politicians, knowing that media control decides
vho wins elections, will do things to please the people who control the
1edia and second, that politicians will do things for money. Our
oliticians do both – usually at once. The growth in the number of
obbyists has severely damaged the quality and honesty of the service
rovided by our politicians (most of whom seem to have forgotten that
1ey are elected to 'serve', rather than appointed to take on the role of
ictator). Corporations, trade groups and unions all have powerful and
ffective lobbyists fighting for their own particular interests (and, often,
1idden agendas) and frequently pressing for legislation which stops people
oing what they want to do. Needless to say there are no lobbyists
ghting for the interests of ordinary electors.

The food industry is, for example, particularly good at lobbying.
round the world there are endless groups campaigning for the right to
at more fat, more sugar, more salt and more meat. The spokesmen

for these groups may well be innocent dupes; slightly dotty citizens wh
genuinely believe that it is every individual's duty to eat thre
cheeseburgers a day. But behind the innocent dupes there are the mone
men; the lobbyists who, with varying degrees of subtlety, manipulat
the organisation. The National Eat A Pound Of Sprouts A Da
Foundation may seem to be run by public-spirited citizens with a fondne:
for sprouts. But the smart offices, the expensive advertising campaig
and the foreign travel budget aren't being paid for by sprout eaters.

Of course, the people controlling the money don't think up (or allo\
their frontmen to think up) names which are as unsubtle as the Nation:
Eat A Pound Of Sprouts A Day Foundation, however much that ma
reflect the views of their corporate supporters. They prefer to give the:
organisations less confrontational names. They like words lik
'independent', 'foundation', 'national' and 'world' because these giv
an organisation a solid sound to it. And they like words like 'consumer
'parent', 'patient' and 'family' because these give an organisation
homely, down-to-earth, caring feel.

The international drugs industry has a number of powerful lobb
groups. The Zionists are powerful because they have become adept :
lobbying. The medical profession (supported by the drugs industry) ha
one of the most powerful and heavy spending lobby groups in the worl
The arms industry and the oil industry routinely influence politiciar
(and significant national and international events) because they can affor
public relations corporations (and, in many cases, 'buy' good medi
exposure) and because they can and do give huge sums of money t
politicians. They are not usually so crude as to hand over a briefcase (
money. Instead they will offer a politician consultancy work, a seat o
the board or a chance to buy shares at a special price. And, of cours
they will often give money to politicians by paying them huge speakin
fees or paying them vast and commercially unsound amounts of mone
to write books that no one is ever likely to want to buy, let alone read

In all these cases the individuals are merely pawns working for th
institutions which they serve.

Fifth, politics has become a career. Politics has become somethin
people no longer choose to do because it is a way to give something t
society, or a way to correct injustices. Today people go into politic
because it offers a good way to earn a living and get on in the worl
Just a few generations ago most of the people who went into politic

did so because they wanted to put something back. They had either been born to wealth and position or they had earned wealth and position through their own talents and hard work. Most were gentlemen and were not easy to bribe (because they were already rich and they already had all the status and social position they needed). Was Alec Douglas-Home (coincidentally the only Prime Minister ever to play first-class cricket) the last British Prime Minister who could be described as a gentleman without risking action under the Trades Description Act? Today's politicians are an entirely different breed to yesterday's men. Which one of today's raggle taggle bunch could possibly be described as a 'Statesman' in the mould of Disraeli or Churchill? Today's average MP has no skills, no job experience and little or no wealth of his or her own. This is particularly true of Labour MPs, though it applies to MPs on both sides of the House; if they lose their jobs their future will be bleak. It is, therefore, perhaps not surprising that most MPs think solely of their careers and allow themselves to be treated as voting lobby fodder.

Our world is run by people who may be formally educated but who have never learned to question what they have been told, and have no valid life experience with which to create judgements. The average citizen has less respect for politicians than any other group other than lawyers. (Is it merely a coincidence that most politicians were trained as lawyers?)

New Labour is controlled by professional politicians who have risen far beyond their meagre potential. They are in power because no one else wanted what they wanted quite as much; no one else was prepared to sacrifice their integrity on the altar of their ambition. New Labour politicians don't understand the world or the needs of ordinary people. They live a life divorced from the real world.

Today's British politicians are in Parliament because they want power. They call it patriotism, service and leadership. But it's really the power they want. And why do they want the power? Simple. They want the power because it is the best (and for them probably the only) way they know to get rich.

Today's politicians are in it for the money and the glory rather than because they want to serve the people.

We don't know what New Labour stands for, though we do know what it is against. We know, for example, that the New Labour storm-roopers are against 'the forces of convservatism'. But although there are many bad things about conservatism there are also many good things. New Labour is clearly determined to throw out our heritage together with the elitism which is more reasonably regarded as the unacceptable face of conservatism.

The New Labour storm-troopers seem to believe in all things modern in progress for its own sake, regardless of whether it is what people want or whether or not it works. Traditions are neither respected nor preserved.

Local councillors are now the same. They used to serve (without pay) out of a sense of public responsibility, and a feeling that they could help make their part of the world a better place. Their reward was the sense of glory; some local fame, their picture in the paper, respect, a chance to wear the gold chain and drive in the mayoral limousine and perhaps, an invitation to a Buckingham Palace garden party. Now, like national politicians, they are in it for the money. Just as unskilled as national politicians they blunder from crisis to crisis; putting up local taxes and cutting services.

It is hardly surprising that when things go wrong most of today's MPs and Ministers lie, and look for someone else to blame, rather than resign. They are in politics for what they can get out of it, rather than what they can put in. They have no passion for improving the world and they have no experience of competence; never having run anything (a business or a professional practice) why should they suddenly be capable of running huge departments? Besides they have no real control over day-to-day issues. The big decisions are made by civil servants not now, in London but in Brussels. The end of the 'gentleman amateur' in politics meant the end of honour and justice in Parliament.

Their immorality (and lack of scruples) has, through spin and deceit led all our institutions down a dangerous spiral into a world where the only thing that seems to matter is who wins. Politicians no longer lead the electorate. Instead of 'leading' they merely try to please enough electors to stay in power. New Labour realised some time ago that they could win an election (and subsequently stay in power) simply by appealing to people who don't pay tax. At the last general election New Labour was voted into office by people who approve of, and have a strong vested interest in, our current illogical and unfair benefits system.

Because they are always looking for money (either for themselves or for their next political election campaign) today's politicians are easily bought' by lobbyists. There are numerous examples of politicians changing public policy to suit their own personal circumstances and taking advantage of their public position to obtain better holidays.

Two recent former British Prime Ministers gained enormously from having been popular in America and there has been an almost endless trail of politicians moving from public life into corporate boardrooms. There is little doubt that many politicians regard political life as some sort of apprenticeship which, when served, entitles them to cash in and earn huge amounts of money in the city of London. Professional, career politicians are prepared to lie and to cheat and to deceive if that is what it takes to be successful. And because so many of them do lie and cheat and deceive then that is now what it does take to be successful. Politicians make promises they know the electors want to hear, even though they have no intention of ever honouring those promises. Modern politicians don't resign if they are caught out. They just lie and cheat some more in the hope that they can get away with whatever it is that they have done. And then, at worst, they just lie low for a couple of years before they make a comeback. Dishonesty is now so rife among politicians that it has become almost impossible for an honest, decent politician to succeed at all. Indeed, politics is now such a discredited part of public life that very few honest, decent people want to have anything to do with it. For the time being at least, the crooks have taken over.

$$* * *$$

Science fiction writers have, in the past, often written about a future in which man loses power over his world because computers and robots have taken control.

That hasn't happened.

But we have, unthinkingly, lost power in a quite different way. We have lost power and handed over control of our lives to an untouchable, nebulous, almost indefinable force.

When we are feeling angry or upset with the world we often blame 'them'. When we feel that we are being forced to do things against our will we blame 'them'. When we feel frustrated or cheated we blame 'them'. When we are hampered by injustice or wounded by unfairness we say that it is 'their' fault.

But there is no 'them'.

The man who seems to represent injustice – and seems one minute to be one of 'them' – will, the next minute, be standing shoulder to shoulder with you sharing your complaints.

The opponents of justice and fair play have no human form.

The truth is that when we are complaining about 'them' we are really complaining about the world we have created for ourselves; we are complaining about the unseen forces which structure our society; we are complaining about things which are now out of our control.

The real problem is that we are no longer in control of our destiny. We have created a world, a society, which now exists to protect itself. We have created a society which exists to improve and strengthen itself at our expense. We have created a social structure in which we now exist as mere pawns.

* * *

The man in a suit who, when sitting behind his desk, seems to be cruel, uncaring and utterly devoid of understanding, will, when he finds himself in a different situation become nervous and uncertain. The woman who works in a government office and treats supplicants with more contempt than compassion (and who seems to her victims to be one of 'them') will find herself becoming a victim if she needs to visit a hospital as a patient. The customs officer who greets passengers with a sneer and a scowl (and therefore seems to be one of 'them') will lose all his authority and power when he has to queue in his local post office to buy stamps.

The men and women who seem to be 'them' aren't really 'them' at all. They are each of them given their temporary 'them' quality by the institutions (the companies or universities) for which they work. It is the institutions which have the real power. The man who sits behind the desk is merely borrowing or representing that power. When he steps out from behind his desk (either temporarily, to go home at night, or permanently, to retire) he loses all his 'themness' and once again becomes an innocent in a cruel and distant world.

If you carefully examine the way the world is being run at the moment you could reasonably come to the conclusion that most multinational corporations and most governments are more or less exclusively controlled by ruthless, James Bond villain style psychopathic megalomaniacs.

What other explanation could there be for the fact that drugs companies make and sell drugs which they know are both dangerous and ineffective? What other explanation could there be for the fact that food companies make and sell food which they must know causes cancer and contains very little of nutritional value? What other explanation could there be for the fact that arms companies sell products deliberately designed to blow the legs off small children? What other explanation could there for the fact that tobacco companies continue to sell products which they know kill a high proportion of their customers?

And what other explanation could there possibly be for the fact that bureaucrats, civil servants and politicians allow all this to happen?

The fact is that for the very first time in history the main opponents of justice and fair play, the proponents of abuse and tyranny, have no human form. We have created new monsters: new monsters which we cannot see or touch (we cannot see or touch them for the excellent reason that they do not exist in reality).

* * *

For the first time in history we have succeeded in creating a world, a society, which now exists solely to defend, protect and develop itself. We have created a society whose institutions have acquired power of their own. These institutions – governments, multinational corporations, multinational bureaucracies and so on – now exist solely to maintain, improve and strengthen themselves. These institutions have their own hidden agendas and the human beings who work for them may think that they are in control – but they aren't.

I now believe that the biggest threat to the survival of the human race (and the planet upon which we live) comes not from the atomic bomb, or the fact that we are steadily destroying the very fabric of our world by polluting our seas, our rivers, the air we breathe and even the space which separates us from other planets, but from the fact that we have created a social structure over which we, as human beings, have very little control. It is this new social structure which is pushing us along at a great speed and 'forcing' us not only to destroy our environment but also to abandon all those moral and ethical values which it is reasonable to expect to be fundamental in a 'civilised' society.

It may be a little difficult to accept the concept of institutions having agendas of their own but the reality is that this is exactly what has happened.

The people who appear to run large institutions, and who themselves undoubtedly believe that they are in charge, are simply institutional servants.

Every multinational company has a constant thirst for cash. In order to satisfy bankers, brokers and shareholders companies need to produce quarterly figures which show a nice big, fat profit on the bottom line. The directors have to do what is in their company's best interests. If they don't then their company will falter and that can't be allowed to happen. The company, the unimaginably powerful corporate demon, must come first.

So, for example, if the directors of a drug company find that one of their products causes lethal side effects they may, as human beings, feel ashamed about this. Individually the directors may want to withdraw the drug immediately and to apologise to the people who have been injured by their product. But this course of action would not be in the company's best short-term interests. Withdrawing the drug would doubtless cost the company money. Research and development costs would have to be written off. And apologising would expose the company to lawsuits. So the directors, acting in the company's best interests, must keep the drug on the market and deny that there are any problems. In these circumstances the company (a non-human entity which only exists on paper) is in control. The decisions are made not in the interests of people (whether they be customers or directors) but in the interests of the corporate 'being'.

The problem is compounded by the fact that, big as they are, multinational companies have no souls and no sense of responsibility. Thirty years ago I wrote an essay which attracted a good deal of mail from readers because it clearly hit a nerve; the essence of the piece was one of the major problems of our society is that responsibility was being separated from authority. I wrote the piece when I was still practising as a doctor and I couldn't help illustrate my essay by pointing out that the young hospital doctor has a great deal of responsibility but virtually no authority whereas the hospital administrator has an enormous amount of authority but virtually no responsibility. I warned that this constant separation of these two would lead to great problems.

The same thing has happened in universities and colleges and charities where activities are run with the same end in sight: profit. Corporation (represented by their slaves – the people who think they are running hem) never think beyond the next set of profit figures; they are ultimately ruthless and (since they are inanimate and bloodless) utterly 'cold-blooded'.

By and large, the men and women who run large drug companies, arms companies, food companies and genetic engineering companies don't really want to destroy the world in which we all live. They know that their families have to breathe the same air as you and I. They know that they too need good food, clean drinking water and a healthy environment.

However, despite the evidence being to the contrary, the people who run these companies probably think that they are doing good and useful work. They have denied the truth to themselves.

Occasionally, this constant denial and self-deceit breaks down and absurdities appear. For example, British Members of Parliament have, as members of an institution, consistently voted to allow multinational corporations to pollute our drinking water and to tamper with and pollute our food. And yet MPs themselves, as individuals, are so conscious of the value of the pure food and clean drinking water that in the House of Commons they have arranged to be given spring water to drink and fed on organic food which has not been genetically modified. The men and women who vote to allow our water to be polluted and our food to be genetically modified are voting as representatives of institutions rather than as representatives of people. They know that they are creating a world in which the food is unfit to eat and the water unfit to drink. But they can't stop it happening because they are operating for the benefit of institutions rather than people.

* * *

Some years ago Dr Albert Schweizer saw the first signs of what has happened. 'Another hindrance to civilisation today,' he wrote, 'is the over-organisation of our public life. While it is certain that a properly ordered environment is the condition and, at the same time, the result of civilisation, it is also undeniable that, after a certain point has been reached, external organisation is developed at the expense of spiritual life. Personality and ideas are often subordinated to institutions, when it is really these which ought to influence the latter and keep them inwardly alive.'

It's all happening. The over-organisation of public life has a

momentum of its own; public individuals and public bodies are pushe
this way and that by corporate lobbyists. The direction they finally tak
depends on who pushes hardest.

No one has control of anything any more.

***

Do you remember the story I told about the youths in the nightclu
I ran? The ones who felt estranged from society?

That's what has happened to ordinary, decent, God-fearing Britis
citizens.

There is one difference.

The ordinary, decent, God-fearing British citizens have not yet reache
the point where they feel they have nothing to lose. They have not ye
reached the point where they just don't care. They have not yet reache
the point where they are prepared to fight for what is left of thei
freedom and what is left of their world. The elderly who want bette
medical care *will* say 'enough'. The young families who realise tha
their children are being denied a decent education *will* say 'enough
Everyone has their breaking point. Everyone has something that matter
to them. Everyone has something they care so much about that when
is threatened they will rise up.

They *will* reach that point.

It *will* happen.

And it will happen sooner than anyone believes. And when it do
New Labour can hire as many policemen as they like, they can pass a
many laws as they likes – they will still lose.

Because the bottom line is that it is the people who work who ar
the engine of a country; they provide the power that drives everythin

Chapter 13

The Citizens' Charter: A Blueprint for a Bloodless Revolution

It is clear that our world is in a mess. And things are going to get worse before they get better.

We have for decades been betrayed by our political leaders. They have let us down time and time again. Our leaders don't have solid principles of their own and they have replaced passion with expediency. Real leaders care for the community they serve. Our leaders care for themselves. Personal greed and vanity have replaced public responsibility.

But this isn't the way it has to be. And it isn't the way it should be. As freedom fighter and USA President Thomas Jefferson said in his inaugural speech: '... a wise and frugal government, which shall restrain men from injuring one another, shall leave them otherwise free to regulate their own pursuits of industry and improvement and shall not take from the mouth of labour the bread it has earned. This is the sum of good government.'

To regain Jefferson's basic principle of good government you and I have to stand together.

During the latter stages of the 20th century our freedom virtually disappeared. If we don't make our voices heard nothing will ever happen.

Why Everything is going to get worse

It's ten minutes to midnight in the battle for our individuality and ou
freedom. But it isn't over yet.

What follows is a blueprint for a bloodless revolution.

If, when you have read through this list, you think: 'That's all fine
And I agree with all/most of it. But it's never going to happen becaus
they will never agree with it' just remember that this is still our country
Although most of them forget it as soon as they get into power, politician
are hired to do what we want them to do – not to tell us what to do.

1. As citizens we are entitled to privacy. Governments do not have
    right to listen to private telephone calls, read private e-mails or t
    peer into every citizen's private bank accounts unless they hav
    clear evidence that a citizen has acted illegally.

2. The principle of innocent until proven guilty should be resurrecte
    – and upheld in all courts. In civilised countries governments d
    not have the right to hold their citizens (or anyone else's) in gac
    merely because they suspect they might do something. And civilise
    governments do not sanction torture.

3. State employees should be held personally responsible for their ow
    incompetence or fraudulent behaviour. Why should taxpayers hav
    to pay up when policemen or nurses or civil servants make mistakes
    Civil servants (of all kinds) should take personal responsibility fo
    their actions – and should pay privately for any insurance cove
    they want to take out. Such a change would dramatically reduc
    the amount of damage caused by public sector employees throug
    incompetence, neglect or deliberate misbehaviour.

4. Proper league tables should be published showing the effectivenes
    (or otherwise) of schools, hospitals and other public institutions
    This information is available to government officials but much of i
    is suppressed and not made available to the public – the very peopl
    most entitled to see it. Citizens should have the right to use th
    information available to help them choose a suitable school o
    hospital for themselves and their family – and to see how thei
    taxes are being spent.

5. A crackdown should be introduced to control and investigate th
    number of state employees taking early retirement on the ground
    of ill health. Many such employees claim to be ill when they aren'

– getting massive pensions from taxpayers and adding to the burden carried by taxpayers.

6. There should be a cash limit of £10,000 on compensation payments for damage which does not entail physical injury. This would dramatically reduce the payout for compensation paid to individuals claiming sexual harassment, racial discrimination or libel.

7. When lawyers share in the 'profits' from legal action they should be limited to 10% of the proceeds. This would dramatically reduce the number of cases brought and result in plaintiffs receiving a fairer share of any award. The costs of all legal cases thrown out of court should be borne by the plaintiffs.

8. Britain should leave the European Union. If Scotland and Wales prefer to stay within the EU (in the misguided belief that this will give them greater independence) then England should declare unilateral independence.

Neither the EU nor the euro have a long-term future.

The idea of Europe surviving as a superstate may be fine in theory but in practice it just won't work. And when the European superstate collapses the fallout will be considerable. France and Germany will, as always, look after themselves. The other countries in the EU will be badly damaged for decades. The economic problems caused by the collapse of the euro will lead to crisis after crisis in many European countries.

Those who claim that it is impossible for the EU to collapse should look around. For years the trend outside the EU has been towards the localisation of power and resources. The USSR, Czechoslovakia and Yugoslavia have split up. Ethiopia has redrawn regional boundaries. Canada may soon break up. And even the American States don't seem quite as United as they once were: Hawaii is on the verge of becoming independent again and Texas is considering leaving the Union.

Even within the EU there has been pressure for the break up of some countries and for the formation of smaller states. Andorra has become independent (with a population of 58,000). In Spain the Basques want independence. Germany and Belgium have both given more power to regions. In France, before the introduction of the euro, there was a powerful movement towards dividing the nation into three republics and five autonomous regions.

Tomorrow's Europe may be broken up into scores, maybe hundreds, of much smaller, independent countries – linking together very loosely for defence and trade. The citizens of all these small countries will be much better off – and much more capable of controlling their own destinies – when political power is in the hands of local or regional politicians who are accountable to the electors.

If Britain leaves the EU now we will be the strongest and richest country in Europe in ten years time.

At the moment the UK is in a uniquely weak position because it has tied itself to both the EU and the USA. The old saying about falling between two stools springs to mind.

Britain has excellent global connections and there are still countries where the British are respected and even admired. (We would be respected and admired much more if we were not seen as America's lapdog.)

Our future lies mainly in resurrecting old alliances and friendships in Asia, Australasia and Africa. There is much we can learn from our old friends. Few countries are growing as fast as India, few respect individual freedom as much as Canada.

It is no exaggeration to say that Britain would have a happier, healthier future if we put more effort into rebuilding our relationships with the other cricket-playing nations. Australia, New Zealand, Canada, India, Pakistan, South Africa and the West Indies would, I feel confident, be forgiving and happy to re-develop a global trading partnership. We have far more in common with these nations than we have with countries such as Slovakia or Greece. We have far more in common with Australia than we have with America. The former Commonwealth countries include some of the fastest growing, and strongest, nations on earth. They all speak English too.

9. Compulsory retirement should be abandoned.

10. Schoolteachers should be told that the priorities for education are reading, writing and arithmetic. Schools do not need to teach social studies or have computer departments.

11. Welfare should be put back into the hands of voluntary groups (who deal with it better and more fairly) and taken out of the hands of government agencies. Spending on social services should be

slashed. Most of this money is wasted and many of the services provided in this way could be provided more economically and more humanely by charitable organisations.

12. Research funds should be cut dramatically and money used to ensure that we take advantage of the knowledge we already have. Expenditure on fashionable diseases such as AIDS (which may not even exist) should be cut in favour of expenditure on the prevention of unfashionable diseases (such as cancer and heart disease) which do kill vast numbers of citizens. We already know how to prevent 80% of all cancers. Heart disease can be treated without drugs or surgery. Funding for preventive medicine programmes should be dramatically boosted. Governments should fund genuinely independent research into the hazards associated with electrical appliances (such as mobile telephones and microwave ovens) transmitter masts and overhead power lines.

13. There should be a permanent moratorium on genetic engineering with severe penalties for those who break the moratorium. We don't need genetic engineering and the risks are too great. It should be a criminal offence for companies to sell genetically engineered food. The same penalties should be used to control xenotransplantation and cloning. It is absurd for governments to claim that genetic engineering is safe because it has not been proven to be dangerous. They should prove it is safe.

14. The abuse of animals should be halted. Activities – such as hunting and vivisection – which are barbaric and indefensible should be halted immediately.

15. The public should have an inviolable and unlimited right to demonstrate peacefully.

16. The police should get back onto the beat. Only in rural communities should the police patrol in cars. The police should be accountable to local communities – and chief police officers should be fired if crime levels rise. Severe automatic penalties should be introduced for policemen who lie in court.

17. Capital punishment should be banned by international law.

18. There should be complete freedom of information on all government matters except military ones.

19. The United Nations should instruct the United States of America to obey international law. If it fails to do this it should be subjected to strict trade embargos.

20. No one in any institution (whether private or public) should be paid more than 20 times the pay of the lowest paid employee.

21. All international arms sales should be banned on the grounds that this activity is immoral and reckless. Countries (such as the USA) which use banned weapons such as landmines or cluster bombs should be publicly reprimanded by the United Nations.

22. Governments should decriminalise and tax the sale of formerly illegal drugs. They should abandon the ineffective, expensive and deadly War on Drugs. If the money wasted on policemen and drug enforcement agencies was spent on drug education there would be far less drug abuse. The War on Drugs is an excuse to remove more and more of our freedoms – it keeps drug prices high, encourages crime, rewards drug barons and does nothing whatsoever to prevent drug abuse.

23. There should be referendums on all major questions – as there are in Switzerland. Referendums give citizens a chance to have a voice on big issues.

24. All income taxes should end and be replaced with a sales tax. Sales taxes would bring in the same revenue but free citizens from audits, bureaucracy and false accusations. Income tax puts governments and citizens at loggerheads. Tax revenues should be steadily reduced and central government expenditure reduced. Many government departments are unnecessary and many government employees are paid by the public to perform political duties. Local council taxes should be replaced by a simple poll tax – by far the fairest way for local residents to pay for the services they receive. It is absurd that an elderly person living alone, and surviving on a fixed pension, should pay as much or more than a family of four adults for the provision of schools, police, roads and rubbish collection.

25. Returning to a gold standard would give currencies more stability and help control inflation. It would limit government deficit spending.

26. Power should be returned to local communities. Federal powers

and control should be reduced and kept to a minimum. Federalism should be avoided and resisted. As a general rule small is better than big. Local leaders tend to be more accountable than distant ones.

27. Bank privacy should be sacrosanct. Citizens have a right to put their legally earned money wherever they want to put it – without governments snooping.

28. Racism which is euphemistically known as affirmative action should be outlawed immediately. Racism is racism, whatever it is dressed up as.

29. Identity cards are an infringement of human rights and all attempts to introduce them as compulsory 'must be carried' items should be abandoned.

30. Criminals should be forced (by law) to make restitution to their victims. Criminal punishment is too often revenge not justice. Prison sentences should, in many cases, be replaced with community service. Prisons should be smaller and tougher. Prisoners should make financial restitution to their victims (and to the State for the costs of their trial) through their prison earnings.

31. Inheritance (estate) taxes should be ended. Why should governments re-tax money that has already been taxed?

32. Company directors should be legally responsible for what they do. Directors should pay large fines when companies break the law (e.g. when polluting rivers etc.). Company directors should be obliged by law to have a considerable amount of their personal wealth in the companies they direct.

33. If we are to solve our problems and reverse the trend towards mindless violence we must weaken the suffocating effect of the welfare society and we must teach people to care and feel compassionate; to have belief in themselves and to believe that they can change and improve the system.

    I believe that the easiest way to do this is to introduce some form of National Community Service.

    Every school leaver should spend a year working full-time in the community with the sick, the elderly or the disabled. Career paths should be rudely interrupted while students are taught about the real world. Dole money should be replaced for twelve months with a wage for working for the National Community Service.

When exposed to real suffering and allowed to take real responsibility, the heartless and selfish children of the welfare state, who are wreaking such havoc in our society, will slowly acquire pride, sympathy and understanding.

When given the chance to explore their own fears and expectations, hopes and passions, millions of young people will discover that they can make a difference and that life has much more to offer than football, lager and an annual two week beach holiday on a nightclub-infested Greek or Spanish island.

34. Political parties should not be allowed to receive Government support or sponsorship. Political parties should not be allowed to accept money from trades unions, commercial organisations or any other groups – they should only be allowed to accept donations from individuals. No individual should be allowed to give more than one hours earnings (at minimum wage level) to a political party.

35. No public money should ever be used to fund organisations which publish or broadcast. The BBC, for example, would be a stronger, more independent organisation if its funding did not depend upon Government approval. The TV licence fee is an anachronism which should be abandoned. Viewers should be invited – not forced – to subscribe.

✳ ✳ ✳

You may not agree with every item on this list.

But I hope you will feel that much of this list makes sense – and that the principles which are clear here are closer to your own ideals than the policy statements made by the major political parties.

Remember that all revolutions (and revolutions should be peaceful) are based on a shared, common cause.

If you believe in the general tone of the items on this list then please pass copies of this book to your friends for discussion. This list will also appear on www.vernoncoleman.com

We live in a world where law abiding citizens often dare not go out-of-doors after dark, where the water is barely fit to drink and where the air is unfit to breathe. We live in a world where the incidence of cancer has been rising steadily for years – despite the fact that we know what causes 80% of all cancers.

We live in a world where politicians routinely lie and cheat, where large corporations ride roughshod over our rights, where authority and responsibility have been separated and where most law abiding citizens admit that they are more frightened of the law enforcement agencies than of the criminals. We live in a world where millions routinely expect to be stopped and searched for no good reason, where privacy is an almost forgotten concept, where government officials paid to be our servants are rude, aggressive and demanding and where petty bureaucracy has, in many areas, virtually put an end to originality and creative thinking.

We live in a country which has a health service which, though once the envy of the world, has effectively collapsed. Our transport infrastructure is the most dangerous and most unreliable in the 'developed' or 'first' world.

It doesn't have to be like this.

Show this book to your friends and relatives and to the people with whom you work so that we can spread the word and build up a solid, campaigning force of like-minded individuals.

As you think so you will become.

Having goals and a purpose is self-fulfilling. The more we want the more we get.

In the next, and final chapter, of this book I will explain to you precisely how we can get our country back, how we can throw out the liars, the cheats, the confidence tricksters and the warmongers and how we can recreate a world in which can we live proudly.

Freedom, dignity, privacy and justice are not optional extras. They are our right.

Chapter 14
How We Can Reshape Our Own Future

In our Cruel New World, ruled by men such as Bush and Blair, standing up for your principles has become very dangerous. If you put your head up above the parapet you are likely to have it shot off.

If you protest you will be filmed and photographed. If you speak out against tyranny the authorities will watch your every move, listen to your every word and read everything you write. If (even in a private conversation or exchange of e-mails) you say anything critical of the Government you will be listed as a terrorist sympathiser. The line between terrorism and legitimate civil disobedience has been deliberately blurred by the Government; which is using a manufactured fear of the former as an excuse to suppress the latter.

We have lost our privacy and we have damned near lost our freedom. Our Government has given itself unbelievable new powers to listen to, read and monitor all our communications and transactions. Personal privacy, the essence of true liberty, no longer exists. And the worst is yet to come. Our ruthless and abusive Government clearly intends to extend its powers still further – and to continue to take away what few rights we have left and what little privacy remains.

Every new piece of legislation is now introduced in the name of terrorism. But the truth is that terrorism is a minor cause of death in the UK. Indeed, there are fewer terrorist attacks in the UK now than there were a few years ago when the American funded IRA was targeting the UK with some regularity.

Surveillance cameras are everywhere. The Government is bringing in ID cards. New legislation reducing our civil liberties is being introduced so quickly that civil liberties groups hardly have time to express outrage at one new piece of fascist legislation before another is being prepared. Thanks to the threats from the authorities, and the ever present armed guards, travel has become a nightmare. Tourists and businessmen have their personal toiletries confiscated lest they be used as weapons.

The Government keeps detailed records of every move we make. They have introduced new legislation which has so damaged our personal security that identity theft is now one of the fastest growing types of crime. Personal privacy for law abiding citizens is now just a memory. The law enforcement agencies have given up protecting the public (the task for which they are paid) and now spend most of their time persecuting motorists (an easy target and a ready source of income).

The warmongers who have taken Britain into an unending, illegal and immoral war regard anyone who opposes them as a terrorist sympathiser. Honesty and integrity no longer exist within the political or financial establishments. Your Government wants you to be afraid and silent, and to hand over all your money without asking any questions.

The Government no longer defends British citizens who have been arrested abroad. Our courts now officially sanction the torture of suspects, who are considered guilty until proven innocent.

Everything they do is secret. Nothing we do is secret. They can arrest us and confiscate our property on the flimsiest of excuses. If you contribute money to a an organisation which is branded 'terrorist' then your belongings can be confiscated. The danger here lies in the fact that it is the Government which decides which organisations should be described as 'terrorist' and they have, for example, long ago decided that animal rights campaigners are terrorists. So, for example, if you protest about vivisection or hunting then you are a terrorist.

If you protest about what is happening you are likely to find yourself in a secret court, condemned as a terrorist (or terrorist sympathiser – which is, these days, regarded as much the same thing) and liable to find yourself imprisoned indefinitely.

The punishments for political crimes, crimes against the State, are now far greater than the punishments for crimes against individuals or against property.

✳ ✳ ✳

When defectors left the former USSR the three words they most commonly used to complain about the Soviet regime were: corruption, cynicism and nepotism. I cannot think of three words which sum up New Labour's regime more accurately.

✳ ✳ ✳

You may think that, as an innocent and law abiding citizen, you have nothing to fear. You are wrong. In a fascist world where the authorities have all the power and individuals have no rights we are all vulnerable. And, make no mistake about it, we are living in a fascist country.

The police, the authorities, the bureaucrats and the politicians are, of course, all exempt from criticism and stand outside the law. Now that we are at permanent war just about everything the authorities do is legal. All they have to do is claim that whatever they did was done in the name of 'national security'.

The state is now everything. The individual is nothing. That is pure fascism.

✳ ✳ ✳

'The most dangerous man to any government is the man who is able to think things out for himself, without regard to the prevailing superstitions and taboos. Almost inevitably he comes to the conclusion that the government he lives under is dishonest, insane and intolerable.'
H. L. MENCKEN

✳ ✳ ✳

I have to warn you, dear reader, that in order to protect yourself and your family you should be very careful when openly criticising the Government or any of its actions.

But we have to do something to make our voices heard and to prove that we cannot be bullied, frightened and intimidated into submission.

We can no longer take our freedom for granted. We have to fight for the privilege of being left alone. And we can make a difference.

BEFORE IT GETS BETTER

If we are not doing what is right then what we are doing is wrong.
Do not allow anyone to force you to compromise on your integrity: once we compromise we do not have any integrity.

* * *

On the following pages I have explained how we can take back control of our country. The suggestions which follow will, I believe, enable us to combat the various forces which have led to the problems we now face.

Our country doesn't love us any more. But we still love it. And we want it back.

* * *

'A piece of freedom is no longer enough for human beings; unlike bread a slice of liberty does not finish hunger. Freedom is like life; it cannot be had in instalments. Freedom is indivisible, we have it all or we are not free.'
MARTIN LUTHER KING JR

* * *

None of the three leading political parties will take the action we need. None of them will loosen the ties holding us to Europe. New Labour, the Conservative Party and the Liberal Democrats all seem convinced that Britain cannot exist without being a member of the European Union. Curiously, the same three main parties also believe that Britain must remain America's panting lapdog.

Britain needs to get rid of its existing three-party political system and start again – from scratch. The big three parties don't exist to protect Britain, or to defend or protect the voters. The big three political parties in Britain exist to defend themselves.

* * *

In many British elections there is a less than 50% turnout.
In 1997 New Labour got a massive landslide victory. Since only about two thirds of the electorate bothered to vote Blair received the support of around one third of the electors. So, in the year when Tony Blair got an overwhelming, unprecedented majority in the House of Commons, two thirds of the British people either didn't vote for him or didn't want him as Prime Minister.

WHY EVERYTHING IS GOING TO GET WORSE

In America, when George W. Bush won a two horse race to become president, he received just 25% of the possibly available votes and became president because five out of nine supreme court justices (mostly appointed by his father) chose to give the presidency to him.

Millions have given up voting in political elections because they don't think their vote is going to make any difference. There are, they believe, three reasons for this.

First, modern politicians lie. They regard campaign promises and manifesto pledges as gimmicks to win elections.

Second, there is no significant difference between the main parties.

Third, once they get into power politicians don't take any notice of the wishes of the people. They turn into dictators.

* * *

'A civilization flourishes when people plant trees under
whose shade they will never sit.'
GREEK PROVERB

* * *

It is a myth that we have a three-party system. We don't even have a two-party system. The political parties we have are all parts of the same party; they all share the same basic beliefs.

Politics today is primarily about politicians rather than voters. The only people who get anything out of elections are the politicians and people don't vote because the politicians aren't worth voting for.

Very few sensitive, thoughtful, caring individuals go into politics these days. Today, the only people who go into politics are the pompous, thick-skinned, greedy, self-centred people who see politics as a way to improve themselves. In the end, the people who run the country are the very people who should *not* be leading the country.

We need leaders who care but instead of caring people we end up with people whose primary concern is not the good of the nation, or the welfare of the people, but simple self preservation and self aggrandisement. It is hardly surprising that there is plenty of fraud in modern politics but very little genuine passion.

Those politicians who are led by an ideology (and there are few enough of those) use their ideology as an excuse to further their control, rather than to improve the state of the world they are supposed to be managing

Before It Gets Better

* * *

Elections are a sham. There are no real choices. It is always the government who wins, and never the people. All our major political parties are fundamentally fascist; they want to tyrannise us and impose their beliefs on us. Instead of wanting to create a free and liberated society where we can all get on with our lives they want to expand their control over our lives and they want to interfere in every aspect of everything we do. All today's political parties want to violate our individual rights and to increase the rights of government. Those views are fundamentally fascist.

* * *

Think of any leading politician. Now imagine him transplanted into another political party. It isn't difficult is it?

There is nothing much to help us distinguish between the three main parties; they have much the same policies and the same arrogance, they display the same indifference to the voters and they make the same mistakes. They share the same taste for power (for its own sake rather than for what it can be used to achieve) and the same denial of reality.

People don't vote in European, parliamentary or local government elections because there doesn't seem much point. There isn't any significant difference between the parties. Politicians don't take any notice of what the voters want. And they don't keep their promises. Politicians are so focused on the next election that they never think of the next generation.

* * *

But although people often don't bother about voting in political elections, people still love voting when they think it is worthwhile and when they think their vote will make a difference. They do it all the time. They vote in their millions to subject minor celebrities to great indignities in the television programme *I'm a Celebrity – Get Me Out Of Here*. They vote for their favourites in *Pop Idol*. They vote to have obnoxious players thrown out of the *Big Brother* house. In these 'elections' people actually pay to cast their vote. In many areas of the country more English people voted for candidates in the *Big Brother* house than voted in the last Parliamentary elections. Over ten million people voted in the final round of *Pop Idol*.

WHY EVERYTHING IS GOING TO GET WORSE

* * *

We must take back the political power which is rightfully ours. We have to take back power from the crooks and the crooked institutions which now rule our lives. We have to take back power from the weak, spineless and unthinking politicians who serve those institutions with such uncritical faithfulness.

The people are now the only force of opposition; the only voice for freedom and justice is the voice on the streets.

What Britain really needs is a House of Commons made up of independent men and women who would keep their promises, who would stick to their manifestos and who would vote honestly and decently according to their consciences.

The biggest problem we have at the moment is that our destiny, our welfare and our history are all in the hands of political parties which have their own vested interests to pursue. Political parties need to grow and thrive in order to survive.

* * *

Charities now commonly exist not to fight for the cause which led to their foundation but to provide salaries, perks and pensions for their employees. If you doubt this just look at the accounts for any successful, professional charity. There is a good chance that between 50% and 75% of the charity's gross income goes towards paying the organisation's costs; in other words the organisation exists largely to sustain itself.

Political parties are much the same; they exist to provide comfortable employment for the paid employees, social support groups for voluntary workers (who usually spend most of their time concerned with constitutional minutiae and fighting one another for power within the organisation) and power, money and status for the party's political representatives: the MPs and the councillors. Political parties exist to win seats and to win elections. That is all they exist for.

The interests of the modern political party no longer match the original aims of the founders; they are far removed from the original concerns and passions which led to their foundation.

The New Labour party doesn't really care about the British people or about Britain. The New Labour Party doesn't care whether England exists or disappears; it doesn't care about Scotland, Wales or Northern

Ireland; it doesn't care about the NHS, the railways or the security of old people in Birmingham, Manchester or Leeds.

The New Labour party is an organisation, and organisations don't have feelings, passions or purposes. Organisations exist only to exist. And as with so many organisations the New Labour Party is run for the benefit of the people who run it: the managers, the office staff and the other employees whose salaries and pensions are paid by it.

The same thing is true of the Conservative Party. And the Liberal Democrat Party. And in the end it will be the same of any large, successful political party.

✳ ✳ ✳

Our first step to freedom must be to free ourselves of the 'party system' and to create a Parliament which consists of honest, caring individuals whose only concerns are the future safety and welfare of the people they represent – and the country of which they are citizens.

And that would be a real revolution.

It is not the duty of a government to micro-manage peoples' lives. It is the duty of a government to provide a safe, effective, unobtrusive infrastructure which allows citizens the freedom to do their own thing. Ayn Rand, the author of *Atlas Shrugged* and founder of the philosophy of objectivism, declared that the only true purpose of politics is to protect individual rights. And she was right.

✳ ✳ ✳

Time is running out and we must act fast. Our existing political parties are giving away more and more power to America and to the EU. We must act before New Labour (or its successors) have given away everything.

So, here's what we do.

Ask yourself if you could stand for Parliament – not as a member of any party but as a concerned and caring individual, standing for freedom, justice and truth. Ask yourself two simple questions.

The first question is 'Why?'

And the answer to that one is easy.

You should stand for Parliament because your country needs you. It needs people who care, who genuinely want to help make the world a better place and who will vote according to their consciences.

The second question is 'Why not?'

Only you can answer that.

If for whatever reason you do not want to stand for Parliament yourself then you should make sure that whenever possible you always vote for an independent candidate or a candidate representing one of the smaller parties. Do not, under any circumstances, vote for a candidate representing one of the main three parties.

We have to break the three-in-one party system which has for so long held a stranglehold over British politics. We must fill Parliament with people who care about nothing but the voters and the country; parliamentary representatives who will think only about the needs and wishes of the voters and the good of the country when they are voting in the House of Commons. We have to vote for representatives who know that if they fail to represent the wishes of the voters, or at least satisfy the voters that they have voted honestly and honourably, then they won't be elected at the next election. Vote not for the party but for the individual.

Even if it takes time to fill the House of Commons with truly independent MPs it will take much less time to build up the success and power of other, smaller political parties. A House of Commons with members divided among half a dozen parties would be infinitely more independent, representative and responsible to the needs of the nation than a Commons dominated by our current three-in-one party system.

Is it possible for us to regain power over our representatives this way?

Yes.

Is there a choice?

Well, there is always a choice.

If you want things to continue to get worse you can carry on voting for the present corrupt and incompetent system.

Or if you want a better life and a better world then you can vote for genuine change. Only the people who are crazy enough to think they *can* change the world *will* change the world.

* * *

The most powerful form of communication in the world is not the television, the Internet, the radio or the newspaper; it is word of mouth. Talk to your friends. Tell them what you know.

BEFORE IT GETS BETTER

The second most powerful form of communication is the book. Books are more powerful than television, the Internet, the radio or newspapers. So, please pass your copy of this book onto a friend. Regard the book as a chain letter – designed to start people thinking. (Bulk copies of this book are available at very low prices from Publishing House.)

There are many who still believe that when the revolution comes it will come through the computer. After all, a billion people are now walking around with computing devices – computers, telephones and personal digital assistants (PDAs) – which are connected and able to communicate with one another at high speed.

But the authorities can and do control what appears on the Internet. They can and do listen in to telephone conversations and they can and do read your e-mails. They can use satellite technology to pinpoint your position when you make a phone call.

The new revolution won't happen through a billion laptops, mobile telephones and PDAs. It will happen the old-fashioned way: through people reading and talking.

And since the big international publishers have a vested interest in maintaining the status quo (and will not, therefore, publish anything which threatens the stability of their economic superiority) the word will be spread through small, independent publishers operating outside the system.

We at Publishing House intend to continue to do what we can to combat fascism and to fight for freedom, justice, privacy and independence.

Our weapons are truth, our fraternity and our conviction that our cause is just. Please help us spread the word. This is a battle which is worth fighting. And time is running out.

For a catalogue of Vernon Coleman's books
please write to:

Publishing House
Trinity Place
Barnstaple
Devon EX32 9HJ
England

Telephone	01271 328892
Fax	01271 328768

Outside the UK:

Telephone	+44 1271 328892
Fax	+44 1271 328768

Or visit our website:

www.vernoncoleman.com